day trips® from austin

Praise for previous editions

"If you're looking for a one- or two-day getaway but you're not sure where to go, then Paris Permenter and John Bigley may have just the ticket for you."
—*Hill Country News*

"No matter how much you love living in the city, there's nothing more refreshing than leaving home for rest, relaxation, and a quick recharge. This book provides twenty-five detailed itineraries for residents and visitors looking for a rejuvenating getaway."
—*Advocate* (Victoria, Tex.)

"If the idea of traveling Texas this summer appeals to you, but you don't have a week or two to devote to wandering the farm-to-market roads searching for interesting Lone Star locales, there is a solution: day trips."
—*San Antonio Current*

"The value of any guidebook is its ease of use, and *Day Trips* is a very user-friendly guide. *Day Trips* has its share of golden nuggets. This guidebook is good for stashing in the car for those spontaneous Sunday drives or when planning a vacation."
—*Austin Chronicle*

help us keep this guide up to date

Every effort has been made by the authors and editors to make this guide as accurate and useful as possible. However, many changes can occur after a guide is published—establishments close, phone numbers change, hiking trails are rerouted, facilities come under new management, and so on.

We would love to hear from you concerning your experiences with this guide and how you feel it could be improved and be kept up to date. While we may not be able to respond to all comments and suggestions, we'll take them to heart, and we'll make certain to share them with the authors. Please send your comments and suggestions to the following address:

The Globe Pequot Press
Reader Response/Editorial Department
P.O. Box 480
Guilford, CT 06437

Or you may e-mail us at: editorial@GlobePequot.com

Thanks for your input, and happy travels!

INSIDERS' GUIDE®

day trips® series

day trips® from austin

fourth edition

getaway ideas for the local traveler

paris permenter

and

john bigley

INSIDERS' GUIDE®

GUILFORD, CONNECTICUT
AN IMPRINT OF THE GLOBE PEQUOT PRESS

**The prices and rates listed in this guidebook
were confirmed at press time. We recommend,
however, that you call establishments before
traveling to obtain current information.**

To buy books in quantity for corporate use
or incentives, call **(800) 962–0973, ext. 4551,**
or e-mail **premiums@GlobePequot.com.**

Text design: Linda Loiewski
Spot photo: © Getty Images

ISSN:1535-8232
ISBN: 0-7627-3865-0

Manufactured in the United States of America
Fourth Edition/First Printing

contents

day trips from austin

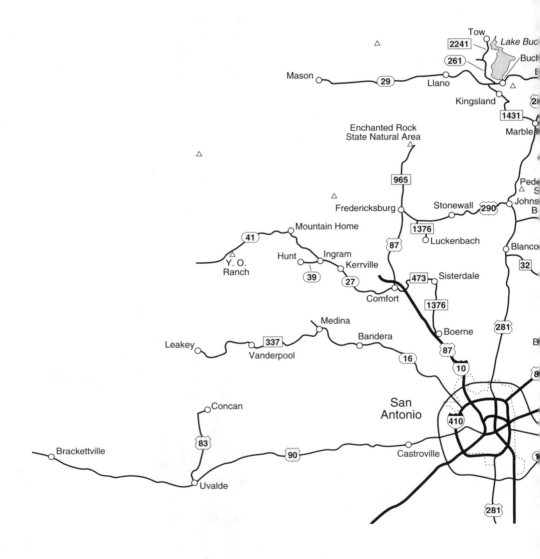

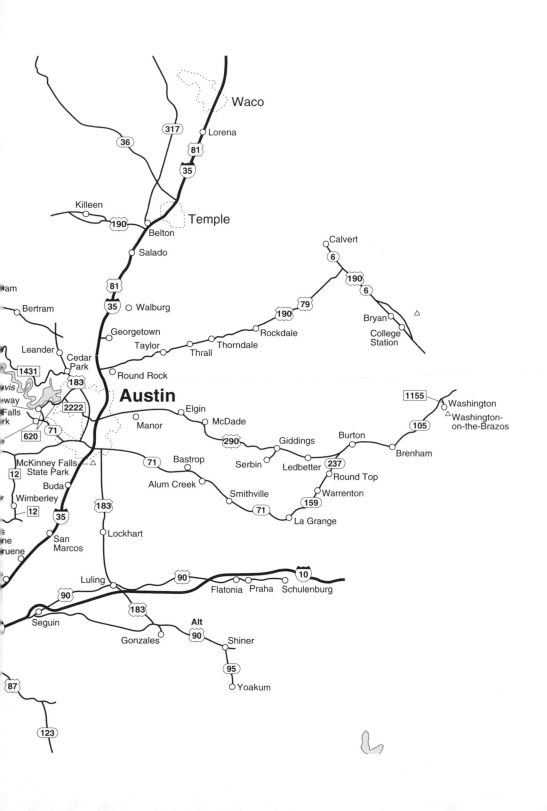

south
day trip 01
painted churches

day trip 02
texas history

day trip 03
shop 'til you drop

day trip 04
concrete city

southwest
day trip 01
the alamo city

day trip 02
old-world fun

day trip 03
kodak country

day trip 04
that's history

day trip 05
cowboy country

day trip 06
alsatian escape

west
day trip 01
willie nelson country

day trip 02
lbj country

day trip 03
hill country escape

northwest

day trip 01

lakeside luxury

day trip 02

granite world

day trip 03

ranch road rambling

day trip 04

rock hound's delight

preface

Most people have a mental image of Texas as miles of rugged, uncivilized land where the outlines of cattle and lonely windmills stretch above the horizon. But that's just one side of the Lone Star State, known as the "land of contrast." Texas also boasts high-tech cities, piney woods, sandy beaches, rolling hills, and fertile farmland—much of it within a two-hour drive of Austin.

The region covered in this book is as diverse as the more than thirty cultures who helped found the state. German, French, Mexican, Polish, and even Alsatian settlers brought their traditions to Texas in the 1800s. The influences of these pioneers are still apparent today in the varied festivals and ethnic foods that vacationers come here to enjoy.

The day trips within this book span terrain ranging from farmland to rocky hills. This difference in topography is the result of an ancient earthquake that created the Balcones Fault, which runs north to south. The fault line, slightly west of Interstate 35, forms the dividing line between the eastern agricultural region and what is known as the Hill Country to the west.

Many of the attractions lie along the route taken by the 350,000 Winter Texans who flock here during the cooler months. So, whether you're heading for the Rio Grande Valley, the coast, or the Mexican border, you'll find a wealth of useful tips and information in this guide. Be sure to check the sections marked "Especially for Winter Texans." This will help you identify special services, festivals, and parks aimed at making you feel right at home.

You'll find that Texans are friendly folk who wave on country roads and nod as they pass you on the sidewalk. Talk to local citizens as you wind through the back roads for even more travel tips and a firsthand look at the varied cultures that make up the pieces of your journey.

texas travel tips

carry a road map

Although we've included directions, it's best to carry a Texas road map as you travel. It's also advisable to carry a county map for a better look at farm-to-market (FM) roads and ranch roads (RR). To get brochures on Texas attractions and a free copy of the Texas State Travel Guide call (800) 888–8TEX or see www.traveltex.com. The guide is available in print and as a CD. The guide is coded to a free Texas state map also provided by the highway department. These maps are also available from any of the Tourist Information Centers located on routes into Texas and at the Texas State Capitol in Austin. The Tourist Information Centers are open daily, except Thanksgiving, Christmas, and New Year's Day.

The expansiveness of Texas sets it apart from other states. Note the scale of the map. With 266,807 square miles of land, Texas is the second largest state in the country. One inch on the state road map spans 23 miles.

Driving varies with terrain: In the western Hill Country, towns are distant and roads can be slow and winding. To the east, population is more dense, and day trips involve quiet, slow drives along farm-to-market and ranch roads.

For questions about travel in Texas, call (800) 452–9292.

be wary of weather conditions

As a general rule, the Austin region enjoys a very temperate climate. Winters are mild, with just about twenty-five freezing days annually. Snow is rare and, when it does occur, causes businesses and schools to close and roads to congest quickly.

The most pleasant seasons in the region are spring and fall. You'll find many Austin-area festivals are scheduled during these pleasant weekends, times when temperatures are in the 70 and 80°F range.

Austin receives less than 30 inches of rain annually, most of it arriving during the spring. Thunderstorms are common from April through September, especially during late afternoon as temperatures rise. Tornados are most common during May and June.

avoid midday heat

In summer, the Texas heat is hotter than sizzling fajitas. In warm weather, it's best to drive in the early-morning hours or after sunset. If you are traveling with children or pets, never leave them in a closed car; temperatures soar to ovenlike heights in just minutes.

heed road signs and weather warnings

Always be on the lookout for road signs, and if you see a notice, observe what they say. Obey flash flood warnings: A sudden rainstorm can turn a wash into a deadly torrent. Never cross a flooded roadway; it may be deeper than you think. This is a serious problem in the Hill Country where deaths occur every year as motorists try to cross flooded roads.

watch out for stray livestock

When driving through open-ranch cattle country on farm-to-market or ranch roads, be on the lookout for livestock and deer wandering across roads, especially near dusk. Deer can be a driving hazard even in populated regions.

using this travel guide

Highway designations: Federal highways are designated US. State routes use Highway. Farm-to-market roads are defined as FM, and ranch roads are labeled RR. County roads (which are not on the Texas state map) are identified as such.

Hours: In most cases, hours are omitted in the listings because they are subject to frequent changes. Instead, phone numbers and Web sites are provided for up-to-date information.

Restaurants: Restaurant prices are designated as $$$ (Expensive: $20 and more per person); $$ (Moderate: $10–20); and $ (Inexpensive: $10 and less).

Accommodations: Room prices are designated as $$$ (Expensive: more than $100 for a standard room); $$ (Moderate: $50–100); and $ (Inexpensive: less than $50).

Credit cards are accepted unless noted otherwise.

 # day trips from austin

Welcome to Austin, the state capital and gateway to attractions in Central Texas. With Austin as your base, you'll have a chance to visit both rugged hills to the west and miles of scenic roads and interesting small towns to the east.

Austin is a high-tech city, with an economy based on computer-related industries and state government. The city of Austin takes in more than 657,000 residents, including a University of Texas population of more than 50,000 students and faculty from around the world. This gives Austin an international feel, with many ethnic restaurants and specialty grocery stores. Many people have relocated here, attracted by the clean industry and beautiful weather. The numerous relocations make Austin the nation's second-fastest-growing city; the city has burst the metropolitan boundaries and now encompasses a sprawl of more than 1.25 million residents in the metropolitan area.

New residents aren't the first to discover the beauty of Austin. When Mirabeau B. Lamar, the president-elect of the Texas Republic, set out to hunt buffalo in the fall of 1838, he returned home with a much greater catch than a prize buffalo: a home for the new capital city. Lamar fell in love with a tiny settlement surrounded by rolling hills and fed by cool springs. Within the coming year, the government arrived and construction on the Capitol building was begun. Austin was on its way to becoming a city.

Since those early days, there's been no looking back. Today Austin is a city on the move. Hollywood has discovered this big city with a small-town atmosphere, and it's not uncommon these days to see film crews blocking off an oak-lined street. High-tech industries have also migrated to Austin, making this area Texas's answer to Silicon Valley.

But, for all the changes that have occurred in this capital city, Austin is still very much a town with roots buried in a past the city is proud to preserve and show off to its visitors.

A visit to Austin should begin downtown, where the Colorado River slices through the heart of the city. Once an unpredictable waterway, the Colorado has now been tamed into a series of lakes, including two within the Austin city limits. The 22-mile-long Lake Austin begins at the foot of the Hill Country and flows through the western part of the city.

Lake Austin flows into Town Lake, a narrow stretch of water that meanders for 5 miles through the center of downtown Austin. Several hotels overlook the beautifully planted greenbelts that line the lakeshores. In the late afternoon hours, locals grab their sneakers and head to the Zilker Park or Town Lake shores for a jog or a leisurely walk. When the sun sets on summer days, attention turns to the lake's Congress Avenue bridge, the location of the country's largest urban colony of Mexican free-tailed bats. The bats make their exodus after sunset to feed on insects in the Hill Country.

Many of Austin's historical buildings are found downtown, and the granddaddy of them all is the State Capitol. Tours introduce you to this pink-granite building that holds the distinction of being the tallest state capitol in the United States.

After a tour of the Capitol, step across the street to the Governor's Mansion for a free tour Monday through Friday, 10:00 A.M. to noon. Your tour will take you past the grand staircase (a former governor was once forced to drive nails through the banister to prevent his children from sliding down it), through the formal parlor, into the library and the state dining room where formal state dinners are held, and finally into the conservatory, a cheery room with lemon-yellow walls and a huge glass cabinet holding memorabilia donated by former governors.

Just blocks from the Governor's Mansion lies the Driskill Hotel, Austin's most historic hotel. Since 1886 this property has been a stopover for dignitaries, heads of state, legislators, and vacationers from around the globe.

The Capitol, the Governor's Mansion, and the Driskill are all historical Austin landmarks, but they're just babes when compared with the French Legation, Austin's oldest existing home. Located in east Austin at 802 San Marcos, this is the only foreign legation in the country ever built outside of Washington, D.C. (Wondering why it was built in Austin? Don't forget: Texas was once a separate country—complete with its own foreign ambassadors!)

Austin's most famous museum is the Lyndon Baines Johnson Presidential Library, located on the University of Texas campus. Special exhibits portray the Vietnam conflict, the Civil Rights movement, and the advances for education that took place during these years. Visitors can also view extravagant gifts received from other countries, a limousine used by the president, and family memorabilia.

After a day of touring, Austin presents plenty of other entertainment options. The heart of Austin's nightlife is Sixth Street, a historic seven-block area that compares itself with New Orleans's Bourbon Street. Here you'll find many nightclubs and restaurants, as well as eclectic shops open during the day. And if you get hungry in the capital city, have no fear—Austin is home to more restaurants and bars per capita than any other city in the nation.

live music capital of the world

Austin has earned its nickname thanks to the large number of live music venues scattered throughout the city. On any given night, about one hundred venues ranging from concert halls to alternative bars to honky tonks move to the sound of live music. The city has drawn many well-known names who select Austin not just for performances but for their home. Today Austin is home to the Dixie Chicks, Shawn Colvin, Willie Nelson, Asleep at the Wheel, Don Walser, and others.

And if all that dining creates a need for a little activity, fun comes in many forms. In the warm months, Austin really lives up to its nickname, "The River City," since everyone takes to Lake Austin and nearby Lake Travis to enjoy swimming, scuba diving, skiing, and boating. Golfers find plenty of challenge in this area as well.

Austin spreads out into the suburban communities of Round Rock, Cedar Park, Oak Hill, and others. But beyond the reach of Austin's bedroom communities, you'll find a Texas that's largely unchanged by the 1990s. Bowling alleys still set pins by hand, businesses close on Friday nights during high school football season, and pickup trucks seem to outnumber every other form of transportation. Some of the best barbecue in the world comes from the small towns that nestle in the Hill Country, a region so-called because of its rugged terrain. The topographical change represents the 1,800-mile Balcones Fault, which has separated the western Hill Country from the flat eastern farmland ever since a 3.5-minute earthquake 30 million years ago.

This part of Texas gives you a chance to slow down, meet some local folks, and enjoy a good old-fashioned chicken-fried steak at the local diner.

For brochures and maps on Austin area attractions, call (866) GO–AUSTIN. To speak with the Austin Convention and Visitors Bureau, call (800) 926–2282 or (512) 474–5171, or write: Austin Convention and Visitors Bureau, 301 Congress Avenue, Suite 200, Austin, TX 78701, or check out www.austintexas.org.

north

day trip 01

north

**round rock, georgetown,
walburg, salado:
small-town texas**

round rock

Now over 80,000 strong, this booming Austin bedroom community located north on Interstate 35 is named for the circular rock formation that lies in the middle of Brushy Creek.

Round Rock was the scene of a Wild West shoot-out a century ago. Sam Bass was a well-known outlaw in these parts back then, a stagecoach and train robber who boasted that he'd never killed a man. Bass planned to make his first bank robbery in Round Rock, but things went awry when the Texas Rangers learned his scheme. They were waiting as Bass and his gang rode into town on July 19, 1878, and they gravely wounded him during a gun battle in the 100 block of East Main Street. Bass fled from town and died two days later.

This colorful figure was buried in the old Round Rock cemetery, situated on what's now known as Sam Bass Road. The grave is near an interesting slave cemetery, a reminder of the cotton industry and plantation system that once dominated this area.

Round Rock was also once a part of the stagecoach route that stretched from Brownsville, Texas, to Helena, Arkansas. Frontiersmen used the round rock to judge the depth of Brushy Creek before crossing. Today visitors still can see coach tracks in the Brushy Creek riverbed, just west of I–35.

Every July Round Rock hosts Frontier Days, recalling its Wild West heritage with a re-enactment of the Sam Bass shoot-out.

north day trip 01

Waco

0   10   20 miles   81
35

Killeen
Belton   Temple
190

Salado
81
35
Walburg
972

Georgetown
Leander   Taylor   Thrall
Cedar   79
Park   Round Rock

183
Austin
2222
Elgin
71   Manor
290
Bastrop
71

Buda

183   Smithville
35

San   Lockhart
Marcos

Luling   Harwood   90
90   10
183
Seguin   Alt
Gonzales   90

Today Round Rock is home to the Round Rock Express (512–255–BALL; www.roundrockexpress .com), a AAA minor league baseball franchise. The city boasts an expansive sports facility off I–35 at Highway 79 near Old Settlers Park. The team comes to the community thanks to Texas baseball great Nolan Ryan.

where to go

Palm House Museum. 212 East Main Street. Built in the 1860s, this historic home now contains a two-room museum and the local Chamber of Commerce. In the kitchen and parlor hang photos and artifacts from Round Rock's early days. Look for the silver bowl that had its lid blown off during the Sam Bass shoot-out. Open daily. Free. (800) 747–3479 or (512) 255–5805.

Texas has more buried treasure than any other state, much of it tied to outlaw Sam Bass. The robber hid from the law in the town of Round Rock. Bass was in Round Rock making plans for a bank robbery, until a final shoot-out with the Texas Rangers on July 19, 1878. Before he died, however, many say that he hid much of the loot from his train, stagecoach, and bank robberies somewhere in the area.

The trail of Sam Bass continues near the state capital, where he allegedly buried $30,000 in the community of McNeil. No treasure was ever recovered, and today there is little remaining of McNeil, located in the northern part of Travis County near Round Rock.

where to eat

Jorge Arredondo's. 118 East Main Street. This is the way Tex-Mex should be served, with chips and salsa brought to your table as soon as you sit down. The menu offers combinations galore and plates piled high with rice and beans, all at very reasonable prices. $. (512) 244–3030.

georgetown

Georgetown is an elegant community of over 38,000 residents that rests on the border of farmland to the east and ranch land to the west. Located 10 miles north of Round Rock on I–35, this was once an active agricultural center. Today Georgetown is home to many Austin commuters and 1,300 students at Southwestern University, the oldest college in Texas.

Georgetown's first residents were the Tonkawa Indians, a resourceful group that drove buffalo off the bluffs of the San Gabriel River. Years later, the town of Georgetown was founded by a group of men that included George Washington Glasscock. After he donated the land for the town, it was named in his honor. Glasscock had come to Texas from the East after running a river-barge business for a time in Illinois with Abraham Lincoln.

Georgetown became a cattle center after the Civil War and the starting point of many northern cattle drives. The community grew but remained a small town into the late 1900s. Austin's runaway growth during the 1980s eventually turned Georgetown into a bedroom community divided by I–35. To the west is "new" Georgetown, with many subdivisions, including nationally known Sun City, along Williams Drive on the way to Lake Georgetown. "Old" Georgetown sits east of the highway, and among its main attractions are the winding North and South San Gabriel Rivers, which join together in shady San Gabriel Park.

In recent years, Georgetown was selected as one of five national winners of the Great American Main Street awards. To view the award-winning revitalization project, take exit 261 off I–35 and continue east to Austin Avenue. Turn left at the light for a look at the restored courthouse square. With its stately oaks and shady lawn, it is so typical of Texas that it's been used as a set for several movies and TV shows.

Georgetown has refined its recipe for community charisma as the city has grown and prospered. Serving as seat of the second-fastest-growing county in the nation, Georgetown continues to hang onto its cozy charm. Even with a growing population, it is proud to say that it's still the kind of place where folks can walk around the square and be welcomed by a smile and a friendly nod. Celebrating more than 150 years of small-town life, Georgetown may have just found the secret ingredient: preservation.

poppy fields

In late March, the fields and yards around Georgetown bloom with the vibrant color of red poppies. Georgetown holds the title of the "Red Poppy Capital of Texas," with both native and cultivated varieties growing throughout the town.

Many of the poppies date back to seeds imported to the town by Henry Purl "Okra" Compton. During his service in World War I in Europe, he collected seeds and planted them around his mother's home upon his return.

Today the poppies brighten yards and highway right-of-ways from late March through May. Look for white signs indicating a "Poppy Zone" as you travel through town.

North of the courthouse square, San Gabriel Park has served for centuries as a gathering site. Native Americans camped on the verdant grounds, pioneers met here, and early Georgetown residents congregated on the riverbanks for parades and meetings, including one event that featured speaker Sam Houston.

Today, park lovers enjoy shady picnics on grounds dotted with oak and pecan trees. Children romp on the playscape while anglers try their luck from the grassy riverbanks. Crystal clear springs bubble up at three sites on the park grounds, and often you can watch these little "salt and pepper" springs spew up chilly spring waters.

Upstream, the North San Gabriel River has been controlled to create Lake Georgetown, a 1,310-acre lake popular with anglers, boaters, water skiers, and swimmers.

where to go

Georgetown Visitor Information Center. 101 West Seventh Street, on the square. Stop by for a copy of a Georgetown map, brochures on area attractions, and walking tour booklets. The center also sells many Georgetown items, from posters to T-shirts. Open daily. (800) 436–8696 or (512) 863–5598.

Inner Space Cavern. West off I–35, exit 259. Discovered during the construction of the interstate, this cave is a cool getaway for summer travelers and was once a hideaway for animals as well. A skull of a peccary (a pig-like hoofed mammal) estimated to be a million years old has been found here, along with bones of a giant sloth and a mammoth.

Guests enter the cavern on a cog railroad car, traveling down from the visitors center to the well-lit, easy-to-follow trail. Along the way, guides point out features of Inner Space, including large stalactite and stalagmite formations. Some of the larger formations of the cavern are "The Warriors," two stalagmites that have grown together, the "Flowing Stone of Time" in the Outer Cathedral, and "Ivory Falls," a beautiful flow of white stalactites. The cavern uses sound and light displays to create special effects, including the grand finale of the tour: a show at the "Lake of the Moon." After reaching cave level aboard a small trolley, follow your guide for a tour of cave formations, a small lake, and evidence of those prehistoric visitors. Kids also enjoy the Inner Space Mining Company with the chance to pan for gems and minerals. Open daily. Fee. (512) 931–CAVE, www.innerspace.com.

Lake Georgetown. FM 2338, 3.5 miles west of town. Built on the north fork of the San Gabriel River, this lake spans 1,310 surface acres. Three public parks offer swimming, fishing, boating, camping, and hiking opportunities. Public facilities include Jim Hogg Park with overnight camping, electric and water hookups, and boat launching ramp; Cedar Breaks Park with picnic facilities and campsites with electric hookups; Russell Park for picnicking and camping; and Tejas Park for picnics and hikes among oak-shaded trails. The 17-mile Good Water Trail follows the upper end of the lake. Free. Fee for camping. (512) 930–5253.

Good Water Trail. A favorite getaway with nature lovers is the 17-mile Good Water Trail, named in honor of the Tonkawa, a people who made the region near the San Gabriel River their home. Known for their flint arrowheads and tools, these Native Americans called this region *takatchue pouetsu* or "land of good water."

The trail is marked by mileposts as it snakes its way along the lake, passing through several historical points of interest. One such spot is Russell Crossing, later known as the Second Bootys Crossing, located near milepost one. In the late 1860s, Frank Russell resided at this crossing, and his rock house served as a postal substation. Mail was carried in saddlebags to the local residents. Between mileposts two and three, hikers can see Crockett Gardens, a natural spring. A flour mill was operated here in 1855, and a few decades later the first strawberries in Williamson County were grown in truck gardens at this site. Today the remains of the springhouse and corrals can still be seen.

Besides man-made attractions, hikers are also surrounded by natural beauties. White-tailed deer, coyote, skunk, raccoon, ringtail cat, armadillo, and opossum thrive in this area. From February to August, the region is home to the endangered golden-cheeked warbler, a small bird that nests in older juniper trees. Free. (512) 930–5253.

Blue Hole. Austin Avenue at Second Street. West of the park at Blue Hole, where river waters reflect limestone cliffs, a revitalization has made this beautiful spot again a place to be appreciated by residents and visitors. At Blue Hole, walkers and joggers journey along the wide paths that wind beside waters as green as fresh spring leaves. On quiet mornings anglers try their luck with just the sound of an occasional cardinal singing its friendly song in the distance. Free.

Firefighters' Museum. 103 West Ninth Street at Fire Station Number One. This museum is home to an authentic 1922 Seagraves fire engine as well as antique fire extinguishers and old photos. Open weekdays. Free. (512) 930–3606.

San Gabriel Park. Off Austin Avenue. This park, just south of the junction of the North and South San Gabriel Rivers, includes children's playscape, picnic sites, a swimming pool, and walking trail. Open daily. Free. (512) 930–3595.

Southwestern University. 1001 East University Avenue. Southwestern holds the title as Texas's first institution of higher learning. Visitors can call for a guided tour. Open daily. Free. (512) 863–6511.

where to shop

Georgetown has more than a dozen antiques shops. For a free map of the shops listing hours and specialties, call (800) GEO–TOWN or (512) 930–3545 for a copy, or stop by the visitors center on the square where other brochures are also available.

The Candle Factory. On I–35 North, exit 259. This year-round factory produces a variety of handcrafted candles, from classic tapers to popular snowball creations. The large operation makes and sells to the public hundreds of styles of candles in an assortment of colors, scents, and sizes, from tiny votives to hand-painted candles, arrangements, and ceramic candleholders. Open daily. (512) 863–6025; www.thecandlefactory.com.

Georgetown Antique Mall. 708 South Austin Avenue. This expansive shop features antiques from many dealers, ranging from collectibles to glassware to furniture. Open daily. (512) 869–2088.

Rough and Ready Antiques. Sixth and Main Streets. This shop specializes in early Texas furniture as well as architectural details. Open daily. (512) 819–0463.

David Love Store. 110 West Eighth Street. This large gift store has a broad selection of fine accessories, wedding gifts, and more. Open Tuesday through Saturday. (888) 819–1800 or (512) 863–6696.

Handcrafts Unlimited. 104 West Eighth Street. This nonprofit store features handicrafts produced by local residents ages fifty and older. Open daily. (512) 869–1812.

Jan Hagara Doll Collectables. 3700 Williams Drive. Jan Hagara Outlet features heirloom-quality Victorian children's products. From hand-sculpted dolls dressed in vintage clothing to collector plates and prints, Jan's collection is hard to resist. Open Monday through Saturday. (800) 228–3739, (512) 869–1365; www.janhagara.com.

The Windberg Gallery. 714 South Austin Avenue. Georgetown is home to the renowned Texas artist Dalhart Windberg. Known for his emotional portrayals of American landscapes and settings, the gallery offers a view of both original art and handsome prints. Open Monday through Saturday. (512) 819–9463.

where to eat

Monica's 701. 701 South Main Street. Located on the courthouse square, this stylish eatery offers downstairs dining as well as an upstairs bar and open-air balcony featuring live music weekly. Menu options range from coconut shrimp to chicken roulade and prime rib to pecan-crusted trout. Open for lunch and dinner Tuesday through Sunday. $$$. (512) 931–2438; www.monicas701.com.

Monument Cafe. 1953 South Austin Avenue. Styled like an old-fashioned diner, this family restaurant serves up favorites ranging from chicken-fried steak to burgers. The eatery is also a popular breakfast stop with excellent breakfast tacos as well as traditional breakfast fare. And, if you need to check e-mail during your day trip, the restaurant also has free wi-fi connectivity. $–$$. (512) 930–9586; www.themonumentcafe.com.

Wildfire. 812 South Austin Avenue. *Time* magazine said that this restaurant's blue cornmeal-encrusted catfish was reason enough to move to Georgetown; judge for yourself with a visit to this upscale eatery, located next door to the former movie theater. Southwestern-inspired cuisine, much of it prepared on an oak-burning grill, rules, although you'll also find dishes such as Jamaican jerk pork chops and New Zealand elk tenderloin rounding out the menu options. $$$. (512) 869–FIRE; www.thewildfire.com.

where to stay

Claibourne House. 912 Forest Street. Walk to the courthouse square from this Victorian home, built in 1896. The four bedrooms are elegantly furnished. $$. (512) 930–3934; www.claibournehouse.com.

Quality Inn. 1005 Leander Road. This family accommodation offers guests complimentary continental breakfast. Guest facilities include a pool, cable TV, and more. $–$$. (512) 863–7504; www.choicehotels.com.

walburg

This small German farming community is located northeast of Georgetown. From Georgetown, travel north on I–35 to exit 268, turn right and continue 4 miles.

where to eat

Walburg Restaurant. North from Georgetown on I–35 to exit 268; right 4 miles to Walburg. This restaurant is housed in the 1882 Walburg Mercantile building and features authentic

German food and music. Behind the restaurant, a converted cotton gin serves as a bier-garten. The menu includes Wiener schnitzel, bratwurst, sauerbraten, and some Texas favorites like chicken-fried steak and catfish. The restaurant hosts several annual celebra-tions, such as Harvestfest and Maifest. Closed Monday and Tuesday. Open for lunch and dinner Friday and Sunday; dinner on Wednesday, Thursday, and Saturday. $$. (512) 863–8440.

salado

Continuing north on I–35, you'll encounter Salado, a shopping stop for interstate travelers. Antiques stores, artists' galleries, and specialty shops fill the historic downtown buildings. Salado (pronounced "sa-LAY-dough") is a Spanish word meaning either "salty" or "amus-ing," although residents prefer the latter interpretation.

This community is located where Salado Creek flows beneath I–35. The site once was a stagecoach stop on the old Chisholm Trail and served the line that stretched from San Antonio to Little Rock, Arkansas.

Today the old rest stop has been converted to the modern Stagecoach Inn, located on the east side of I–35. Visitors' accommodations are found in a new addition, and the origi-nal building, where Sam Houston once delivered an antisecession speech, has become an elegant restaurant.

The former stagecoach route, now called Main Street, is lined with historic structures housing antiques shops and specialty stores. In all, eighteen of these buildings are listed in the National Register of Historic Places, and twenty-three boast Texas historical markers.

where to go

Central Texas Area Museum. Main Street, across from Stagecoach Inn. This museum traces the history of the Salado area and all of the Brazos Trail—the rich farming area near the Brazos River. Open by appointment and during festivals. Fee. (254) 947–5232.

Pace Park. Downtown, off Main Street. This beautiful area filled with tall oaks is an excel-lent spot to bring a picnic lunch and wade in the creek. Don't miss the statue of Sirena, located in the middle of the creek. Local artist Troy Kelley created the statue cast in bronze of the legendary Indian maiden who was transformed into a mermaid by a magical fish. Mornings you can see fog rising from the chilly waters of the pure springs near the statue. Free. (254) 947–5040.

Driving Tape Tour. Prepared by the Bell County Historical Commission, this cassette tour directs you past twenty-two historic Salado sites. You'll see DRIVING TAPE TOUR signs through-out town that correspond to an explanation on the cassette. Budget about two hours for the excursion, which explains the history and background behind each location. The tapes are available for rent at the Stagecoach Inn, Salado Galleries, and the Inn at Salado. Fee. (254) 947–5040.

where to shop

Shopping is the main drawing card of Salado, and many stores are open daily. Most sell one-of-a-kind, handmade items.

Salado Galleries. Main Street, across from Stagecoach Inn. Fine art, including many paintings of central Texas bluebonnet fields, fill this gallery. Open daily. (254) 947–5110.

Truly Texan Metal Art and Custom Design. 74 Van Bibber Lane. This unique store specializes in one-of-a-kind home accents with a true Texas touch. Here you'll find metal art in every shape and form, from tabletop cowboys atop bucking broncos and wall signs to shelving and end tables. The store also offers handcrafted rustic furniture, candles, jewelry, and etched glassware. (254) 947–8986.

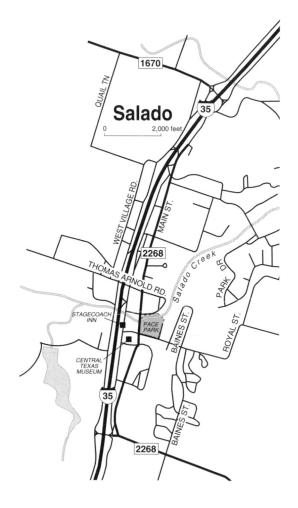

Salado Pottery. Beside the Stagecoach Inn. Here you'll find beautiful Salado-made pottery, from water pitchers to bird feeders. Open daily. (254) 947–5935.

Shady Villa. Main Street, across from Stagecoach Inn. This open-air mini-mall sells everything from unique kaleidoscopes and collectibles to Victorian jewelry and gifts from around the world. Most shops are open daily.

Magnolias of the Square. Main Street on the Square. This shop is actually twenty-two vendors with a complete variety of specialty gifts and home accessories. Open daily. (254) 947–0323.

Salado Haus. Main Street and Salado Creek. This gift store offers Fenton art glass as well as many other fine collectibles and home gifts. Open daily. (877) 947–1868 or (254) 947–1868.

where to eat

Stagecoach Inn. I–35, east side. This tiny restaurant features servers who come to your table and recite the day's offerings by heart. Entrees include chicken-fried steak, baked ham, whole catfish, roast prime rib of beef, and T-bone steak. Don't miss the hush puppies or banana fritters. Open daily for lunch and dinner. Reservations recommended. $$–$$$. (254) 947–9400.

Robertson's Hams and Choppin' Block. I–35, exit 285. Enjoy a deli sandwich of sugar-cured ham, then shop for kitchen collectibles in the extensive gift shop. $. (800) 458–HAMS or (254) 947–5562.

The Salado Mansion. 200 South Main Street. This popular restaurant is housed in a historic building in downtown Salado. With both indoor and outdoor seating, the restaurant offers a variety of Southwest favorites such as mesquite-grilled trout and steaks. Open daily. $$–$$$. (254) 947–5157.

where to stay

Stagecoach Inn. I–35, east side. This reminder of Salado's early days started out as the Shady Villa Inn, an important rest stop on the Chisholm Trail. Today guests stay in a modern addition, and the original building, where Sam Houston once delivered an antisecession speech, is now an elegant restaurant. Notable guests have included George Armstrong Custer, Robert E. Lee, and outlaw Jesse James. $$. (254) 947–5111.

The Inn at Salado. North Main Street at Pace Park. This lovely white two-story bed-and-breakfast is located in the main shopping district. Room rates include a full breakfast. $$. (800) 724–0027 or (254) 947–0027; www.inn-at-salado.com.

Inn on the Creek. On Center Circle. Seven guest rooms with 1892 Victorian elegance. Some rooms boast brass beds; all have private baths. A block away the Reue House has four bedrooms, mid-1800s style. All guests receive a full breakfast. $$. (877) 947–5554 or (254) 947–5554; www.inncreek.com.

day trip 02

north

>>> belton, killeen,
the grove, temple:
military history

Beyond Georgetown and Salado (see North Day Trip 1 for attractions in those towns), Interstate 35 continues its northward journey to two larger central Texas communities. If you're a military buff, take a short detour to Killeen, home of the largest military base in the free world, Fort Hood.

belton

Built on the Leon River and Nolan Creek, this community was once named Nolanville, a place where merchants sold goods from wagons and tin cups of whiskey from a barrel. Today Belton is a small town of over 15,000 residents, best known as home of the University of Mary-Hardin Baylor. The Baptist college began here over a century ago and was once the women's school for Waco's Baylor University.

Two lakes, Stillhouse Hollow and the larger Belton Lake, lie outside the city limits. Both provide fishing, boating, camping, and a quiet retreat only a few minutes from busy I-35.

where to go

Bell County Museum. 201 North Main. This National Register property was first a Carnegie library. Today the Beaux Arts–style building houses exhibits on Bell County's first century, 1850–1950. Special displays remember Miriam "Ma" Ferguson, Texas's first woman

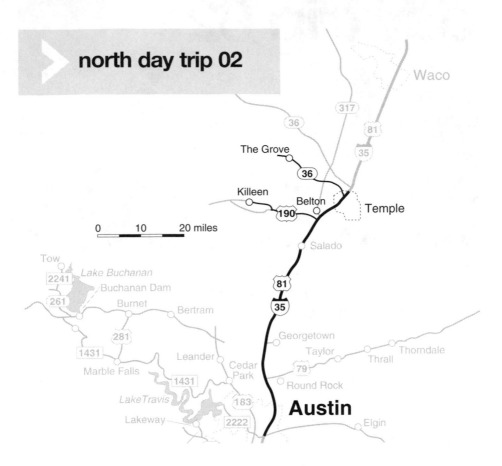

> **north day trip 02**

governor, as well as the history of Camp Hood, later to become Fort Hood. Open Tuesday through Saturday afternoons. Free. (254) 933–5243; www.bellcountytx.com/museum.

Summer Fun USA. 1410 Waco Road. This 6.5-acre water theme park offers more than 900 feet of water slides to help you cool off in the Texas heat. Hop in an inner tube and enjoy the 750-foot Lazy River ride, or slide into the water from a 40-foot tower. There's a picnic area and concession area as well. Open seasonally. Fee. (254) 939–0366.

Stillhouse Hollow. U.S. Highway 190, 4 miles southwest of Belton. Six public parks surround this lake. You'll find the most facilities at Stillhouse Park, the first you'll come to on US 190. Free. (254) 939–2461.

Belton Lake. Highway 317, 5 miles northwest of Belton. Built on the Leon River, this winding 7,400-acre lake features thirteen public parks within its 110 miles of shoreline. Trailer sites, camping, nature trails, and boat ramps are available. Call (254) 939–1829, or write: Reservoir Manager, 3110 FM 2271, Belton, TX 76513.

Mother Neff State Park. From I–35 take exit 315 to Highway 107 west to Moody, continue 6 miles west on FM 107, then take Highway 236 for 2 miles to the park. Named for Isabella Neff, the mother of Governor Pat Neff, this park is nestled along the shady bottomland along the Leon River. A nice place for a quiet day of picnicking and walking, the park also offers periodic trailer rides to point out historical areas. Free. (254) 853–2389; www.tpwd .state.tx.us.

killeen

Military buffs should take a detour at this point in the journey and head west on US 190 to the city of Killeen. Twenty-five miles west of Belton, this small town is dwarfed by Fort Hood, one of the world's largest military posts and the largest training post on the globe.

where to go

Fort Hood. US 190. Established in 1942, Fort Hood spans 339 square miles, encompassing more people and machines than any other post in the free world. The post is home to more than 42,000 soldiers. Access to the base is restricted, but the public is welcome at two museums: The First Cavalry and the Fourth Infantry Division Museums.

The First Cavalry Division Museum. Building 2218, Headquarters Avenue. Fort Hood is home to the First Cavalry Division Horse Detachment. Wearing authentic nineteenth-century uniforms, this group performs at exhibitions throughout Texas. This museum traces the history of this division from its days on the western frontier through its berm-busting attacks during Desert Storm. An outdoor area displays more than three dozen pieces of military equipment, including aircraft and tanks. To visit the museum, all visitors without Department of Defense decals need to enter at the Clear Creek gate (about 1 mile west of the main gate) to obtain a day pass. Open Monday through Friday 9:00 A.M. to 4:00 P.M., Saturday and Sunday noon to 4:00 P.M. Free. (254) 287–3626.

The Fourth Infantry Division Museum. Building 418, Battalion Avenue at Twenty-seventh. Activated in response to the United States' Declaration of War against Germany in 1917, the Fourth Infantry Division participated in four major campaigns during World War I. This museum allows the visitor to explore the history of the Fourth Infantry Division through a series of self-guided exhibits that use artifacts, texts, and photographs showing the soldiers in service through three wars. To visit the museum, all visitors without a Department of Defense decal need to enter at the Clear Creek Gate (about 1 mile west of the main gate) to obtain a day pass. Open Monday through Friday 9:00 A.M. to 4:00 P.M., Saturday 10:00 A.M. to 4:00 P.M., and Sunday noon to 4:00 P.M. Free. (254) 287–8811.

Belton Lake Outdoor Recreation Area. Sparta Road northeast of Fort Hood. This 890-acre park offers woodland hiking and lakeside recreation. Fishing, boating, paddleboating, and swimming are available at the lake. Landlubbers can enjoy a nature path and equestrian trails. Open daily. Fee. (254) 287–4907.

where to stay

Killeen has over 1,500 guest rooms, with daily rates ranging from $45 to $89. For a complete listing, call the Killeen Convention and Visitors Bureau. (800) 869–8265 or (254) 526–9551 or see www.killeen-cvb.com.

La Quinta. 1112 South Fort Hood Street. This family accommodation has a pool, continental breakfast, and more. $$. (254) 526–8331.

the grove

Once a colony founded by Wendish settlers in the mid-1800s, The Grove is a community frozen in time. This agricultural center was once home to many businesses and almost 400 residents, but eventually the community became a ghost town. Today The Grove Country Life Museum is privately owned and open on weekends for visitors to tour.

To reach The Grove, turn west from Temple on Highway 36. The community is open to travelers on Saturday and Sunday for a small admission fee. You're welcome to have a look at the W. J. Dube General Store. With its coffee grinders and tin boxes still in place, it looks like the storekeeper has just walked out for a few minutes. Nearby, the Planters State Bank, which was in business from 1917 through 1932, also looks like it's open for business. A United States post office, doctor's office, and blacksmith's shop also interest visitors. Open weekends 10:00 A.M. to 6:00 P.M. Fee. (254) 986–3437.

temple

From Killeen and Fort Hood, return to I–35 and continue north to Temple. With more than 111,000 residents in the Greater Temple area, this city is the medical center for Central Texas and an important industrial producer. Temple was established by the Gulf, Colorado, and Santa Fe Railroad and named for its chief construction engineer, B. B. M. Temple. Temple is also nicknamed "The Wildflower Capital of Texas." Visitors lucky enough to arrive in late March and April are greeted by a variety of native blooms.

zabcikville

It's a little too lively to be a true Texas ghost town, but the Czech community of Zabcikville, located 10 miles east of Temple on Highway 53, is the next closest thing. During its boomtown days in the 1940s, the population reached about 80; today you'll find just a few dozen residents. There's still one good reason to make a detour to this town, though: Green's Sausage House. The only business in town packs in area diners eager to lunch on sausage burgers, hamburgers, and home-made kolaches. An adjacent meat market sells sausage, ham, turkey, bacon, and more. For hours, call (254) 985–2331.

where to go

Czech Heritage Museum. 520 North Main Street. The Czech people played an important role in settling Central Texas, and their contributions are remembered in this museum housed in the SPJST (*Slovanska Podporujici Jednota Statu Texas*, or Slavonic Benevolent Order State of Texas) Insurance Company. The museum contains Czech costumes, a circa 1530 Bible, quilts, a handmade dulcimer, and household items. Open weekdays during work hours. Free. (254) 773–1575.

Railroad and Pioneer Museum. 710 Jack Baskin Street. The old railroad depot once located in nearby Moody was transported here—boards, floor, and all. It's now a museum and library. Open afternoons, Tuesday through Saturday 10:00 A.M. to 4:00 P.M., Sunday noon to 4:00 P.M. Fee. (254) 298–5172.

where to eat

Clem Mikeska's Bar-B-Q Restaurant. 1217 South 57th Street. A member of the legendary Mikeska family, often referred to as the "first family of Texas barbecue," Clem Mikeska has been serving up 'que since 1965. Clem and his family specialize in sirloin rather than brisket barbecue. You'll also find popular favorites like homemade sausage, cole slaw, potato salad, and banana pudding. Open daily. $. (800) 344–4699 or (254) 778–5481; www.clembbq.com.

Clem Mikeska's Grill. 1217 South 57th Street. Located directly behind Clem Mikeska's Bar-B-Q Restaurant, this eatery specializes in Texas food, from chicken-fried steaks to fried catfish. An expansive salad bar rounds out the offerings. Open daily. $. (800) 344–4699 or (254) 778–5481; www.clembbq.com.

Doyle Phillips Steak House. 4011 South General Bruce Drive. This family-operated steak-house has served up chicken-fried steak, sirloin, and catfish for nearly half a century. One of the roadstop's best known dishes—chicken and dumplings—is available on Thursdays only. $–$$$. (254) 778–9951.

day trip 03

lorena, waco:
heart of texas

lorena

Located 80 miles north of Austin on Interstate 35 (see North Day Trips 1 and 2 for attractions along this drive), the community of Lorena was formerly a railroad town. Named for the daughter of a local businessman, Lorena was a thriving town before the Depression. From the 1920s until the late 1960s, Lorena was especially quiet. In 1968 renovation began on several historic structures and the town returned to life. Today the old part of the city (known as "Olde Town") is home to several antiques and specialty shops.

where to shop

The Village Lamplighter. 109 East Center Street. This shop, in business for over three decades, showcases lamps and lights of all types. Open Monday through Saturday. (254) 857–4435; www.villagelamplighter.com.

waco

Continue north on I–35 to Waco, a city of more than 113,000 named for the Waco Indians who resided here before the days of recorded history. The Wacos were attracted to this rich, fertile land at the confluence of the Brazos and Bosque Rivers.

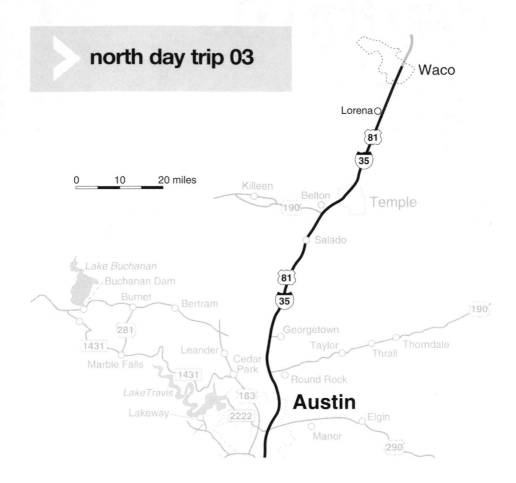

Although Spanish explorers named this site "Waco Village" in 1542, over 300 years elapsed before permanent settlement began. At that time, Waco was part of the Wild West, with cattle drives, cowboys, and so many gunslingers that stagecoach drivers called the town "Six-Shooter Junction." (Drivers routinely asked passengers to strap on their guns before the stagecoach reached the rowdy community!)

In the 1870s Waco became a center of trade with the completion of a 470-foot suspension bridge across the Brazos, the longest inland river in Texas. The bridge still stands and was designed by the same engineers who constructed New York City's Brooklyn Bridge years later.

Today Waco's Wild West heritage is tempered by a strong religious influence. The city is home to Baylor University, a Baptist liberal arts college of 12,000 students. The university has several excellent museums open to the public.

Some of the most scenic areas in Waco fall along the Brazos River. This waterway slices the city in half and provides miles of shoreline parks, shady walks, and a winding river walk. The river walk begins at Fort Fisher Park and extends to Cameron Park.

where to go

Fort Fisher Park. I–35, exit 335B. This park was once the site of Fort Fisher, an outpost of the Texas Rangers built in 1837. The lawmen established a post here to protect the Brazos River crossing. Today the park contains the City of Waco Tourist Information Center and the Texas Ranger Hall of Fame and Museum. Free. (800) WACO–FUN for information.

City of Waco Tourist Information Center. Fort Fisher. The visitors center provides helpful maps and brochures, and staff members give advice on Waco attractions, accommodations, and restaurants. Open daily. Free. (800) WACO–FUN.

Texas Ranger Hall of Fame and Museum. Fort Fisher. If you're interested in the taming of Texas, budget a couple of hours for this large museum. Visitors here can see guns of every description used by the Rangers, who had the reputation of lone lawmen who always got their man. Dioramas in the hall of fame recount the early days of the Rangers, including their founding by Stephen F. Austin. A fifty-five-minute film shows at 9:30 and 11:00 A.M., and 12:30, 2:00, and 3:30 P.M. Open daily. Fee. (254) 750–8631.

Dr Pepper Museum and Free Enterprise Institute. 300 South Fifth Street. The famous Dr Pepper soft drink was invented by pharmacist Dr. Charles Alderton at the Old Corner Drug Store in Waco, which once stood at Fourth Street and Austin Avenue. Today the drugstore is gone, but the original bottling plant remains open as a museum. Interesting exhibits and films offer a look at some early promotional materials, as well as the manufacturing process of the unusual soft drink. (Also of note: the popular advertising slogan promoting Dr Pepper as an energy booster to be consumed at "10-2-and-4.") After a look through the museum, visit the re-creation of the Old Corner Drug Store fountain for an ice cream soda or (what else?) a Dr Pepper. Open daily. Fee. (254) 757–1025; www.drpeppermuseum.com.

Armstrong-Browning Library. Eighth and Speight Streets, Baylor University campus. The works of Elizabeth Barrett Browning and husband Robert Browning fill this two-story library. The building also boasts the world's largest collection of secular stained-glass windows, which illustrate the works of both writers (including Robert Browning's *The Pied Piper of Hamlin*). Take a guided tour to see the upstairs rooms furnished with the couple's belongings. Open daily except Sunday and some university holidays. Free. (254) 710–3566; www.browninglibrary.org.

Homestead Heritage. Elm Mott. From I–35, take exit 343 and turn west on FM 308, continue 3 miles to FM 933. Turn north on FM 933 and continue 1½ miles to Halbert Lane. Turn left (west) onto Halbert Lane and continue for ½ mile. This 510-acre Christian homesteading community is the home of a 200-year-old Dutch-style barn that showcases the crafts of the village's woodworkers as well as unique quilts, wrought iron, oil lamps, and more. You can take a walking tour of the village to see the Potter's House, herb gardens, blacksmith's shop, and the restored 1760 gristmill. A deli serves all-natural sandwiches and ice creams. Open 10 A.M. to 6 P.M. Monday through Saturday. Free. (254) 829–0417; www.homestead heritage.com.

Mayborn Museum Complex. 1300 South University-Parks. This expansive museum complex includes exhibits on natural and social history of this region. Learn more about Waco with a visit to the Waco at the Crossroads of Texas Natural History Exhibits, which includes three walk-in dioramas of a limestone cave, Texas forest, and Waco mammoth experience. A popular area with children is the new Discovery Center, where sixteen themed rooms offer hands-on learning in areas that range from vertebrates to TV weather to Native Americans. Beyond the museum walls, the learning continues in fifteen wood-frame buildings found on the 13-acre Governor Bill and Vara Daniel Historic Village, a recreation of a nineteenth-century cotton town. It includes a schoolhouse, a mercantile store, and, of course, a Wild West saloon. The buildings, once the property of the Governor, were moved to this site from a plantation community in Liberty County, Texas, and restored by Baylor University. Open 10:00 A.M. to 5:00 P.M. Monday through Saturday, 1:00 P.M. to 5:00 P.M. Sunday. Fee. (254) 710–1110; www.maybornmuseum.com.

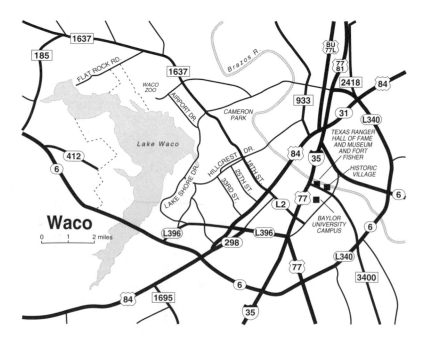

Texas Sports Hall of Fame. University Parks Drive and I–35. Waco's popular attraction is a tribute to the athletes of the Lone Star State. Sports memorabilia highlight more than 350 sports heroes, including an autographed baseball by Texas Ranger Nolan Ryan, Earl Campbell's letter jacket, and one of Martina Navratilova's Wimbledon rackets, as well as displays featuring prominent Texas high school athletes. Open daily. Fee. (800) 567–9561 or (254) 756–1633; www.tshof.org.

Cameron Park. Brazos River at Herring Avenue. This 416-acre municipal park is one of the largest in the state and holds Miss Nellie's Pretty Place, a beautiful wildflower garden filled with Texas bluebonnets. Free. (800) WACO–FUN.

Cameron Park Zoo. North Fourth Street west of I–35. This zoo features natural habitats and displays including the African savanna, Gibbon Island, Sumatran tigers, and Treetop Village. Open daily. Fee. (254) 750–8400; www.cameronparkzoo.com.

Suspension Bridge and River Walk. University Parks Drive, between Franklin and Washington Streets. Spanning the 800-mile-long Brazos River, this restored suspension bridge was once the longest in the world. Built in 1870, it eliminated the time-consuming process of having to cart cattle across the water by ferry. Today the structure is used as a pedestrian bridge bearing the motto FIRST ACROSS, STILL ACROSS. Open daily. Free. (800) WACO–FUN.

The Art Center. 1300 College Drive. This exhibit hall and teaching center is located in the Mediterranean-style home of the late lumber magnate William Waldo Cameron. Exhibits focus on Texas artists in all media. Open daily except Monday. Free. (254) 752–4371; www.artcenterwaco.org.

Historic Home Tours. Historic Waco Foundation, 810 Fourth Street. Although a devastating tornado in 1953 destroyed many of Waco's historic structures, some still remain. Visitors see four historic homes as well as the McLennan County Courthouse on this tour, all in the downtown area. One of the most interesting stops is "East Terrace," an Italian villa on the east bank of the Brazos. Here guests once slept in unheated dormitories to discourage them from overstaying their welcome! Call for hours. Fee. (254) 753–5166.

Red Men Museum and Library. 4521 Speight Avenue. This historic museum features a little bit of everything: a painting by Adolf Hitler, guns that belonged to Bonnie and Clyde, and even historic papers from various presidential periods. Open weekends and by appointment. Free. (254) 756–1221.

Lake Waco. FM 1637, 2 miles northwest of the city on North Nineteenth Street. This lake, part of the Bosque River, is a favorite with anglers and boaters. Several marinas and boat ramps offer access. Fee. Open daily. (254) 756–5359.

the western white house

The tiny community of Crawford, with a population of under 700 residents, drew international attention with the 1999 arrival of two new residents: George W. and Laura Bush. The then governor purchased the 1600-acre ranch, located northeast of town on Prairie Chapel Road, and constructed a home that soon became host to world leaders.

Today Crawford remains a quiet town except when the President is at the Prairie Chapel Ranch. Visitors can drive by the ranch, located about 8 miles northeast of town on Prairie Chapel Road. You'll know you're getting close when you see signs warning "no stopping, no standing, no parking." The ranch is located on the right side of the road heading north. To reach Crawford from Waco, head west on Highway 6 for 18 miles to the intersection of Highway 185.

Nell Pape Garden Center. 1705 North Fifth Street. Operated by the Waco Council of Garden Clubs, this center promotes garden education through programs and exhibits. The center is housed in a 1879 colonial home and is used by area garden clubs. Call for tours. (254) 752–2667.

where to shop

The Market Place. 4700 Bosque Boulevard. This shopping area, located just west of Waco Drive between Bosque and Valley Mills Drive, is filled with unique specialty stores. Shops sell furniture, religious items, china, jewelry, lamps, silver, antiques, and fine art.

Cameron Trading Company. 618 Austin Avenue. This shop, which calls itself Waco's largest antiques mall, sells all types of items ranging from fine antiques to imports and flea market finds. Open daily. (254) 756–7662.

Craft Gallery Antique and Craft Mall. 7524 Bosque Boulevard in Bosque Square. This shop is home to more than 225 vendors offering antiques, collectibles, candles, jewelry, garden accessories, stained glass, and more. Open daily. (254) 751–0693.

Spice Furniture and the Shops of River Square Center. Mary Avenue in downtown Waco. This shop, housed in a restored warehouse, sells a variety of items ranging from antiques and collectibles to specialty furniture. Open daily. (254) 757–1066.

where to eat

Lake Brazos Steakhouse. 1620 North Lake Brazos Parkway. This casual eatery serves up a Texas favorite—steak—as well as seafood, including many dishes from the Gulf. Open daily for lunch and dinner. $$. (254) 755–7797.

where to stay

Best Western Old Main Lodge. I–35 at Fourth Street. This family accommodation is located near Baylor University and includes a pool. $$. (254) 753–0316; www.bestwestern .com.

Clarion Inn. 801 South Fourth Street, off I–35. The atrium in this two-story hotel encloses a swimming pool, a hot tub, and a restaurant. $–$$. (800) 275–9226 or (254) 757–2000; www.clarionhotelwaco.com.

Comfort Inn. 1430 I–35 South. This family accommodation includes a complimentary continental breakfast and a pool. $$. (254) 752–1991; www.staycomfort.com.

Courtyard by Marriott. 101 Washington Avenue. Located across from the convention center, this hotel offers a heated pool, covered whirlpool spa, and more. $$$. (800) 321–2211 or (254) 752–8686; www.marriott.com.

La Quinta Inn. 1110 South Ninth Street. Located near Baylor University, this motel includes a complimentary continental breakfast and a pool. $$. (254) 752–9741; www.lq.com.

Lexington Inn. 115 Jack Kultgen Freeway. Close to Baylor University, this motor inn provides guests with a complimentary continental breakfast, pool, hot tub, and more. $–$$. (800) 92–SUITE or (254) 754–1266; www.lexres.com.

Hilton-Waco. 113 South University Parks Drive. Located by the convention center and Indian Spring Park, this hotel offers guests a pool, hot tub, tennis, restaurant, and more. $$. (254) 754–8484; www.waco-hilton.com.

northeast

day trip 01

northeast

>>> **taylor, thrall, thorndale, rockdale, calvert: farming heartland**

taylor

To reach Taylor, follow Interstate 35 north into Round Rock (see North Day Trip 1), then take the U.S. Highway 79 East exit and drive past the farming communities of Hutto and Frame Switch to Taylor. The route draws you through acres of cotton fields and blackland farms that stretch for miles.

Taylor's claim to fame is its International Barbecue Cook-off in August and its controversial National Rattlesnake Sacking Championship and Roundup held every March. (See "Festivals and Celebrations" at the back of this book.)

Taylor was the hometown of former Texas governor Dan Moody as well as Bill Pickett, an African-American cowboy born in the area in 1860. Pickett originated the practice of "bulldogging"—throwing a bull by twisting its head until it falls. The well-known cowboy also had a habit of biting the steer's upper lip, a trick called "biting the bull" that he practiced on the rodeo circuit.

where to go

Moody Museum. 114 West Ninth Street. Governor Dan Moody was born in this 1887 home, which today is filled with his furniture and personal belongings. He went to law school

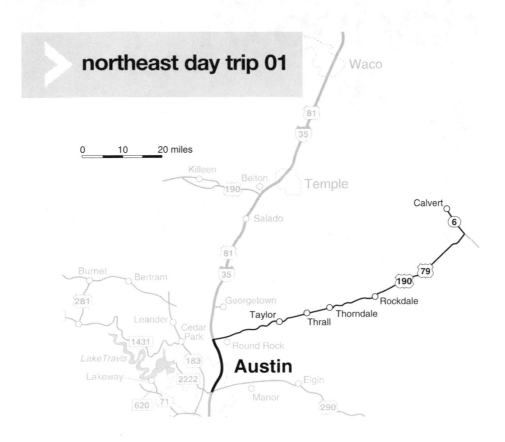

northeast day trip 01

Waco

0   10   20 miles

Killeen
Belton
Temple
190
Calvert
6
Salado
81
Burnet
Bertram
35
79
190
281
Georgetown
Rockdale
Leander
Taylor
Thorndale
Cedar
Park
Thrall
1431
Round Rock
LakeTravis
183

Austin

Lakeway
2222
Elgin
Manor
620 71
290

at the University of Texas, served in World War I, then returned to become governor at the age of thirty-three. The hometown hero was best known for prosecuting members of the Ku Klux Klan in Williamson County. Open by appointment. Free. (512) 352–5134.

where to eat

Rudy Mikeska's Bar-B-Q. 300 West Second Street. This popular restaurant tempts diners with sausage, lamb ribs, pork ribs, ham, and baby back ribs. The Mikeskas are the most famous family in a state renowned for barbecue pit masters. This restaurant has catered numerous governors' inaugurations and even served Prince Philip at a state event. Open for lunch and dinner, Monday through Saturday; lunch only on Sunday. $–$$. (800) 962–5706 or (512) 365–3722; www.mikeska.com.

Louis Mueller Barbecue. 206 West Second Street. One of the most authentic barbecue joints in Texas, this restaurant is cooled by ceiling fans and a breeze through the screen door. Diners eat off white butcher paper on simple tables, in a room decorated with free calendars and a corkboard filled with business cards (all imbued with enough smoke to give them the color of a grocery sack). But none of that matters. What matters is the barbecue: brisket, sausage, pork ribs, and steak. $–$$. (512) 352–6206.

Taylor Cafe. 101 North Main Street. This local eatery has all the atmosphere of a small-town diner—from its ceiling fans to its pool tables to the members of the local police force who often have lunch here. Barbecue is the house specialty. $. (512) 352–8475.

thrall

When oil was discovered in 1915, Thrall's population skyrocketed as more than 200 wells were drilled. As the saying goes, what goes up must come down, and Thrall was back on its way down as soon as oil production diminished. Today it's once again a quiet spot on US 79, composed of a few blocks of homes that run parallel to the railroad.

where to go

Stiles Farm Foundation. US 79, east of Thrall. This 3,200-acre farm is administered by Texas A&M University. Here new techniques are demonstrated to area farmers and ranchers. Visitors can take guided tours to see everything from hog raising to cotton growing. This is a great chance to have a look at an operating Texas farm and ranch. Call for appointment. Free. (512) 898–2214.

the mikeska dynasty

In Texas the Mikeska name is synonymous with barbecue, thanks to brothers Rudy, Maurice, Clem, Jerry, Mike, and Louis. Each man founded his own barbecue restaurant, spread throughout the state. This accomplishment made Texas Monthly proclaim the brothers "The First Family of Texas Barbecue." Their restaurants were no chain of pits, however; each brother had his own preferences and his own way of preparing barbecue. "We're a very close family," explained CEO Tim Mikeska to us, "but we all do things a little different." Through the years, we've visited all the locations, but found that each had unique menus and their own special way of preparing their specialty.

The Taylor pit was the creation of Rudy Mikeska. During his lifetime, Rudy Mikeska was the dean of Texas pitmasters. If there was a political function to be held, whether it was a policemen's fund–raiser or a governor's inauguration, Rudy Mikeska and his barbecue meats were there.

Rudy died in 1989, but he left a legacy of legendary barbecue that his children, Tim and Mopsie, continue.

smokin' in taylor

Don't be alarmed during an August visit if you see smoke rising from the central Texas town of Taylor, located northeast of Austin. That just means it's time again for the annual International Barbecue Cookoff, and contestants from around the Lone Star State are firing up their pits. With military-like precision, using recipes so carefully guarded it would make the Pentagon jealous, these cooks try their hand at preparing the best smoky delectables.

In a state where you can hardly throw a sausage link without hitting a cookoff, Taylor's is one of the largest and also one of the most prestigious for competitors. The cookoff draws some of the best pitmasters from around the Lone Star State. Although there are no cash prizes, up to one hundred teams show up every year to compete for twenty-seven cooking trophies plus prizes for showmanship. Besides the prestige of being able to claim the best brisket, poultry, lamb, goat, pork ribs, seafood, or wild game, the teams come for the pure enjoyment of the competition.

Using secret spices, the pitmasters season the meats and start the slow process of smoking over their chosen wood. Many cooks stay up through the night, basting or "mopping" the meat with marinade to keep it from drying.

Judging takes place on Saturday afternoon, and once the judging is completed, the real fun begins. Cooks are encouraged, although they are not required, to provide the public with a sample of their craft. In the relaxed atmosphere after the judging is completed, cooks also enjoy talking about the art of barbecueing, sometimes even sharing tips and secrets.

thorndale

Tiny Thorndale lies northeast of Thrall on US 79. It's another farming community built alongside the railroad tracks. As you drive through town, you can't miss the enormous cottonseed processing mill on the right, another of the many industries that make up this agricultural part of Central Texas.

rockdale

Unlike most of the other towns on this day trip, Rockdale is not known so much for farm-ing but for what lies beneath the soil. This region is rich in lignite, a soft brown coal used as a fuel to generate electricity. The resulting energy in turn fuels Alcoa, America's largest aluminum-producing facility.

where to go

Alcoa (Aluminum Company of America). Between Thorndale and Rockdale on US 79, look for a roadside park sign that says TO ALCOA; turn and follow signs to the plant. Alcoa, the largest smelter in North America, is not open to the public because of open flames and molten metal. Visitors, however, can take a drive-by tour of the facility, which is lit up like Christmas at night. The twenty-four-hour operation has a 914-acre man-made lake and power plant on one side, and the smelter plant and mine on the other. Tours offered every Wednesday and Saturday at 9:00 A.M. take visitors via bus to view the mining and plant operations. To set up a tour, call the Rockdale Chamber of Commerce. Advance registra-tion is required. (512) 446–2030.

calvert

To reach Calvert, continue northeast on U.S. Highway 79 to the intersection of U.S. Highway 190 in Hearne. Turn left and continue on US 190 (which becomes Highway 6) to the town.

In 1868 Calvert was the end of the line for the Houston and Central Railway. With more than 10,000 residents, it was the fourth-largest city in the state. P. C. Gibson, a cotton trad-er, came to the area and built the world's largest cotton gin in the 1870s. A 1965 fire and a tornado a decade later all but demolished the once-grand business. Today Calvert is home to 1,400 residents.

One of Calvert's most colorful figures was Myra Bell Shirley, better known as Belle Starr. Some say that Shirley was a Confederate spy; others say she befriended outlaws like Jesse James. Belle Starr's demise is the stuff of legend: She was shot in the back by her Indian lover, Sam Starr.

Calvert's boomtown status faded when the railroad was extended to Dallas. Things stayed quiet in Calvert for many years, but because of its many Victorian homes and refur-bished downtown businesses, the town was declared a National Historic District in 1978. Today Calvert welcomes visitors to browse in shops containing woodwork, candles, fine art, and pottery. Many travelers obtain a driving-tour brochure from the Chamber of Commerce for a drive-by look at the town's historic homes. Every Saturday, one home is open for tour-ing; call the Chamber of Commerce for the week's home tour. (979) 364–2559.

where to shop

Boll Weevil Antiques. 506 Main Street. This fine antiques shop specializes in eighteenth- and nineteenth-century furniture and porcelain. Open Friday through Sunday and by appointment. (979) 364–2835.

where to stay

Pin Oak Bed and Breakfast. 503 Pin Oak Street. This two-story home, built in 1901, is located in the city's historic district. Guests choose from five rooms (two with shared baths). Rates include breakfast. $$. (888) 367–8096 or (979) 364–2935; www.pinoakbb.com.

The Calvert Inn. 406 East Texas. This elegant bed-and-breakfast is especially known for its fine dining; the facility also has dining by reservation. $$. (800) 290–1213 or (979) 364–2868; www.calvertinn.com.

day trip 02

northeast

**bryan–college station:
presidential corridor**

bryan-college station

To reach the combined cities of Bryan–College Station, follow U.S. Highway 79 east of Round Rock to the town of Hearne on Highway 6. Turn south on Highway 6 and continue for 18 miles to Bryan–College Station, one of the largest educational centers in the state. Another route is to follow U.S. Highway 290 east of Austin. (See East Day Trips 1 and 2 for attractions along this drive.) From Brenham continue east on US 290 to Hempstead, then turn north on Highway 6 to Bryan–College Station. The US 290 drive is nicknamed the Presidential Corridor because it links Austin's LBJ Library with Bryan–College Station's Bush Library. (For more on the attractions of the Presidential Corridor, see www.rtis.com/corridor.) Home of Texas A&M University, these adjoining communities are home to more than 133,000 residents and several attractions to interest travelers.

Bryan was chartered in 1855, located in the area where early colonists led by Stephen F. Austin first settled. Agriculturally rich, the city still has an emphasis on farming thanks to Texas A&M University, the first public institution of higher learning in Texas. The college is well known for its agricultural, veterinary, and engineering programs, as well as its military Corps of Cadets.

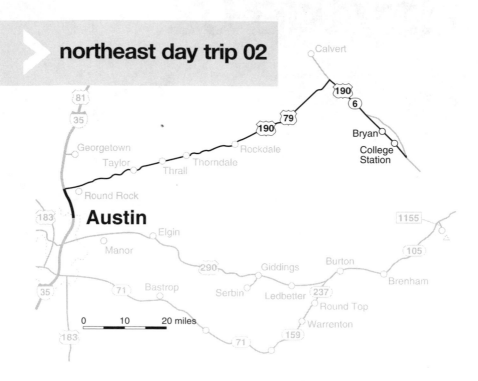

northeast day trip 02

Calvert

81
35

190
6

79
190

Georgetown
Rockdale

Bryan
College
Station

Taylor
Thorndale
Thrall

Round Rock

183

Austin

1155

Elgin

Manor

105

290
Giddings
Burton

Brenham

35

71
Bastrop

Serbin
Ledbetter
237

Round Top

0   10   20 miles

183

71

159

Warrenton

where to go

Messina Hof Wine Cellars and Vineyards. 4545 Old Reliance Road, Bryan. One of Texas's most celebrated wineries offers free tours and tastings by reservation. Started in 1983, the winery includes forty-five acres of vineyards and demonstrates the wine-making skills of the Messina, Italy, and Hof, Germany, regions. Call for hours and tour times. Free. (979) 778–9463; www.messinahof.com.

Brazos Valley Museum of Natural History. 3232 Briarcrest Drive, Bryan. Bring the whole family to this collection of natural history with exhibits on life in the Brazos Valley more than 12,000 years ago. Open daily. Fee. (979) 776–2195; http://bvmuseum.myriad.net/.

George Bush Presidential Library Center and Museum. 1000 West George Bush Drive, College Station. The state's newest presidential library contains exhibits on the first Bush presidency as well as research materials in the library center. Open daily. Fee. (979) 691–4000; http://bushlibrary.tamu.edu.

Texas A&M University. Several sites at this large college in College Station are of special interest to visitors including the Floral Test Garden (Houston and Jersey Streets). Stroll among hundreds of varieties of flowers planted and studied by university students. (979) 845–3211; www.tamu.edu.

Sam Houston Sanders Corps of Cadets Center. Learn more about the Corps of Cadets through College Station's displays that trace the graduates' service in World Wars I and II, Korea, Vietnam, the Gulf War, and more recent conflicts. (979) 862–2862; http://aggiecorps .tamu.edu/home/corpscenter.

D. A. "Andy" Anderson Arboretum. Bee Creek Park, 1900 Anderson Street, College Station. Learn more about the local flora and fauna at this wetlands arboretum. Free. (979) 764–3410.

The Children's Museum of the Brazos Valley. 111 East 27th Street, Bryan. Teaching through hands-on exhibits, this museum gives kids the opportunity to do everything from shopping for groceries to creating a puppet show. Open Monday through Saturday. Fee. (979) 779–KIDS; www.mymuseum.com.

Benz Gallery of Floral Art. Texas A&M University in the Horticultural and Forest Sciences Building on the west side of campus. This museum features everything related to floral art. Open weekdays. Free. (979) 845–1699.

MSC Forsyth Center Galleries. Texas A&M University in the Memorial Student Center. This gallery features both touring exhibits and an extensive glass display. Open daily. Free. (979) 845–9251.

J. Wayne Stark University Center Galleries. Texas A&M University in the Memorial Student Center. This gallery features Texas art and artists. Open Tuesday through Friday and weekend afternoons. Free. (979) 845–8501.

bonfire memorial

Throughout the state, the Texas Aggies had long been known for their pre-game bonfires, a tradition that dated back to 1909. On November 18, 1999, the tradition came to a halt when twelve students were killed by the collapse of a massive bonfire. To memorialize the fallen students and the longtime tradition, the university constructed the Bonfire Memorial, a circular ring with doorways representing each of the lost students. The History Walk leading up to the memorial traces the longtime tradition with a timeline, leading up to the 170-foot diameter circle, one that represents the size of an actual Aggie bonfire. The memorial is located on the Polo Fields at the TAMU campus.

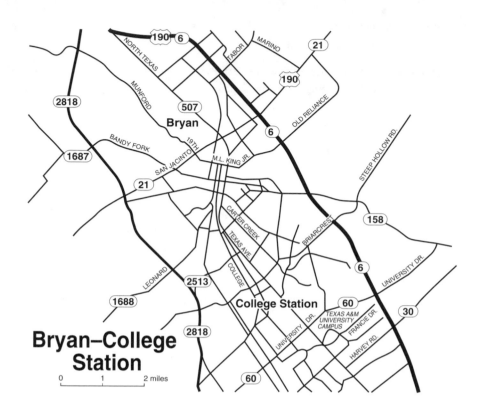

Bryan–College Station

0   1   2 miles

Benjamin Knox Gallery. 405 University Drive East, College Station. This gallery features the work of Benjamin Knox, known locally as the "University Artist." Along with fine art, the gallery sells gift items.

where to shop

The Texas Store. 1500 Harvey Road in the Post Oak Mall, College Station. This shop features Texas goods from western hats to foods from the Lone Star State. Open daily. (979) 693–2061.

The Garden District. 106–108 North Avenue, Bryan. This unique shopping area is housed in a neoantebellum home. Shops stock unique gift and specialty items including designer jewelry, candles, children's heirloom clothing, and collectibles. Open Monday through Saturday.

where to eat

Cenare. 404 University Drive, College Station. This restaurant features Italian cuisine ranging from veal marsala to homemade pastas. $$–$$$. (979) 696–7311.

Christopher's World Grille. 5001 Boonville Road, Bryan. Bryan chef Christopher Lampo spent ten years wandering the globe before returning to the region to restore a hundred-year-old ranch home and transform it into a fine dining destination. Mediterranean, South Pacific, and Louisiana touches grace the menu, which includes chile-cocoa rubbed ribeye on andouille sausage grits, Zihuatanejo Snapper, and roasted Halibut Provencale. Open for lunch and dinner daily; reservations encouraged. $$$. (979) 776–2181; www.christophers worldgrille.com.

where to stay

Villa Bed and Breakfast. 4545 Old Reliance Road. One of Texas's unique bed-and-breakfast properties, the Villa is located above the Messina Hof Winery. Featuring a full-size bed, private bath, and television, it is a place where couples can enjoy an evening alone in the vineyards at this romantic hideaway. Book early for this popular getaway on weekends and holidays. $$. (979) 778–9463; www.messinahof.com.

Bed and Breakfast Texas Style, Inc. Call this reservation service for local bed-and-breakfast inns, guest cottages, and ranches. Prices vary with accommodation. (800) 899–4538 or (409) 860–9100; www.bnbtexasstyle.com.

Hilton Hotel and Conference Center. 801 University Drive East, College Station. This hotel offers guests a pool, exercise facilities, restaurant, private balconies, and more. $$. (979) 693–7500; www.hilton.com.

east

day trip 01

east

>>> manor, elgin, mcdade, giddings, serbin: sausage country

manor

To reach Manor, drive east from Austin on U.S. Highway 290. Manor was named for settler James Manor, who came to the state with Sam Houston. This community was a quiet suburb until a few years ago, when Texas legalized pari-mutuel wagering. Today the town is home to Manor Downs, a quarterhorse track that holds fall races from September through December and a spring season starting in February. Races are held on Friday, Saturday, and Sunday afternoons. Call for race times. Fee. (512) 272–5581; www.manordowns.com.

elgin

Continue east from Manor on US 290 to Elgin. This city began as a railroad stop in 1872, named for the railroad commissioner. Often mispronounced (it rhymes with *again*), Elgin is known for two products: bricks and sausage. Red Elgin bricks are seen throughout Texas, and Elgin sausage is so prevalent the city has been named by the Texas Legislature as the "sausage capital of Texas."

Much of the city lies along US 290, but its real history is found off the highway in its historic downtown. Named a Main Street City for its preservation efforts, the downtown is home to several renovated buildings that now house shops.

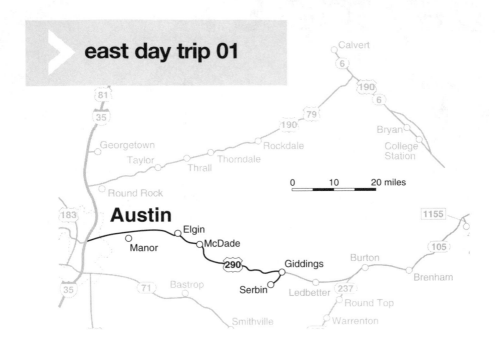

east day trip 01

where to go

Historic Tour. Pick up a copy of the free historic tour brochure at the Chamber of Commerce office at 114 Central Avenue. (512) 285–4515.

where to shop

Meyer's Elgin Sausage. 188 US 290. Stop here to buy a gift box or a freezer full of Elgin's most famous product: sausage. (512) 281–5546.

Elgin Antique Mall. 1100 US 290. This multidealer mall, spanning more than 10,000 square feet, is filled with everything antique and collectible, from furniture to dolls to housewares. The merchandise changes continually, brought to the mall by more than fifty dealers. Open daily. (512) 281–5655.

where to eat

Southside Market and B-B-Q. 1212 US 290 West. This casual barbecue eatery has been the source of Elgin sausage since 1882. The back dining room is filled with Formica tables, the smell of smoke, and happy customers. Open for lunch, early dinner, and takeout. Closed Sunday. $. (512) 281–4650; www.southsidemarket.com.

City Cafe. 19 North Main Street. Stop by for the lunch buffet at this downtown diner that serves up traditional small-town cookin' at its best. $. (512) 281–3663.

mcdade

About 5 miles outside of Elgin lies the small community of McDade. The town was named for a Brenham lawyer in 1871 and has always depended heavily on farming and ranching. The town is especially noted for its watermelon crop. An annual watermelon festival is held the second Saturday in July.

giddings

From McDade, continue east on US 290 to Giddings. This town began as a railroad community in the 1870s. At that time, most of the residents of Giddings were Wendish immigrants (Germans of Slavic descent); these founders later moved to the community of Serbin. Today Giddings remains a quiet railroad town, although oil production has taken over as the major economic activity.

hot guts

Yes, it's true; Elgin sausage is sometimes (make that often) referred to as Elgin Hot Guts. No, it's not an appetizing moniker. Nonetheless, this spicy sausage is the standard against which other Texas sausages are judged.

We both grew up cutting our teeth on this hot links, a staple at Sunday dinners, picnics, and any special event throughout the state. The best known of Elgin's smokin' stops is the Southside Market (1212 US 290 West), probably one of the most recognized names in Texas barbecue lore. In business since 1882, the market is known for its sausage. The mainstay in many barbecue restaurants around the state, the Southside's product is what many people have in mind when they order sausage. Spicy but not hot, the concoction is all beef.

For generations, Southside was located in a smoky den that spoke volumes about the history of barbecue. Sadly, the business outgrew its old home and now sits in a red tin building with a concrete floor—less atmospheric but now one of the largest barbecue restaurants in the state. The building may have changed, but the product remains the same. It's one we pick up fresh whenever we pass through Elgin; the smoky scent serves as a fragrant billboard long before you reach the Southside building.

where to go

Fireman's Park. Two miles west of Giddings on US 290. This park includes an RV park, picnic grounds, ball field, adjacent rodeo grounds, and even an antique carousel. The carousel, restored by local citizens, was left in Giddings during the Depression by a traveling carnival as a debt payment. Today it is run only during city events. Open daily. Free.

Lee County Museum. Grimes and Industry Streets. This small museum contains numerous local history displays. It is located in the former house of a pioneer doctor. Open Tuesday and Friday afternoons 2:00 to 5:00 P.M. No phone.

serbin

Turn south on U.S. Highway 77, then south again on FM 448, continuing for 5 miles. At the intersection of FM 2239, turn right and continue 2 miles to the hamlet of Serbin.

This town was settled by the Wendish, who came to Texas in the 1850s and brought with them the Gothic architecture of their homeland. From 1865 to 1890 this was a thriving town, boasting dry goods, jewelry, music stores, a drug store, three doctors, and two dentists. When Serbin was bypassed by the railroad, it quickly declined.

where to go

St. Paul Lutheran Church. Off FM 2239. The historic St. Paul Lutheran Church, a smaller version of the elaborate German cathedrals of the eighteenth and nineteenth centuries, was built in 1859 of native sandstone. To replicate marble, the parishioners painted the plaster walls using turkey feather brushes. This church once had an unusual seating arrangement: Men sat in the balcony across from the pulpit, women and children took the pews on the floor. Open daily. Free. (979) 366–9650.

Texas Wendish Heritage Museum. Off FM 2239, near St. Paul Lutheran Church. You'll find antique furniture and household items as well as photos of the early days in this local history museum. Open 1:00 to 5:00 P.M. Tuesday through Sunday. Fee (students free). (979) 366–2441.

day trip 02

east

>>> ledbetter, burton, brenham, washington-on-the-brazos: birthplace of texas

This day trip is an extension of East Day Trip 1, for travelers looking for a more extended getaway. This trip is filled with history.

Begin by taking U.S. Highway 290 East from Austin beyond Elgin and Giddings, following a route nicknamed the Presidential Corridor.

ledbetter

From Giddings, drive east on US 290 for 9 miles to the tiny community of Ledbetter. Once the first town in the county to boast a railroad, its importance declined when nearby La Grange became a freight center.

where to go

Stuermer Store. South side of US 290. This metal building has served as a general store since 1870. At one time, the current owner's grandfather ran a saloon next door. Now the businesses are joined, creating a general store, museum, and soda shop all in one. A working museum exhibits the tools of the early grocery, from cheese cutters to coffee grinders. Today the wildest drink in the saloon is an old-fashioned malt. You can order up some local Blue Bell ice cream or fresh sandwiches at the fountain and listen to a free tune on a jukebox packed with oldies. Open Monday through Saturday. Free admission. (979) 249–3066; www.ledbettertexas.com.

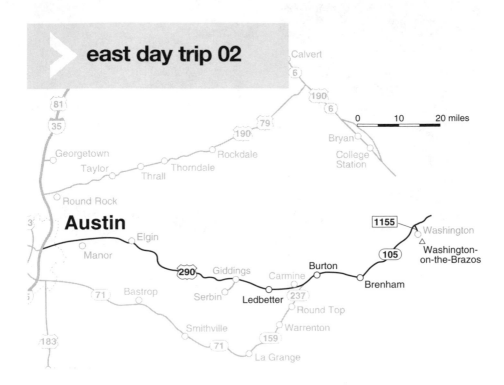

east day trip 02

burton

Follow US 290 east past the tiny town of Carmine, which is full of antiques shops (open Saturday only), to the tiny agricultural community of Burton, located just off US 290 on FM 390. With a population of slightly more than 300, this town has a surprising number of shops and businesses, many open only on weekends.

Take some time to walk around the historic buildings and drop in to the Burton Cafe. Here you can make arrangements for a guide to take you on a tour of the restored cotton gin, railroad depot, and old caboose.

where to go

Burton Cotton Gin. Main Street, across from the Burton Cafe. Stop in the Burton Cafe to arrange for a forty-five-minute tour of this restored gin, a National Historic Landmark. You'll see the engine room, the mechanical floor, the ginning floor, and an old cobbler shop where harnesses were made for the horses that pulled the cotton wagons. Tours can be conducted in German. Open on a walk-in basis. Fee. (979) 289–3378; www.cottongin museum.org.

brenham

Return to US 290 and continue east to Brenham. In this state, Brenham means the Blue Bell Creamery. This is one of the biggest independent manufacturers of ice cream in the country, selling more than twenty-five million half-gallon containers a year. It's as Texan as bluebonnets and two-stepping, and expatriates have been known to carry back picnic freezers full of Brenham's product.

Brenham has a host of other less-fattening attractions as well, including a historic downtown that's filled with antiques and specialty shops, and residential streets that showcase splendid antebellum and Victorian homes.

A free visitors' guide of historic sites is available from the Washington County Chamber of Commerce, 314 South Austin Street in Brenham. (888) BRENHAM or (979) 836–3695.

where to go

Blue Bell Creamery. FM 566 off US 290 West. Blue Bell has been making ice cream since 1911, when it packaged its product in wooden tubs and delivered it by horse-drawn wagon. The "tasting room" here is an antique soda shop, where visitors can choose from among twenty-five flavors. After a free dish of your personal favorite, you can have a look around the Country Store, which sells everything from strawberry-scented pencils to piggy banks in the shape of the company's early delivery trucks. Open daily. Tours conducted Monday through Friday; call for times. Fee. (800) 327–8135 or (979) 830–2197; www.bluebell.com.

Monastery of St. Clare Miniature Horse Ranch. Highway 105, 9 miles northeast of Brenham. This monastery is occupied by a group of Catholic nuns who raise and sell miniature horses to support themselves. The tiny horses, some less than 34 inches tall, bring in anywhere from $3,000 to $30,000. On self-guided tours visitors see the barn and grooming facilities (with miniature carriages and harnesses) and the Mini Mansion where the horses are reared. The Art Barn brims with thousands of ceramics made by the nuns, including tiny reproductions of the horses. Open daily 2:00 to 4:00 P.M. Free. (979) 836–9652.

Ellison's Greenhouses. Horton and Stone Streets, south of Blue Bell Creamery on Loop 577. Ellison's produces African violets, Easter lilies, mums, tulips, and many other decorative flowers. Every year it grows 250,000 poinsettia cuttings and 80,000 finished poinsettias, some of which find their way to the State Capitol and Governor's Mansion. Open Monday through Saturday; guided tours Friday and Saturday 11:00 A.M. and 1:00 P.M. Fee. (979) 836–0084.

Pleasant Hill Winery. 1441 Salem Road, just south of US 290 and Highway 36 intersection. Travel just a few hundred yards west and a hillside vineyard will appear. Free tours and tastings are offered inside the carefully reconstructed old barn at the top of the hill. Enjoy the spectacular view of the vineyard below. Spend some time studying the corkscrew collection and winery artifacts, or just enjoy the warmth and beauty of the barn's interior. The tour will take you through the path of the grape as it makes its transformation from vine to wine. Gift shop with Texas wines and souvenirs for sale. Open Saturday 11:00 A.M. to 6:00 P.M. and Sunday noon to 5:00 P.M. Groups may request other tour times by appointment. Fee. (979) 830–VINE; www.pleasanthillwinery.com.

John P. Coles Home Tours. Guided tours of the area's earliest homes (built during the days of independence) are available on weekends during spring months as well as other times by appointment. The tours include a look at early dogtrot-style cabins, a 1900 one-room schoolhouse, and more. Fee. (979) 830–0230.

Baptist Historical Center. Twelve miles north of Brenham at the intersection of FM 50 and Highway 390 in Independence. This Baptist church was once attended by Sam Houston. It is one of the state's oldest Baptist churches as well as the birthplace of Baylor University. Open daily 9:00 A.M. to 4:00 P.M. Free. (979) 836–5117.

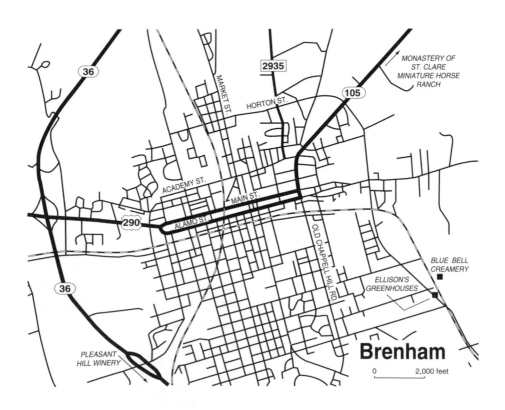

where to stay

The Brenham area is home to more than thirty bed-and-breakfasts, many located in historic homes or on local farms. The city also has several motels. For more information on accommodations, call (888) BRENHAM or write Brenham-Washington County Convention and Visitor Bureau, 314 South Austin Street, Brenham, TX 77833 or see www.brenham texas.com.

James Walker Homestead. Old Chappell Hill Road, a few miles east of Brenham. This structure was built in 1826 as the home of James Walker, one of the first 300 colonists who came to Texas with Stephen F. Austin. Today the original log construction is still visible inside the home, which is furnished with Texas antiques. The bed-and-breakfast does not allow children, and no smoking is permitted in the house. Lodging includes one bedroom with sleeper bed for extra guests. $$$; (979) 836–6717.

Nueces Canyon Equestrian Center and Resort. 9501 US 290 West. This expansive equestrian center offers group activities on a working ranch. Guests can watch cutting horses at work, enjoy a hayride, and relax with a barbecue dinner. The center also hosts cutting horse shows most weekends. Accommodations are available as well. Advance reservations are required for all tours and activities. $$. (800) 925–5058 or (979) 289–5600; www.nuecescanyon.com.

washington-on-the-brazos

To reach this community, alternately called Washington and Washington-on-the-Brazos, take Highway 105 northeast of Brenham for 14 miles, then turn right on FM 912.

The town dates back to the days of a ferry landing on the Brazos River that operated at the site from 1822. Washington has become best known, however, as the birthplace of Texas. On a cold March day in 1836, founders gathered here and signed the Declaration of Independence, establishing Texas as a sovereign nation.

From 1842 to 1845, Washington served as the capital of the republic, also gradually becoming a commerce center on the busy Brazos. When the seat of government was moved to Austin, the town hung on, kept alive by its position on the river. Eventually, though, in the 1850s, Washington was bypassed by the railroads, and the community dwindled to a tiny dot on the map.

One of the hidden treasures of the Texas parks system is the Washington-on-the-Brazos State Historical Park. Today the park includes a new visitor center and interpretive trails to introduce visitors to the importance of this site where the early Texans declared an independent and sovereign nation.

Near the center, the Star of the Republic Museum, built in the shape of a star, highlights the history of the Republic of Texas with exhibits and special collections. Exhibits cover all aspects of commerce during the nineteenth century, including displays on the general store, blacksmithing, steamboats, and carpentry.

The park's interpretive trail winds from Independence Hall—a replica of the original building where the signing of the Texas Declaration of Independence took place—to the historic Washington town site. To reach Washington-on-the-Brazos State Historical Park from Brenham, take Highway 105 northeast of the city for 14 miles, then turn right on FM 912 to reach the park. The facility is open daily from 8:00 A.M. to sundown.

where to go

Washington-on-the-Brazos State Historical Park. Located on the banks of the Brazos, this quiet park is shaded by acres of walnut and pecan trees. This is a day-use park, with picnic tables along the river. Free. Its three main sections include the following points of interest:

Independence Hall. The original building where the signing of the Texas Declaration of Independence took place did not survive the nineteenth century. In 1901 a group of citizens erected a monument at the site. The simple frame building reconstructed here holds long, mismatched tables and unadorned chairs. Open daily. Fee. (936) 878–2214.

Barrington Living History Farm. This was once the home of Anson Jones, the fourth and last president of the Republic of Texas. This site includes a two-story home that has been relocated, an orchard, demonstration garden, carriage shed, corn crib, kitchen, and more. Open Wednesday through Saturday 10:00 A.M. to 5:00 P.M. and Sunday 11:00 A.M. to 5:00 P.M. Fee. (936) 878–2214.

Star of the Republic Museum. Built in the shape of the Lone Star State, this museum covers the republic period. Visitors can start with a twenty-minute film narrated by Bill Moyers for an overview of the period. Upstairs, exhibits cover all aspects of commerce during the nineteenth century, including displays on the general store, steamboats, blacksmithing, and carpentry. Open daily. Fee. (936) 878–2461; www.starmuseum.org.

southeast

day trip 01

southeast

>>> **bastrop, alum creek, smithville, la grange: lost pines**

bastrop

To reach Bastrop, take Highway 71 southeast from Austin. Unlike the juniper-dotted hills to the west or the rolling farmland to the east, the Bastrop area is surrounded by a pine forest called Lost Pines. Here grows the westernmost stand of loblolly pines in America. Scientists believe that these trees were once part of the forests of East Texas, but climatic changes over the last 10,000 years account for the farmland now separating the Lost Pines from their cousins to the east.

Bastrop holds the honor as one of the oldest settlements in the state, built in 1829 along the Camino Real, a road also known as the King's Highway and the Old San Antonio Road. This was the western edge of the "Little Colony" established by Stephen F. Austin. Settlers came by the wagonload from around the country to claim a share of this fertile land and to establish a home in this dangerous territory. Even as homes were being erected, Indian raids continued in this area for many years.

Bastrop is a popular day trip for Austinites looking for a chance to shop and savor some quiet country life in a historic setting. Outdoor lovers can enjoy two nearby state parks and also the Colorado River, which winds through the heart of downtown. Canoe rentals and guided trips along the river are available.

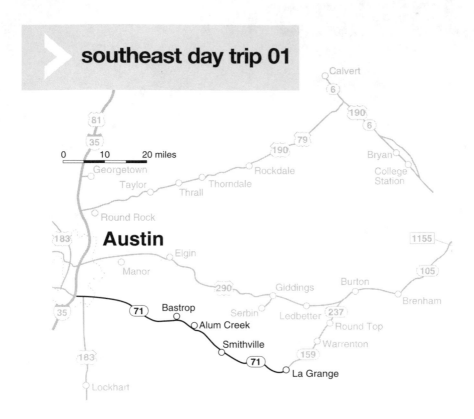

> ## southeast day trip 01

Calvert
6
190
6
81
35
190
79
0   10   20 miles
Georgetown   Rockdale   Bryan
Taylor   Thorndale   College
Thrall   Station
Round Rock
183   **Austin**   1155
Elgin
105
Manor
Burton
290   Giddings   Brenham
35   71   Bastrop   Serbin   Ledbetter   237
Alum Creek   Round Top
Smithville   Warrenton
183   71   159
La Grange
Lockhart

where to go

Chamber of Commerce. 927 Main Street. Stop by this office for maps and brochures, including "A Walking Tour of Historic Bastrop." The Chamber of Commerce can assist in coordinating day and overnight tours of homes, churches, historic sites, and other attractions. (512) 303–0558; www.bastropchamber.com.

Lock's Drug. 1003 Main Street. This drugstore features an antique mirrored fountain where you can belly up for a thick, creamy malt. Built-in cabinets are still labeled with the names of their original contents, and old apothecary tools sit in the front windows. Open daily except Sunday. (512) 321–2551.

Bastrop County Historical Society Museum. 702 Main Street. This 1850 frame cabin contains Indian relics and pioneer exhibits. Open afternoons daily. Fee. (512) 303–0057.

Bastrop State Park. Highway 21, 1.5 miles east of Bastrop. Beautiful piney woods are the main draw at this 3,500-acre park, the fourth busiest state park in Texas. Facilities include an eighteen-hole golf course, campsites, and a ten-acre fishing lake. The 1930s-built stone and cedar cabins are very popular and should be booked well in advance. They feature fireplaces, bathrooms, and kitchen facilities. Guided bus tours every other Saturday during summer months introduce visitors to the park's unique ecology and to an endangered resident, the Houston toad. Fee. (512) 321–2101 for park information or (512) 389–8900 for reservations; www.tpwd.state.tx.us.

Bastrop Opera House. 711 Spring Street. Built in 1889, this building was once the entertainment center of town. After a major renovation in 1978, it's again the cultural center of Bastrop, the site for live theater ranging from mysteries to vaudeville. Call for show schedule. (512) 321–6283.

Central Texas Museum of Automotive History. South on FM 304 to FM 535; left 1 mile to Rosanky. This private museum is dedicated to the collection and preservation of old cars and accessories. The vehicles on display include a 1935 Rolls Royce Phantom, a La France fire engine, and a 1922 Franklin. Open Friday through Sunday October to March; Wednesday through Sunday April to September. Fee. (512) 237–2635; www.ctmah.org.

McKinney Roughs LCRA Preserve. Eight miles west of Bastrop at 1884 Highway 71. A favorite with both hikers and equestrians, this 1,100-acre park preserves several ecosystems as well as an extensive riverbank. Open Tuesday through Saturday 8:00 A.M. to 5:00 P.M., Sunday 1:00 to 5:00 P.M. Fee. (512) 303–5073; www.lcra.org.

Riverwalk. Enjoy this nature walk along the banks of the Colorado River. Opened in 1998, the half-mile trail features a variety of trees, native plants, and wildflowers. It is accessible from either Fisherman's or Ferry Park. Free.

where to shop

Park your car and enjoy an afternoon of browsing through the many antiques and specialty stores along Main Street.

Apothecary's Hall. 805 Main Street. Shop in this downtown store for antiques ranging from collectibles to furniture. (512) 321–3022.

Old Town Emporium. 815 Main Street. You'll find all kinds of crafts and specialty gifts in this large store. (512) 321–3635.

alum creek

Continue east from Bastrop on Highway 71 and soon you'll reach the crossing of Alum Creek. In 1828, this was the site of a fort used by several families during the area's most active Indian days. Years later this spot was used as a stagecoach stop. Today all that's left of the community of Alum Creek is a collection of more than a dozen antiques and junk shops. It's a fun stop for avid collectors. The shops are located on the left side of the road as you head east; many are open weekends only.

smithville

Continue east from Bastrop on Highway 71 to Smithville, a small town that's built alongside the railroad tracks at the edge of the piney woods and home of Buescher State Park. Smithville was once a riverboat ferry stop on the Colorado River. In the 1880s, the railroad replaced the ferries as the main mode of transportation, and tracks were laid across town. Today the railroad still plays an important part in Smithville's economy.

Smithville gained national attention as the site of the filming of the Sandra Bullock movie *Hope Floats.* Many local citizens had small parts in the film.

where to go

Jim Long Railroad Park Museum. 100 West First Street. Built beside the tracks, this park has two cabooses and a depot relocated here from West Point, a community east of town. The Chamber of Commerce office is housed in the depot as well. Open daily; hours vary, so call ahead. Free. (512) 237–2313.

Buescher State Park. 3 miles north of town, via Highway 71 and FM 2104, or access from Park Road 1. Buescher (pronounced "BISH-er") neighbors Bastrop State Park, but the two boast different environments. Oaks dominate this park, along with a few pines. The park is especially popular for its thirty-acre lake. Visitors can enjoy ample campsites and screened shelters, as well as a playground and picnic area. Fee. (512) 237–2241; www.tpwd .state.tx.us.

Smithville Heritage Society Museum. 602 Main Street. This 1908 home contains the Smithville archives and a museum of local memorabilia. Open Tuesday mornings. Free. (512) 237–4545.

Rocky Hill Ranch Mountain Bike Resort. FM 153, 2 miles northeast of Buescher State Park. Beginner, intermediate, advanced, and expert trails tempt mountain bikers with more than 1,200 acres that include gentle slopes and challenging grades as well as stream crossings. More than 30 miles of trails are available for use by helmeted bicycle riders. The ranch includes a casual restaurant with horseshoes, shuffleboard, and beach volleyball; campsites are available along small creeks and spring-fed water holes. Fee. (512) 237–3112.

la grange

Just 4 miles southeast of Smithville on the left side of Highway 71 is a scenic overlook, an excellent place to pull over for a picnic. From here you can gaze at the miles of rolling hills and farmland that attracted many German and Czech immigrants a century ago.

Continue on Highway 71 to the infamous community of La Grange. For generations this was a quiet town in the center of a farming region. In the 1970s, however, La Grange caught the attention of the public with the unveiling of the Chicken Ranch, a brothel that became the subject of the Broadway musical and movie *The Best Little Whorehouse in Texas*. Today the Chicken Ranch is gone, but La Grange still has other sights to see.

where to go

Monument Hill-Kreische Brewery State Historic Site. U.S. Highway 77, 1 mile south of La Grange. Located on a 200-foot bluff high above town, this site is the home to two combined parks.

Monument Hill Historical Park is the burial site for the Texans who died in the Dawson Massacre and the Mier Expedition, two historic Mexican conflicts that occurred in 1842, six

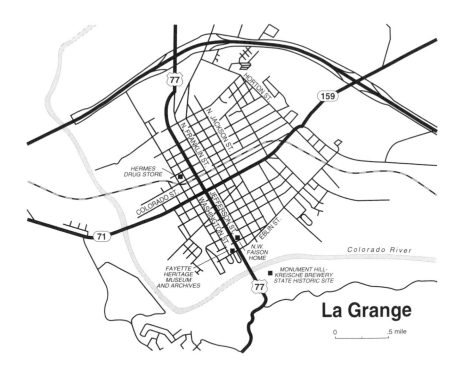

La Grange

0   .5 mile

years after the Texas Revolution. The Dawson Massacre took place near San Antonio when La Grange citizen Nicholas Dawson gathered Texans to halt the continual Mexican attacks. Dawson's men were met by hundreds of Mexican troops, and thirty-five Texans were killed.

The Mexican village of Mier was attacked in a retaliatory move, resulting in the capture of Texas soldiers and citizens by Mexico's General Santa Anna, who ordered every tenth man to be killed. The Texans were blindfolded and forced to draw beans: 159 of them white and 17 black. Men who drew white beans were imprisoned; those who drew black ones were executed.

The Kreische Brewery State Historical Site recalls a far more cheerful time in Texas history. Heinreich Kreische was a German who immigrated here from Europe. In 1849 he purchased the hilltop and the adjoining land, including the burial ground of those Texas heroes, for his brewery site. Before closing the brewery in 1884, Kreische became the third largest beer producer in the state. Open daily until 5:00 P.M. Fee (one admission covers both adjacent sites). (979) 968–5658; www.tpwd.state.tx.us.

Hermes Drug Store. 148 North Washington Street. Established in 1856, this is the oldest drugstore in continuous operation in Texas. Visitors can see authentic old-time structures, beveled mirrors, and more. Open Monday through Saturday. (979) 968–5835.

the chicken ranch

La Grange drew international attention in 1973 when the story of what many believe was the country's oldest continually run brothel was exposed by consumer-affairs reporter Marvin Zindler from KTRK-TV in Houston. The report would inspire a Broadway musical and movie as well as lot of curiosity about the site, which was located on eleven acres outside of La Grange. The house, which was added on many times as the number of women increased, was nicknamed the Chicken Ranch during the Great Depression. When customers grew fewer, the proprietor, a woman known as Miss Jessie, began allowing men to pay in chickens. Soon the ranch was overrun with both poultry and eggs, both of which they sold locally.

As economic times improved, the ranch returned to a cash basis and ownership changed in 1952 to Edna Milton, a madam who become one of La Grange's largest philanthropists.

When the Chicken Ranch closed, the building was moved to Dallas and, for a while, became a chicken restaurant.

N. W. Faison Home. 822 South Jefferson Street. N. W. Faison was a survivor of both the Dawson Massacre and the Mier Expedition in 1842. The Faison family resided in this home for more than twenty years, and today it contains the family's furniture as well as exhibits from the Mexican War. Open by appointment. Fee. (800) 524–7264.

Fayette Heritage Museum and Archives. 855 South Jefferson Street. Housed with the public library, this museum contains displays on the area's rich history. Call for hours. Free. (979) 968–6418.

day trip 02

southeast

**warrenton, round top:
petite getaway**

This day trip continues the journey through Bastrop and La Grange. Follow Highway 71 through these communities, then join up with this day trip for a look at historic and cultural attractions plus some excellent shopping.

warrenton

From La Grange, head northeast on Highway 159 to Highway 237. Continue on TX 237 through Oldenburg to this tiny community. Warrenton is best known as the home of the smallest Catholic church in the world. St. Martin's, on the left side of the road as you head north, is a simple white frame building. Inside the Lilliputian house of worship, plain wooden benches serve as pews before an ornate altar. Step inside for a look; visitors are welcome.

where to go

Sterling McCall's Old Car Museum. 4212 Highway 237. Car buffs enjoy this museum, which traces the evolution of automobiles. Open Thursday and Friday 11:00 A.M. to 5:00 P.M., weekends 10:00 A.M. to 5:00 P.M. Fee. (979) 249–5089; www.oldcarcountry.com.

round top

St. Martin's is a preview of another pint-size attraction along this day trip: the smallest incorporated town in Texas. Continue north on Highway 237 to Round Top. Officially founded in 1835 by settlers from Stephen F. Austin's second colony, this town is filled with restored homes, log cabins, and country stores.

Round Top is also home to a world-class music facility. Festival Hill, located just outside of town, offers performances by visiting symphony orchestras under the summer stars.

"Downtown" Round Top consists of several blocks flanking the old courthouse. Today the county seat is located in nearby La Grange, but the lawn of the Round Top courthouse is still faithfully maintained by the DYD (Do Your Duty) Women's Club, as it has been since the 1930s.

where to go

Henkel Square Museum Village. Highway 237, on the town square. This is one of the finest restorations of pioneer buildings in the state. This collection of forty historic homes and businesses, dating from 1824 to 1915, was assembled from around Fayette County. The

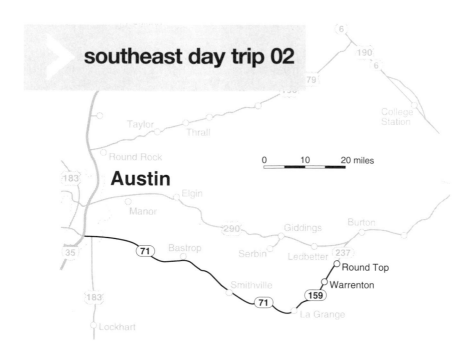

southeast day trip 02

0   10   20 miles

apothecary shop now serves as a visitor center, where tours of the schoolhouse-church, log house, and the Henkel house originate. Open Thursday through Sunday noon to 5:00 P.M. Fee. (979) 249–3308.

Festival Hill. Highway 237, 5 blocks north of Henkel Square. This music and theater center was founded by noted pianist James Dick. During the school year, Festival Hill presents monthly concerts. In the summer, the center hosts students from around the world who entertain guests with musical performances. The center is housed in historic buildings, including an 1870 farmhouse and a former African-American school.

The focal point of Festival Hill is the concert hall, a 1,000-seat limestone structure whose interior, when not hosting a concert, is still a construction zone. In its grandiose scale and its dedication to craftsmanship, the concert hall rises from its rural surroundings like a grand cathedral looming above a European town. Work continues on the concert hall and the rest of the Festival Hill on a pay-as-you-go basis.

Even if you don't have the opportunity to attend a concert, call to schedule a tour of the center. Your look at Festival Hill can include the David Guion Museum Room, housing a collection of belongings and music of this Texas composer, and the Oxehufwud Room, a collection of Swedish decorative arts that recall the life of a Swedish noble family whose final member retired in La Grange. Bring a picnic lunch and enjoy the one-hundred-acre grounds, which are planted with thousands of trees and include walking trails and a recently completed stonework bridge, constructed to resemble a Roman footbridge. Fee. (979) 249–3129; www.festivalhill.org.

Winedale Historical Center. Four miles east of Round Top via FM 1457; north on FM 2714. Operated by the University of Texas at Austin, this center hosts annual Shakespeare productions. A cast of students from assorted disciplines have come to Winedale every summer for the past two decades to perform the works of the Bard in an old hay barn. For fifteen to eighteen hours a day, the students make costumes, prepare lighting, and practice for the performances that draw visitors from Austin and Houston. Public performances are held Thursday through Sunday evenings in late July and early August. (979) 278–3530; www.shakespeare-winedale.org.

Although Shakespeare at Winedale is a summer-only activity, the center is a year-round attraction. The 215-acre complex is home to a collection of historic structures, a research center, a nature trail, and a picnic area. Weekend tours take visitors through homes furnished with period antiques and details such as stenciled ceilings that recall the German culture of the area. Fee. (979) 278–3530.

The Jersey Barnyard. Highway 159, about 1.4 miles northeast of Highway 71 bypass. Children enjoy this attraction, a dairy farm that offers them a chance to feed barnyard animals and take a hayride. Open daily. Fee. (979) 249–3406.

where to shop

Round Top General Store. Highway 237. Since 1848 this general store has been serving the community in many ways. Besides its role as general store and hardware store, it has operated as a barber shop, funeral home, and hotel. Today it offers an impressive array of gift items and antiques, and a confectionery up front serves homemade fudge (try the jalapeño!) prepared in the store. (979) 249–3600.

Round Top Inn Stores. Highway 237. Located on the grounds of the Round Top Inn, you'll find specialty stores offering everything from pottery to home items.

Emma Lee Turney's Round Top Antiques Fairs. At the Big Red Barn on Highway 237. These megafairs draw antiques lovers from around the state to more than 300 booths. The three-day shows are scheduled for the first full weekend in April and October. (281) 493–5501; www.roundtopantiquesfair.com.

Painted Pony Antiques. On the Square. This shop offers items ranging from vintage fabrics to primitives to dinnerware. (979) 249–5711.

where to eat

Royers Round Top Cafe. On the Square. You wouldn't expect to find shrimp scampi, fresh fettuccine, or pasta with fresh marinara sauce at a small-town diner, but here it is. This lively joint serves up some of the best cooking in Central Texas, in a fun atmosphere that's popular with locals and visitors. It's all topped off with homemade pies that include butterscotch tollhouse, buttermilk, and that Texas favorite, pecan. Royers operates a mail-order and wholesale sauce business, featuring pepper sauce, citrus vinegar, mint vinegar, and marinades. Open Thursday through Saturday for lunch and dinner; Sunday 11:00 A.M. to 3:00 P.M. $–$$; (979) 249–3611 or (877) 866–PIES for mail order; www.royersroundtopcafe.com.

Klump's Restaurant. Highway 237. Klump's started out as a grocery store serving barbecue on the weekends. Folks started asking for that 'que, though, and the Klump family decided to start a restaurant. Today barbecue is the special every Saturday, with Tex-Mex night on Wednesday, catfish on Friday, and fried chicken on Sunday. Open for breakfast daily, lunch served Tuesday through Sunday, dinner served Wednesday through Saturday. $. (979) 249–5696.

where to stay

Round Top Inn. Highway 237. Stay in historic structures that have been painstakingly restored to the days of Round Top's earliest pioneers. The inn spans a city block, formerly the property of Johann Traugott Wandke, an herbalist and organ maker known to have handcrafted seven pipe organs from local cedar during his residence here. His home is part of the inn, with a living room and modern-day bathroom downstairs and a picturesque bedroom tucked under the eaves upstairs. Rockers invite guests to sit out on the porch and enjoy small-town life. Other structures at the inn date back from 1840 to 1879, and all are filled with period antiques and accessories that recall the area's early days. $$. (877) 738–6746 or (979) 249–5294; www.andersonsroundtopinn.com.

Heart of My Heart Ranch. County Road 217, 2 miles from Round Top. This Victorian home is tucked into the countryside surrounding Round Top and offers a quiet weekend getaway for city dwellers. Sit in the porch rockers for a spell, or go fishing at the pond just in front of the home. Bicycles, a small, flat-bottom fishing boat, paddleboats, and inner tubes are provided for guests looking for recreation. Accommodations have antique furnishings, and guests share the downstairs living room with hosts Frances and Bill Harris. $$. (800) 327–1242; www.heartofmyheartranch.com.

south

day trip 01

south

mckinney falls state park, lockhart, luling, flatonia, praha, schulenburg: painted churches

mckinney falls state park

McKinney Falls State Park. Thirteen miles southeast of downtown Austin off U.S. Highway 183, take McKinney Falls Parkway south. A favorite with those looking for a quick getaway from the city, this park includes plenty of chances to view the area's wildlife, including white-tailed deer, raccoons, squirrels, and armadillos. Campers can choose from several types of sites as well as screened shelters. Fee. (512) 243–1643; www.tpwd.state.tx.us.

lockhart

Lockhart is a conglomeration of the stuff of Texas legends: Indian battles, cattle drives, cotton, and oil. This small town, located 23 miles south of Austin on US 183, contains a state park and lots of history.

The biggest event in Lockhart's past was the Battle of Plum Creek in 1840. More than 600 Comanches raided the community of Linnville and were on their way home when they passed through this area. A group of settlers joined forces with the Tonkawa Indians to attack the Comanches, driving them further west and ending the Indian attacks in the region. This battle is reenacted every May at the Chisholm Trail Roundup.

south day trip 01

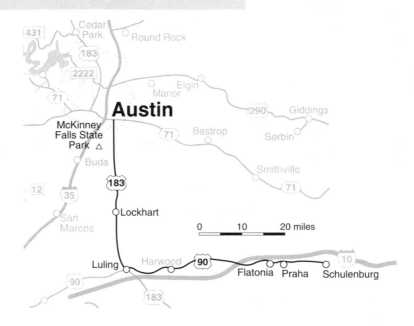

Lockhart is also well known as the home of Mebane cotton. Developed by A. D. Mebane, this strain is resistant to the boll weevil, an insect that can demolish not only whole fields but also entire economies.

where to go

Lockhart State Park. One mile south of Lockhart on US 183 to FM 20, head southwest for 2 miles to Park Road, continue 1 mile south. This 263-acre park has a nine-hole golf course, fishing on Plum Creek, picnic areas, a swimming pool, and campsites for both tents and trailers. Many of the facilities were built by the Civilian Conservation Corps in the 1930s. Open daily. Fee. (512) 398–3479; www.tpwd.state.tx.us.

Dr. Eugene Clark Library. 217 South Main Street. Built in 1889, this is the oldest continuously operating library in Texas. Modeled after the Villa Rotunda in Vicenza, Italy, it has stained-glass windows, ornate fixtures, and a stage where President William Taft once spoke. Open daily. Free. (512) 398–3223.

where to eat

Kreuz Market. 619 North Colorado Street. Vegetarians, head elsewhere. This barbecue restaurant is a meat-only kind of place, offering spicy sausage, pork loin, prime rib, and pork ribs, all served in an atmosphere that's little changed since the present owner took over in 1948. The meat market is up front for take-out orders; the dining area sits in the back. The two are connected by a smoke-filled hallway and dinner counter. Open Monday through Saturday, early morning to evening. $–$$. (512) 398–2361; www.kreuzmarket.com.

Black's Barbecue. 215 North Main Street. This cafeteria-style restaurant is reputedly the oldest barbecue joint in Texas under the same continual ownership. Beef brisket is the specialty of the house, along with sausage, ribs, chicken, and ham. There's also a fully stocked salad bar. Open daily for lunch and dinner. $–$$. (512) 398–2712.

luling

Continue south on US 183 for 17 miles to the oil town of Luling. Oil was discovered here in 1922, and fields pumping this "black gold" can still be seen throughout the Luling area. Even before that time the town had a reputation as "the toughest town in Texas," frequented by gunfighters like John Wesley Hardin and Ben Thompson. Luling was also a cattle center and the end of a railroad line to Chihuahua, Mexico.

When oil was discovered, the economy of the town shifted to this profitable industry. Today 184 wells pump within the city limits. As part of a beautification effort, the Chamber of Commerce commissioned an artist to transform several of the pumpjacks into moving sculptures in the shapes of cartoon characters. There's even a Santa Claus and a butterfly to brighten up the streets.

where to go

Palmetto State Park. Six miles southeast of town on US 183, then southwest on Park Road for 2 miles, along the banks of the San Marcos River. Palmetto State Park is a topographical anomaly amidst gently rolling farm and ranch land. According to scientists, the river shifted course thousands of years ago, leaving a huge deposit of silt. This sediment absorbed rain and groundwater, nurturing a marshy swamp estimated to be more than 18,000 years old. Now part of the state park, the swamp is filled with palmettos as well as moss-draped trees, 4-foot-tall irises, and many bird species. Nature trails wind throughout the area.

The park has full hookups and tent sites. There's also picnicking, but during the warmer months bring along mosquito repellent. Open daily. Fee. (830) 672–3266; www.tpwd .state.tx.us.

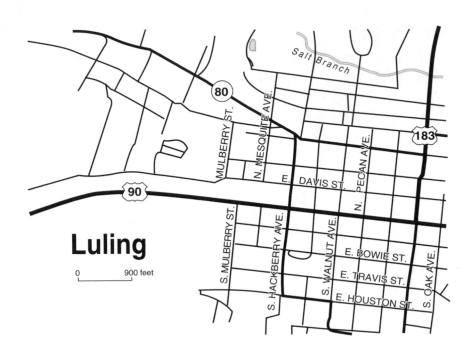

Francis-Ainsworth House. 200 block of South Pecan Avenue. Enjoy a tour of this 1894 home. Managed by the Daughters of the Republic of Texas, the residence is filled with period antiques. Open Thursday and Saturday afternoons. Free. (830) 875–5297.

Central Texas Oil Patch Museum & Luling Chamber of Commerce Visitors' Center. 421 Davis Street. Luling's oil businesses, starting with Rafael Rios No. 1 (an oil field 12 miles long and 2 miles wide), are explored in this museum. Call for hours. Free. (830) 875–3214.

where to eat

Luling City Market. 633 Davis Street. This is small-town barbecue the way it ought to be: served up in a no-frills meat market, with ambience replaced by local atmosphere. The Luling City Market turns out smoked brisket, sausage, and ribs. $. (877) LCM–BBQ1 or (830) 875–9019; www.lulingcitymarket.com.

flatonia

Return to U.S. Highway 90 and continue east to the small town of Flatonia. This community was settled by English, German, Bohemian, and Czech immigrants, many of whom came to the United States in the 1850s and 1860s to avoid Austro-Hungarian oppression.

where to go

E. A. Arnim Archives and Museum. US 90, downtown. This local history museum contains exhibits on Flatonia's early days and its settlement by many cultural groups. Open Saturday afternoon. Free. (512) 865–2451.

praha

Three miles east of Flatonia on US 90 is Praha (the Slovakian spelling for "Prague"). Named for its European counterpart, Praha holds a predominantly Czech population, descendants of immigrants who came here in 1855.

The main structure in Praha is the Assumption of the Blessed Virgin Mary Church, often called St. Mary's. Built in 1895, it is one of a half dozen painted churches in the area. Although few examples remain today, it was not unusual for nineteenth-century rural churches to boast painted interiors. Guided tours from nearby Schulenburg visit all the churches, but you can see most of the structures on a self-guided trip. A free brochure and map is available from the Schulenburg Chamber of Commerce. (979) 743–4514.

St. Mary's has a beautifully painted vaulted ceiling, the work of Swiss-born artist Gottfried Flury. Never retouched, the 1895 murals on the tongue-and-groove ceiling depict golden angels high over a pastoral setting. This Praha church, as well as ones in High Hill and Ammannsville, are listed in the National Register of Historic Places. The churches are open Monday through Saturday 8:00 A.M. to 5:00 P.M., although it is not guaranteed that the doors will be unlocked at all times. Free. (No phone.)

schulenburg

Continue east on US 90 to the agricultural community of Schulenburg (meaning "school town" in German). Carnation Milk Company's first plant was built in Schulenburg in 1929, and even today dairy products generate a major source of income for the area. Schulenburg is known as the "home of the painted churches," although the elaborately painted structures are actually located in nearby small communities (Dubina, Ammannsville, Swiss Alp, High Hill, and Praha). These beautifully painted buildings are reminders of the area's rural traditions and ethnic background.

In Ammannsville, St. John the Baptist Church has stained-glass windows illustrating the Czech heritage of the parish. High Hill's St. Mary's Church boasts marbleized columns, religious statuary, and a history of a European-style seating arrangement, with women on the left and men on the right. The murals in Dubina's Sts. Cyril and Methodius Church were covered over during a 1952 remodeling. In 1981 the paintings, depicting winged angels and elaborate stencil patterns, were renovated by a local parishioner.

where to go

Painted Churches Tour. With a two- or three-week notice, the Schulenburg Chamber of Commerce provides guides for tour groups of ten or more. You can always enjoy a self-guided tour; maps of the church locations are available at the Schulenburg site at 618 Main Street. (866) 504–5294.

where to eat

Oakridge Smokehouse Restaurant. Interstate 10 and Highway 77. Hungry travelers between San Antonio and Houston know all about Oakridge Smokehouse. In business nearly half a century, this family-owned company churns out barbecue and sausage to please travelers and mail-order customers. The comfortable restaurant is popular with families, not just for its extensive menu, but also for its large gift shop up front. $–$$. (800) 548–6325.

day trip 02

south

>>> **gonzales, shiner, yoakum:
texas history**

This history-filled day trip offers a look at a historic battleground, one of Texas's most popular breweries, and one of the world's biggest leather producers.

To begin this trip, head south on U.S. Highway 183 through Lockhart and Luling (see South Day Trip 1 for information on attractions in those cities).

gonzales

Continue south on US 183 for 13 miles to Gonzales, one of Texas's most historic cities. This is the "Come and Take It" town where the Texas Revolution began in 1835.

Plagued by constant Indian attacks, Gonzales's citizens received a small brass cannon for protection by the Mexican government in 1831. Four years later, when relations between Texas and Mexico soured, more than 150 Mexican soldiers staged a battle to retrieve the weapon. The soldiers were faced with eighteen Gonzaleans, who stalled the army while other citizens rolled out the small fieldpiece and prepared for action. Meanwhile, other townsfolk sewed the first battle flag of Texas, which pictured a cannon beneath the words "Come and Take It," a motto by which Gonzales is still known. The Texans fired the first shot and the Mexican troops retreated. Although the confrontation was brief, this act began the Texas Revolution.

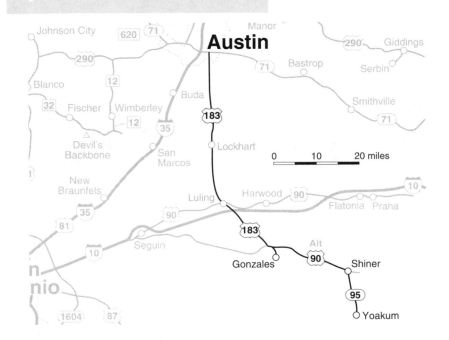

south day trip 02

The site of this historic first conflict is marked by a monument located 7 miles south-west of Gonzales on Highway 97. The first shots were fired ½ mile north of the present monument.

where to go

Chamber of Commerce. 414 St. Lawrence Street. Located in the Old Jail Museum, this office has brochures on local attractions and events. Open weekdays. (830) 672–6532.

Old Jail Museum. 414 St. Lawrence Street. This unusual museum is housed in the old Gonzales jail, built in 1887 and used until 1975. Downstairs you can tour the room where female prisoners and mentally ill persons once were incarcerated together. Exhibits include jail weapons created from spoons and bedsprings.

The walls of the second floor are chiseled with graffiti of past residents. The large room is rimmed with iron cells, all overlooking a reproduction of the old gallows that carried off its last hanging in 1921. According to legend, this prisoner continually watched the clocks on the adjacent courthouse, counting the hours he had left to live. He swore that he was innocent and said that if he were hanged the clocks would never keep accurate time again. Although the four clock faces have been changed since then, none of them has ever kept the same time again.

The museum, located in the Chamber of Commerce building, is open daily (afternoons on Sunday). Free. (830) 672–6532.

Memorial Museum. 414 Smith Street, between St. Lawrence and St. Louis Streets. This museum is dedicated to the history of Gonzales. Exhibits on the town's early days include the "Come and Take It" cannon. Open Tuesday through Sunday. Free. (830) 672–6350.

Gonzales Pioneer Village. One-half-mile north of town on US 183. This living history center takes visitors back to Gonzales's frontier days. The village is composed of log cabins, a cypress-constructed home, a grand Victorian home, a smokehouse, a blacksmith shop, and a church. The village also stages reenactments, including the "Come and Take It" celebration in October. Open weekends (and Friday in summer months); group tours by appointment. Fee. (830) 672–2157.

shiner

Take U.S. Highway 90A east of Gonzales for 18 miles to the tiny town of Shiner, best known as the home of Shiner beer. If you make the trip during the week, stop by the Spoetzl Brewery for a free tour and a sample of the hometown product.

where to go

Spoetzl Brewery. 603 Brewery Street, off Highway 95 North. This tiny but historic brewery was founded in 1909 by Kosmos Spoetzl, a Bavarian brewmaster. Here several Shiner beers are produced in one of the smallest commercial brew kettles in the country. Across the street, a museum and gift shop overflow with Shiner memorabilia, antiques, and photos of Spoetzl's early days. Brewery tours are conducted on weekdays at 11:00 A.M. and 1:30 P.M. Hospitality room open following tour. Free. (361) 594–3852.

City Hall. US 90A, downtown. This two-story building houses the fire department, police department, and city offices. Enter on the left side for city brochures and a free map. (361) 594–4180.

Wolters Memorial Museum. 306 South Avenue I off Highway 95 South. This museum is filled with home implements, weapons, fossils, and even a country store representing the community's early days. Open weekdays 8 A.M. to 5 P.M. (closed noon to 1 P.M.) and the second Sunday afternoon of the month. Free. (361) 594–3774.

where to stay

The Old Kasper House. 219 Avenue C. This bed-and-breakfast is located in the former home of a cotton ginner and his wife from Austria and Czechoslovakia who was best known as a relative of Gregor Mendel, discoverer of genetic information (remember those Mendel pea models in Biology I?). Today the two-story house is a great small-town getaway, offering seven rooms with private baths and a cottage. Behind the bed-and-breakfast there's an RV park with eight full-service hookups. $–$$. (361) 594–4336.

yoakum

From Shiner, drive south on Highway 95 for 8 miles to U.S. Highway 77A. Turn right and continue for 2 miles. Yoakum was the starting point of many cattle drives along the Chisholm Trail, and in 1887 it became the junction for the San Antonio and Aransas Pass Railroad. When the railroad came to town, meat packinghouses followed. In 1919 the first tannery opened, producing leather knee pads for cotton pickers. Soon other leather businesses arrived, and eventually Yoakum earned its title as "the leather capital of the world."

Today twelve leather companies produce belts, saddles, bullwhips, gun slings, and wallets. Although the companies do not sell directly from their factories, the Leather Capital

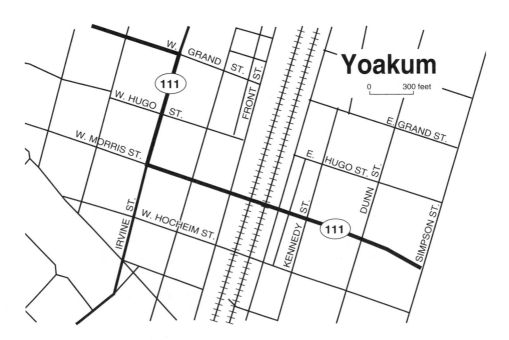

Store operates as a showroom and factory outlet for many Yoakum manufacturers. Tours of the leather companies are offered during the annual Land of Leather Days festival, the last weekend in February.

where to go

Yoakum Heritage Museum. 312 Simpson Street. This two-story museum is filled with Yoakum memorabilia, from railroad paraphernalia to household items. The most interesting exhibit area is the Leather Room, with its displays on the leather factories. Open Tuesday, Thursday, and Friday 1:00 to 5:00 P.M. and Sunday 2:00 to 5:00 P.M. Free. (361) 293–7022.

where to shop

The Leather Capital Store. 123 West Grand Street. This shop is a leather museum and store rolled into one. Its display windows are painted with silhouettes of Texas history scenes. Inside, thousands of belts, purses, and boots—even gun slings and holsters—are offered for sale. Upstairs the facade of a Wild West village brightens a floor filled with saddles and Southwestern and Western art. Deer shoulder blades etched with Indian scenes are produced by owner Leo Smith, who for many years worked as a commercial illustrator for one of the leather companies. Open Monday through Saturday. (361) 293–9339.

Return home from Yoakum by retracing your steps or by heading north on Highway 95 to Flatonia. From here, go west on either Interstate 10 or US 90.

day trip 03

south

buda, san marcos:
shop 'til you drop

buda

Head south from Austin on Interstate 35 to the small town of Buda, located on Loop 4 to the west of the highway. This sleepy railroad town is a busy spot on weekends, when shoppers come to hunt antiques.

Buda is one of the most mispronounced communities in Texas (and with names like Gruene, Leakey, and Boerne around, that's saying a lot). To sound like a local, just say "b-YOU-da." The name has caused more than one foreign visitor to come here expecting an old-world Hungarian settlement. Though possibly a reference to Budapest, it's more likely of Spanish origin. According to legend, several widows cooked in the local hotel restaurant that was popular with employees of the International–Great Northern Railroad. The Spanish word for "widow" is *viuda*. Since the "v" is pronounced as a "b" in Spanish, Buda may be a phonetic spelling for *viuda*.

Buda is still a railroad town, with double tracks running parallel to Main Street.

where to shop

Many Buda stores are closed Monday through Wednesday, although some are open by appointment. Most shops are located in a 2-block stretch of Main Street.

south day trip 03

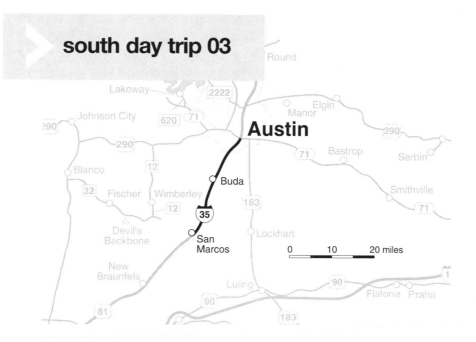

alice's restaurant

There's not a lot in Niederwald these days. Come to think of it, there never has been a lot in Niederwald. Founded by German pioneers and named "brushwood" for the mesquite that dots the area, the town was a stop on the old Austin-San Antonio road. Now it's still a stop on today's Austin-San Antonio road, I–35.

But there's one good reason to make a day trip detour to Niederwald: Alice's Restaurant. This eatery, housed in a frame house and accompanied by a small biergarten, combines good food and good music in one entree, with a healthy side serving of Austin funkiness. The menu ranges from pork chops to shrimp skewers but as much a draw is the live music. Austin talent, including many singer-songwriters, headline here three nights a week.

To reach Alice's Restaurant, in Buda turn east off I–35 on FM 2001 (exit 220) and continue 9 miles to the intersection of Highway 21. Alice's is just a quarter mile east of the intersection on Highway 21 at 14100 Camino Real. (If you'd prefer to take this detour from San Marcos, continue on this day trip and then head east on Highway 21 in San Marcos for 14 miles.) For a schedule of performers, call (512) 376–2782 or see www.alicesrestauranttx.com. Alice's is open Thursday 10:00 A.M. to 10:00 P.M., Friday and Saturday 10:00 A.M. to midnight, and Sunday 11:00 A.M. to 3:00 P.M.

Texas Hatters. Exit 220 on the east side of I-35. This store's founder, the late Manny Gammage, was "Texas's Hatmaker to the Stars." His hats topped the heads of Roy Rogers, Willie Nelson, Ronald Reagan, Burt Reynolds, and many other celebrities whose pictures decorate the shop walls. Besides the obligatory cowboy hats, this store also sells hand-blocked high rollers, Panamas, and derbies. Open Tuesday through Saturday. (512) 295–HATS.

san marcos

Head south on I-35 to San Marcos, the home of Texas State University, two amusement parks, and the crystal-clear San Marcos River.

Like the neighboring community of New Braunfels, San Marcos is best known for its pure spring waters. The San Marcos River, used by humans for more than 13,000 years, flows through town, providing the city with beautiful swimming and snorkeling spots and a family educational park.

Permanent settlement of the area began in 1845. Today San Marcos is a popular tourist town and the home of Texas State University. On the third weekend of every month, the downtown courthouse lawn is used for Market Days. Shop for arts and crafts, antiques, and specialty food and gift items at this old-fashioned outdoor market.

When the city of San Marcos looked around for a slogan, it decided to choose one that naturally fits the riverside city. "San Marcos, A Texas Natural" is more than a nickname, it's a description of the attractions that draw visitors to this city of just more than 41,000 permanent residents. One of the best-known attractions is Aquarena Center, which features the ecological and archaeological riches of the region. Nearby, another park offers a look at San Marcos's natural attractions both above and below the ground. Scientists believe Wonder Cave was created during a violent earthquake thirty million years ago.

There's no better way to see San Marcos during warm weather than from the river. Across from Texas State University, the Lions Club rents inner tubes from May through September so that you can float down the San Marcos Loop. The floating excursion, in 72°F water, takes about an hour and a half. Snorkeling is popular here as well, and you might see a freshwater prawn (which can reach 12 inches in length), the rare San Marcos salamander, or one of fifty-two kinds of fish.

Of course, not all of San Marcos's attractions are natural. Plenty are of the man-made variety. However, the theme of the city as a Texas Natural continues in many of these as well. Downtown, shops are encouraged to feature Texas-made items. "We're trying to connect the products with the consumer and to get people to think Texas," explains Kelly Franks, Main Street manager. Look for "Taste of Texas" foods, "Uniquely Texas" arts and crafts, "Naturally Texas" clothing, and more at the many one-of-a-kind boutiques in downtown San Marcos. While you're downtown, you'll notice the fresh face the area boasts, thanks to more

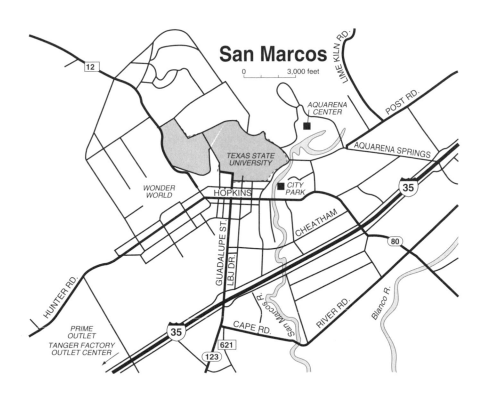

than $16 million in renovations in the last decade, transforming it into a shopping and dining area.

The Texas theme even carries into the only downtown bed-and-breakfast. The Crystal River Inn offers accommodations in rooms named for Texas rivers. It also offers popular murder mystery weekends where costumed guests work to solve a mystery using clues based on actual events in San Marcos history.

where to go

Tourist Information Center. Use I–35 on the northwest side of town at exit 204B (C. M. Allen Parkway). Traveling from the north, take exit 204B. From the south, take exit 205. Stop here for brochures on area attractions and accommodations, as well as free maps. Open daily. Free. (888) 200–5620 or (512) 393–5930; www.sanmarcostexas.com.

Aquarena Center. 921 Aquarena Springs Drive. Take Aquarena Springs exit from I–35 and follow signs west of the highway. This resort dates back to 1928, when A. B. Rogers purchased 125 acres at the headwaters of the San Marcos River to create a grand hotel. He added glass-bottomed boats to cruise Spring Lake, fed by more than 200 springs that produce 150 million gallons daily. This 98 percent pure water is home to many fish (including white albino catfish) and various types of plant life. Today visitors can still enjoy a cruise in the glass-bottom boats and will see the site of an underwater archaeological dig that unearthed the remains of Clovis Man, one of the hunter-gatherers who lived along the San Marcos River more than 13,000 years ago.

Formerly a family amusement park, now Aquarena Center focuses on ecotourism, with exhibits and activities aimed at introducing visitors of all ages to the natural history and natural attractions of this region. This family park features glass-bottom boat rides, an endangered species exhibit, the San Xavier Spanish Mission, an 1890s general store, historic homes from San Marcos's earliest days, and plenty of educational fun. The park offers special guided trips that feature the park's historic attractions as well as other excursions focusing on endangered species, archaeological sites, bird-watching, and the flora and fauna of the area.

Open daily, although hours change seasonally. Free, fee for glass-bottom boats. (512) 245–7570; www.aquarena.txstate.edu.

Wonder World. Exit at Wonder World Drive on the south side of San Marcos and follow signs for about a mile. A guided tour lasting nearly 1½ hours covers the entire park, including the 7½-acre Texas Wildlife Park, Texas's largest petting zoo. A miniature train chugs through the animal enclosure, stopping to allow riders to pet and feed white-tailed deer, wild turkeys, and many exotic species.

The next stop on the tour is Wonder Cave, created during a 3½-minute earthquake thirty million years ago. The same earthquake produced the Balcones Fault, an 1,800-mile line separating the western Hill Country from the flat eastern farmland. Within the cave is the actual crack in the two land masses, containing huge boulders lodged in the fissure. At the end of the cave tour, take the elevator ride to the top of the 110-foot Tejas Tower, which offers a spectacular view of the Balcones Fault and the contrasting terrain it produced.

The last stop is the Anti-Gravity House, a structure employing optical illusions and a slanted floor to create the feeling that you're leaning backward. In this house, water appears to run "uphill," creating yet another illusion. Fee. (877) 492–4657 or (512) 392–3760 for group and tour reservations; www.wonderworldpark.com.

Millie Seaton Collection of Dolls and Toys. 1104 West Hopkins. For thirty years, Millie Seaton has collected dolls from around the world. The number of dolls grew and grew— until finally the avid collector bought a three-story Victorian home just to house the 4,000 dolls! Tours are given Monday through Friday 10:00 A.M. to 2:00 P.M. by appointment. Call to set up a time with Millie or one of her docents for a guided walk through this cherished collection. Free. (512) 396–1944.

John J. Stokes San Marcos River Park. From Highway 80, turn right on River Road for about 1 mile; turn left on County Road to the island where the park is located. Operated by the city of San Marcos, this day-use park is also known as Thompson's Island and is located across the river from the A. E. Wood State Fish Hatchery. The park offers river access but no facilities. Free.

The Calaboose Museum of African American History. Martin Luther King Drive and Fredericksburg Street. Housed in the 1873 building that served as Hays County's first jail, this museum preserves the history of the African Americans of San Antonio, starting in the nineteenth century. Along with an extensive collection of books and artifacts, the museum also schedules frequent educational programs and public events. Open by appointment. Fee. (512) 393–8421.

Living History Trolley Tour. Tanger Outlet Center Visitor Center, exit 200 from I–35 south of San Marcos. These guided tours are scheduled for 2:00 P.M. on the first Saturday of each month, departing from the Tanger visitor center. The trolley tours include stops at sites featured in the novels True Women and Hill Country, as well as along Courthouse Square, the San Marcos River, Aquarena Springs, and historic mansions. Reservations required. Fee. (512) 396–3739.

Millennium Driving Tour of Old San Marcos. The Heritage Association of San Marcos designed this self-drive tour of Old San Marcos, including the Courthouse Square, historic homes, and the Belvin Street National Register District filled with Victorian homes. For a free copy of the driving tour, contact the Convention and Visitors Bureau; www.century inter.net/smheritage.

Central Texas Wing of the Confederate Air Force. 1841 Airport Drive. Housed in a vintage wooden hangar at the San Marcos Municipal Airport, this collection contains World War II artifacts and several historic aircraft. A unique display is a replica of the CAF Japanese "Kate," built for the movie Tora, Tora, Tora. Open Monday, Wednesday, Friday, and Saturday 9:00 A.M. to 4:00 P.M. Donation. (512) 396–1943.

where to shop

Prime Outlets San Marcos. Exit 200 from I–35 on the south side of San Marcos. This open-air mall ranks as the state's third-largest tourist destination. Luggage, shoes, leather goods, outdoor gear, china, kitchen goods, and other specialties are offered for sale. Chartered buses from as far as Dallas and Houston stop here regularly. Open daily. (800) 0628–9465 or (512) 396–220; www.primeoutlets.com.

Tanger Factory Outlet Center. Exit 200 from I–35 south of San Marcos. More than one hundred shops feature name-brand designers and manufacturers in this open-air mall. Housewares, footwear, home furnishings, leather goods, perfumes, and books are offered. Open daily. (800) 408–8424; www.tangeroutlet.com.

Centerpoint Station. Exit 200 from I-35 south of San Marcos. This charming shop, built like an old-fashioned general store, is filled with Texas and country collectibles, T-shirts, gourmet gift foods, cookbooks, and more. Up front, there's counter service for sandwiches, malts, and ice cream. (512) 392-1103; www.centerpointstation.com.

where to stay

Crystal River Inn. 326 West Hopkins Street. The Crystal River Inn has elegant Victorian accommodations in rooms named for Texas rivers. Owners Cathy and Mike Dillon provide guests with a selection of special packages, including tubing on the San Marcos and popular murder mystery weekends where costumed guests work to solve a mystery using clues based on actual events in San Marcos history. $$-$$$. (888) 396-3739 or (512) 396-3739; www.crystalriverinn.com.

day trip 04

south

seguin:
concrete city

seguin

You can reach Seguin (pronounced "se-GEEN") by driving south on Interstate 35 from Austin through San Marcos (see South Day Trip 3 for city attractions). It's a 36-mile trip to this town on the Guadalupe River named for Lieutenant Colonel Juan Seguin, a hero of the Texas Revolution. Prior to the Mexican invasion of 1837, Seguin was ordered by his superiors to destroy San Antonio. He refused, thus saving the city.

Many towns boast nicknames, from Austin's "River City" to San Antonio's "Alamo City." Seguin, though, has one of the most unusual: "The Mother of Concrete Cities." A Seguin chemist held several concrete production patents, which accounts for the use of the material in more than ninety area buildings by the end of the nineteenth century.

The most beautiful area of Seguin is Starcke Park. It offers picnic tables under huge pecan, oak, and cypress trees, and a winding drive along the Guadalupe River. The tree Seguin is best known for is the pecan. The town even calls itself the home of the "World's Largest Pecan," a statue located on the courthouse lawn at Court Street.

where to go

Chamber of Commerce. 427 North Austin Street. Stop by the Chamber for brochures and maps. Open weekdays. (800) 580–PECAN or (830) 379–6382.

Sebastopol State Historical Park. 704 Zorn Street. From I–35, take Highway 123 South in San Marcos and follow Business 123 into Seguin, turn right onto Court Street to 704 Zorn Street. This is one of the best examples of the early use of concrete in the Southwest. Sebastopol was once a large home, constructed of concrete with a plaster overlay. Today it is open for tours and contains exhibits illustrating the construction of this historic building and its restoration in 1988. Guided tours on weekends; call the Chamber of Commerce to set up group tours at other times. Fee. (830) 379–4833; www.tpwd.state.tx.us.

True Women Tours. Fans of Janice Woods Wendle's *True Women* can take a guided tour of the sites mentioned in this best-seller and seen in the television miniseries. Led by local docents, the tours take a look at sites that play an important role in the historical novel: the live oak-shaded King Cemetery, the old First Methodist Church where two *True Women* characters were married, and the river where horses were daringly rescued in the tale.

One of the most memorable stops is the Bettie Moss King Home, near the King Cemetery. The home, with its wraparound porch and shady lawn, was where several generations of the King family were raised and was also the childhood home of author Janice Woods Windle. Today Windle's mother, Virginia Woods, still lives there and often opens her home to tour groups. Woods points out her ancestors' belongings, including the dining-room table that played a part in *True Women,* both in the story and in the writing of the family saga.

Call the Seguin Chamber of Commerce for tour times or pick up a map for a self-guided drive (427 North Austin Street). Fee for guided tour. (800) 580–PECAN; www.seguin tx.org.

flower power

Is it spring? Grab the car keys in one hand, your camera in the other, and get ready for a bloomin' good time! Starting in late March and extending into early summer, wildflowers line the roadways throughout Central and South Texas. The best way to find the top fields is with a quick call to the Texas Department of Transportation's wildflower hotline (800–452–9292). The hotline is active from mid-March until early May, and you can request information by region (Central Texas and Hill Country covers most of this book's scope). Maps showing the best spots for viewing wildflowers are available through the TxDOT Web site (www.dot.state .tx.us/wflwr/main.htm).

south day trip 04

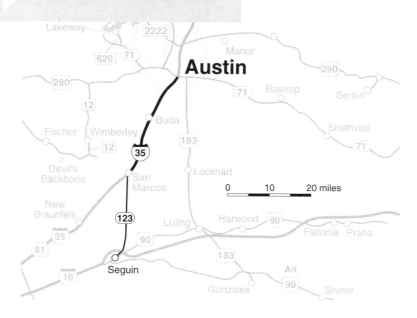

Starcke Park. South side of town, off Highway 123. Make time for this pleasant park, where visitors can enjoy golf, tennis, and baseball as well as many riverside picnic spots. Large waterpark is open seasonally. Free. (830) 401–2480.

Seguin's Lakes. Seguin is surrounded by four lakes on the Guadalupe River that offer bass, crappie, and catfish fishing, including lighted docks for night fishing. RV facilities are available as well. The lakes include Lake Dunlap—Interstate 10 to Highway 46 exit west of Seguin, then 8 miles on Highway 46; Lake McQueeney—I–10 to FM 78 exit, then west for 3 miles to FM 725, then turn right and continue for 1 mile; Lake Placid—I–10 to FM 464 exit, stay on access road; and Meadow Lake—I–10 to Highway 123 bypass, then south for 4 miles.

Los Nogales Museum. 415 South River, just south of the courthouse. Los Nogales, which means "walnuts" in Spanish, houses local artifacts. The small brick adobe building was constructed in 1849. Next door, The Doll House is filled with period children's toys you can see through the windows. This white miniature home was built between 1908 and 1910 by local cabinetmaker Louis Dietz as a playhouse for his niece. Later he used it to promote his business. For tour information, call the Chamber of Commerce. (800) 580–PECAN.

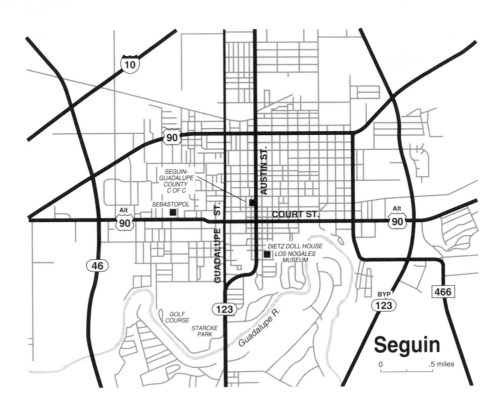

Texas Theatre. 427 North Austin Street. This 1931 theater has been used for scenes in two movies: *Raggedy Man* and *The Great Waldo Pepper*. It still sports its original marquee and recalls the old days of small-town Texas theaters. For information, check with the Chamber of Commerce at 427 North Austin Street.

Wave Pool. Starcke Park East. In this Texas-size pool, youngsters can cool off under the Mushroom Shower or splash in the simulated waves. Nearby, the sprawling Kids Kingdom Playscape makes an excellent stop for energetic young travelers as well. Open seasonally. Fee. (830) 401–2482.

where to stay

Weinert House Bed and Breakfast. 1207 North Austin Street. Kick back and enjoy small-town life amid 1890s elegance in this historic Victorian home. Four guest quarters are decorated with period antiques. The Senator's suite includes a fireplace and screened sunporch. $$. (888) 303–0912; www.weinerthouse.com.

southwest

day trip 01

southwest

>>> san antonio:
the alamo city

san antonio

San Antonio has the reputation of a fun-loving town. Located 80 miles south of Austin on Interstate 35, the city always has something going on to attract visitors. No matter when you choose to visit, you can bet that somebody, somewhere, is hosting a festival. Perhaps it has something to do with the sunshine or the fresh air. Whatever it is, you can feel it. It sizzles up like *fajitas* out of the city's Latino heritage, which abounds with colorful traditions and vivid memories.

San Antonio's rich cultural past dates back to the early Indians who settled the area. They were followed by the seventeenth-century Spaniards, who came here in search of wealth. Later a group of Franciscan friars established a chain of missions designed to convert the Indians of the Southwest to Christianity. In 1718 Mission San Antonio de Valero (better known as the Alamo) became the first of five such structures in the city.

Except for the Alamo, the missions are found in the San Antonio Missions National Historical Park, located within the city limits. The National Park Service has assigned interpretive themes to each of the four—the active parish churches of Mission Concepción, Mission San Juan Capistrano, Mission San Francisco de la Espada, and Mission San José. The latter, established in 1720, hosts a colorful "Mariachi Mass" each Sunday at noon.

San Antonio is also a foodie's paradise. This is the city that heralded the birth of *fajitas*—strips of marinated charcoal-grilled skirt steak. Here you'll also find to-die-for guacamole,

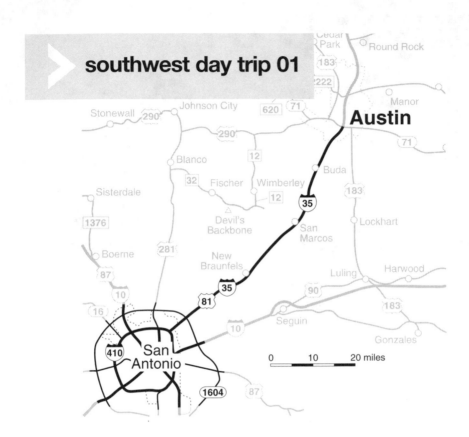

southwest day trip 01

pico de gallo (a Mexican condiment of onions, tomatoes, and chiles), and fresh flour tortillas.

With two excellent theme parks, a world-class zoo, and wonderful museums, San Antonio offers much more to see and do than this book can possibly list. For a complete rundown of possibilities, contact the San Antonio Convention and Visitor Bureau, P.O. Box 2277, San Antonio, TX 78298; (800) THE–ALAMO or (210) 207–6700. Stop in the visitor center at Alamo Plaza (across from the Alamo), where you can pick up information on the VIA streetcars that connect major tourist sites. Open daily.

downtown: river walk area

The River Walk stretches for 2.5 miles from South St. Mary's Street to Alamo Street, and along Crockett and Market Streets. The Paseo del Rio, as it's also called, is a European-style river walk that lies below street level. Part of an urban renovation project six decades ago, the River Walk is now a top San Antonio attraction. Its winding sidewalks, which follow an arm of the San Antonio River, are lined with two-story specialty shops, sidewalk cafes, luxury hotels, art galleries, and bars. Like New Orleans's Bourbon Street, this area of San Antonio has an atmosphere all its own. Arched bridges connect the two sides of the walk, so visitors never have to venture up to street level.

One of the busiest sections of the Paseo del Rio extends from the Hyatt Regency Riverwalk at Crockett Street to the Hilton Palacio del Rio Hotel at Market Street. This stretch of walk boasts most of the sidewalk restaurants and shops. From Commerce Street you can head up to the Henry S. Gonzales Convention Center and the Rivercenter Mall.

A great way to get around in this congested area is aboard the VIA downtown trolleys. For just 50 cents you can hop aboard one of four routes for transportation to most major sites. (210) 362–2020; www.viainfo.net.

king william

Imagine San Antonio without the River Walk. Without the Tower of the Americas. Without the bustling business that fills this modern metropolis.

It is the late 1800s. Texas is still a new frontier, gaining statehood after its years as an independent republic and a territory of Mexico. After years of subsistence on a rugged frontier, San Antonio residents are finally ready for comforts, culture, and a community spirit that emphasized education, music, and the language of their homeland.

With these goals in mind, the King William district was born. Started by the founder of the utopian community Comfort (see Southwest Day Trip 4), this elegant neighborhood on the banks of the San Antonio River soon reached its status as a superior neighborhood. Going back to the mid-1800s, when this district was populated by the Alamo City's most successful businessmen and their families, many of these frontier citizens were German immigrants with names like Guenther, Wulff, and Heusinger. With their wealth gained in merchandising and investing, they set about building the most lavish homes in the city, most in the grand Victorian style.

For visitors seeking a romantic getaway in San Antonio, a place to enjoy historic elegance in a quiet neighborhood that's within easy walking distance of the River Walk, King William is an ideal destination. Tucked in a quiet neighborhood beneath towering live oak trees, this area is home to numerous bed-and-breakfast establishments. Ranging from country comfort to antebellum elegance, there's a bed-and-breakfast for every taste.

where to go

The Alamo. Alamo Plaza, between Houston and Crockett Streets. Located in the very heart of San Antonio, the Alamo was once surrounded on all sides by the forces of Mexico's General Santa Anna. Now it's enveloped by high-rise office structures and a central plaza.

This "Cradle of Texas Liberty," situated on the east side of Alamo Plaza, is probably the most famous spot in Texas. Established in 1718 as the Mission San Antonio de Valero, it plunged into history on March 6, 1836, when 188 men died after being attacked by the Mexican forces of General Santa Anna. Among the most famous defenders were Jim Bowie, William B. Travis, and Davy Crockett.

A symbol of the state's independence and courage, the Alamo draws continuous crowds throughout the year. Visitors entering the main building, the Shrine, can see exhibits such as Bowie's famous knife and Davy Crockett's rifle "Old Betsy." Those interested also can take a self-guided tour of the museum, the Long Barracks, and the beautiful courtyard. Open daily except Christmas Eve and Christmas Day. Free. (210) 225–1391; www.thealamo.org.

Yanaguana Cruises. River Walk. One of the most pleasurable and inexpensive attractions in town, these open barges take passengers on narrated cruises through the heart of San Antonio from morning until late evening. Special dinner cruises afford a romantic look at the city and are arranged by River Walk restaurants. The boats operate on environmentally friendly compressed natural gas. Open daily; hours change by season. Fee. (800) 417–4139 or (210) 244–5700; www.sarivercruise.com.

Tower of the Americas. HemisFair Park. This 750-foot tower is topped by a rotating restaurant that serves lunch and dinner. An observation deck offers an unbeatable view of the city. Open daily. Fee. (210) 207–8615; www.toweroftheamericas.com.

University of Texas Institute of Texan Cultures at San Antonio. HemisFair Park. This fascinating museum features exhibits and a multimedia presentation showcasing the twenty-six different ethnic groups who came here from around the world to settle the new frontier called Texas. Open Tuesday through Sunday 9:00 A.M. to 5:00 P.M. Fee. (210) 458–2300; www.texancultures.utsa.edu.

San Antonio IMAX Theatre. 849 East Commerce Street, Rivercenter Mall. This theater features *Alamo . . . The Price of Freedom,* a forty-five-minute movie about the battle of the Alamo. The six-story screen and six-channel sound immerses you in the glory of the struggle, and it's a good thing to see before visiting the historic site. The theater alternates this movie with other IMAX features, so call for show times. Open daily. Fee. (800) 354–4629 or (210) 247–4629; www.imax-sa.com.

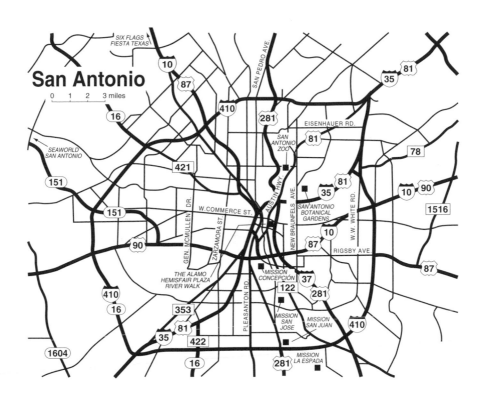

Steves Homestead. 509 King William Street. This grand home was built in 1876 and is currently the only one in the elegant King William Historic District that is open to the public. The Victorian mansion's interior is filled with original furniture, and the grounds include several antique carriages and the gardener's quarters, now a visitor center. Open daily. Fee. (210) 227–9160.

Plaza Wax Museum. 301 Alamo Plaza. This attraction has wax figures of movie and TV celebrities as well as a theater of horrors. The "Heroes of the Lone Star" section is interesting, with realistic scenes depicting the fall of the Alamo. Ripley's Believe It or Not! is located in the same building, and you can buy separate or combination tickets to the two attractions. Open daily. Fee. (210) 224–9299; www.plazawaxmuseum.com.

San Antonio Children's Museum. 305 East Houston Street. This museum specializes in hands-on activities for all ages. A highlight of the museum is its historic San Antonio exhibits. Open daily. Fee. (210) 212–4453.

The Texas Adventure. 307 Alamo Plaza. This state-of-the-art attraction calls itself the world's first Encountarium F-X Theater. The six-minute preshow does a good job of telling the story of the events that led up to the battle of the Alamo, then guests are ushered into a bench-lined room where holographic versions of Davy Crockett, William B. Travis, and Jim Bowie tell their stories. It's interesting for all but the youngest of children, who may be frightened by "figures" materializing and disappearing throughout the presentation. Open daily. Fee. (210) 227–8224.

where to shop

La Villita. Exit through Hilton Hotel, then 1 block right on South Alamo Street. This area on the east bank of the San Antonio River was developed in the mid-to-late eighteenth century by Mexican settlers who lived, without land title, on the outskirts of the Alamo mission. Today La Villita is San Antonio's finest crafts area, filled with weavers, glassblowers, sculptors, and even boot makers. Within the restored buildings, shops sell everything from woven wall hangings to silver jewelry, and the historic Little Church is often the site of weddings. Most shops open daily. Free.

Rivercenter Mall. Bounded by Commerce, Bowie, Crockett, and Alamo Streets. This three-story mall is home to several anchor stores as well as specialty shops and restaurants. On the enclosed bridge over the river vendors sell crafts and specialty items. The River Walk makes a U-turn in an outdoor dining area. Two hours free parking. Open daily.

where to eat

Schilo's Delicatessen. 424 East Commerce Street. This deli is located on the street, not on the River Walk, but what it lacks in atmosphere it definitely makes up for in history. Founded by Papa Fritz Schilo, the German immigrant opened a saloon in 1917, but when Prohibition came along he converted the operation to a deli. It was a lucky break for diners; mere suds could never match the subs and sandwiches that keep this spot packed with locals. Try a Reuben or a ham and cheese, or for dinner go all out with entrees like *Wiener schnitzel* or bratwurst. $. (210) 223–6692.

Boudro's. 421 East Commerce Street. Ask many San Antonians for their favorite River Walk eatery and you'll hear this name. This steak and seafood restaurant offers the finest in Southwestern cuisine, usually with a twist that makes it unique even among San Antonio's plethora of excellent eateries. Start with a cactus margarita, a frozen concoction with a jolt of red cactus liqueur. Follow that eye-opener with an appetizer of smoked chicken or crab quesadillas, or crab and shrimp tamales. Save room, though, for Boudro's specialties— coconut shrimp, pecan-grilled fish fillet, and the specialty of the house, blackened prime rib. Seating is available on the River Walk or in the dining room. $$. (210) 224–8484.

Little Rhein Steakhouse. 231 South Alamo. Located on the River Walk near the Arneson River Theater, this restaurant offers an excellent selection of fine steaks served on terraces overlooking the river. On less pleasant days, you may choose to dine inside the historic steak house, built in 1847, which witnessed the development of San Antonio under six flags. The stone building also survived the battle of the Alamo, only a few blocks away. From the extensive menu, you can choose anything from T-bones to rib eye to porterhouse steak, all served with Texas caviar (a mixture of black-eyed peas and chopped onion). Reservations are recommended. $$–$$$. (210) 225–2111.

where to stay

Hyatt Regency San Antonio. 123 Losoya Street. This beautiful hotel, with its open atrium and glass elevators, is located directly on the River Walk. A stream flows through the hotel outside to the River Walk, where an open-air jazz bar provides nightly entertainment. $$$. (800) 233–1234 or (210) 222–1234; www.hyatt.com.

Ramada Inn Emily Morgan Hotel. 705 East Houston Street, next to the Alamo. General Santa Anna was enamored with a mulatto slave named Emily Morgan, who acted as a spy for the Texas army. Thanks in part to her efforts, Sam Houston's troops defeated Santa Anna's men at San Jacinto on April 21, 1836, winning the Texas Revolution. Emily Morgan came to be known as "The Yellow Rose of Texas," and is the namesake of this 177-room hotel. The rooms overlook the Alamo courtyard or Alamo Plaza, and most have Jacuzzis. $$. (888) 298–2054 or (210) 225–8486.

Plaza San Antonio. 555 South Alamo Street. This elegant establishment has the most beautiful grounds of any downtown hotel: six acres dotted with gardens, Chinese pheasants, and historic buildings. Most of the 252 rooms have a private balcony. The hotel received international attention in 1992 by hosting the initializing ceremony of the North American Free Trade Agreement on the grounds. $$$. (800) 727–3239 or (210) 229–1000; www.plazasa.com.

Wyndham St. Anthony Hotel. 300 East Travis Street. This historic hotel a few blocks off the River Walk offers 352 rooms and access to a restaurant, health club, and swimming pool. $$$. (210) 227–4392; www.wyndham.com.

downtown: market square

Colorful Market Square, bounded by San Saba, Santa Rosa, West Commerce, and Dolorosa Streets, is a busy shopping and dining area from early morning to late evening. It is also the scene of many San Antonio festivals.

To reach Market Square from the River Walk, follow Commerce Street west across the river to just east of Interstate 10. Or, leave your car and take an inexpensive ride on the VIA streetcars, the open-air trolleys that stop at many downtown San Antonio attractions. (For information on VIA routes, stop by the San Antonio Visitor Information Center mentioned earlier.)

The history of Market Square goes back to the early 1800s, to a time when Mexico ruled the settlement of San Antonio de Bejar. Fresh produce and meats filled the farmer's market, and pharmaceutical items were available at Botica Guadalupana, today the oldest continuously operating pharmacy in town (and a very interesting place to browse, even if you're feeling healthy).

Chili con carne, the state dish of Texas, was invented here over a century ago. Back then, young girls known as "chili queens" sold the spicy meat-and-bean concoction from kiosks.

Today Market Square includes the renovated Farmers' Market Plaza (rife with Mexican imports and crafts rather than produce), an open-air restaurant and shopping area, and El Mercado, the largest enclosed Mexican-style marketplace in the country. Also located nearby are two historic structures: the Spanish Governor's Palace and Navarro House, home of a Texas patriot.

where to go

El Mercado. 514 West Commerce Street. Styled after a typical Mexican market, El Mercado's fifty shops sell a profusion of goods, from silver jewelry, Mexican dresses, and *piñatas* to onyx chess sets, leather goods, and much more. Prices are slightly higher than in the Mexican markets, and you can't bargain with the vendors like you can south of the border. Open daily. Free. (210) 207–8600.

Spanish Governor's Palace. 105 Plaza de Armas. Part of an old Spanish fort that was built at the site in 1722, this structure was converted to a military commander's residence in 1749. San Antonio was once the capital of the Spanish province of Texas, and the Spanish governors occasionally resided here. The walls are 3 feet thick, and the home is filled with Spanish colonial antiques. Open daily. Fee. (210) 224–0601.

Casa Navarro State Historical Park. 228 South Laredo Street. This was formerly the residence of José Antonio Navarro (1795–1871), a signer of the Texas Declaration of Independence. The adobe and limestone structure includes an office used by Navarro, who was a lawyer and legislator. Open Wednesday through Sunday. Fee. (210) 226–4801; www.tpwd.state.tx.us.

where to eat

Mi Tierra. 218 Produce Row. This is the place to head for an unbeatable Tex-Mex meal that includes homemade tortillas, enchiladas, and *chiliquiles,* a spicy egg and corn tortilla breakfast dish served with refried beans. Decorated year-round with Christmas ornaments, this San Antonio institution is open 24 hours a day, 365 days a year. $–$$. (210) 225–1262.

hot tamales

Tamales, both mild and spicy varieties, are also found on just about every Tex-Mex menu throughout the state, but they're most popular during the Christmas season. Stores and restaurants sell tamales by the dozen during the holidays when it's popular to bring them to office parties and home get-togethers.

Making tamales at home is a time-consuming job, one often tackled by large families as a holiday tradition. Tamales start with the preparation of a hog's head, boiled with garlic, spices, peppers, and cilantro. After cooking, the meat is ground and then simmered with spices.

As the filling is prepared, other family members ready the hojas, or corn husks, used to wrap the tamale. Others prepare the masa, a cornmeal worked with lard and seasonings, spread thinly on the shucks before filling with meat. Finally, the tamales are steamed in huge pots.

La Margarita. 120 Produce Row. This establishment also is owned by Mi Tierra and is best known for its excellent *fajitas,* which are brought to your table in cast-iron skillets. Open for lunch and dinner. $–$$. (210) 227–7140.

within the city

Although the downtown area has plenty of attractions, other stops lie on the outskirts of the city, including a zoo, missions, and botanical gardens.

where to go

San Antonio Missions National Historical Park. This national park stretches for 9 miles along the San Antonio River and is comprised of four remaining missions (outside of the Alamo) constructed by the Franciscan friars in the eighteenth century. The missions are active parish churches today, and all are open to the public. For a map of the mission locations, visit the National Park Service Web site at www.nps.gov/saan/. Each of the four illustrates a different concept of mission life:

Mission San José. 6539 San José Drive. The most complete structure in the tour, Mission San José was built in 1720. It has beautiful carvings, eighty-four rooms that once housed Indians, a restored mill with waterwheel, and what may be the only complete mission fort in existence. Make this mission your first stop; it is also home to the Visitors Information Center. (210) 932–1001.

Mission Concepción. 807 Mission Road. Built in 1731 this mission holds the title as the oldest unrestored stone church in the country. (210) 534–1540.

Mission San Juan Capistrano. 9102 Graff Road. This mission was relocated here from East Texas in 1731 but never completed. (210) 534–0749.

Mission San Francisco de la Espada. 10040 Espada. Established in 1731, its original chapel was in ruins by 1778 and the building was reconstructed around 1868. (210) 627–2021.

San Antonio Zoological Garden and Aquarium. 3903 North St. Mary's Street. This world-class zoo features barless "habitat cages" for many of its animals. The cliffs of an abandoned quarry are home to more than 3,000 birds, fish, mammals, and other fauna, making the zoo one of the largest animal collections in North America. There's a children's petting area, a reptile house, and an aquarium. Open daily year-round; call for seasonal hours. Fee. (210) 734–7184; www.sazoo-aq.org.

Japanese Tea Gardens. 3800 North St. Mary's Street, by the zoo. San Antonio's semi-tropical climate encourages the lush flowers, climbing vines, and tall palms found inside this quiet, serene place. The ponds, with beautiful rock bridges and walkways, are home to koi (large goldfish). Open daily. Free. (210) 207–3211.

San Antonio Botanical Gardens and Halsell Conservatory. 555 Funston Place, near Fort Sam Houston. Roses, herbs, a garden for the blind, and native plants are found within the lovely setting of these thirty-three-acre gardens.

The centerpiece here is the $6.9 million Halsell Conservatory. A futuristic-looking, 90,000-square-foot structure is composed of seven tall glass spires. A self-guided tour of these seven areas takes visitors through the plants and flowers found in different environments, from desert to tropics. The conservatory sits partially underground for a cooling effect in the hot Texas summers. Open daily. Fee. (210) 207–3255; www.sabot.org.

Fort Sam Houston Self-Guided Tour. North New Braunfels Avenue and Stanley Road. This National Historic Landmark, an army base dating back to 1870, has nine times as many historic buildings as Colonial Williamsburg. These include the residence where General John J. Pershing lived in 1917; the Chinese Camp, once occupied by Chinese who fled Mexico to escape Pancho Villa; and the home where Lieutenant and Mrs. Dwight Eisenhower lived in 1916. Visitors can stroll past the structures (they are not open to the public). Call for hours. Free. (210) 221–1886.

The post also includes two museums. The Fort Sam Houston Museum is filled with exhibits about the site's early days. Open Wednesday through Sunday. Free. (210) 221–1886. The U.S. Army Medical Department Museum houses exhibits on military medical practices dating back to the Revolutionary War. Open Wednesday through Saturday. Free. (210) 221–6358.

Buckhorn Saloon and Museums. 318 East Houston Street. There's nothing more Texan than Lone Star beer, and you can sample the product at the Buckhorn Saloon. This historic bar once was frequented by short-story writer William Sydney Porter (O. Henry), whose home has been relocated to the brewery grounds 2 blocks from the Alamo.

The Buckhorn Saloon building also contains the Buckhorn Hall of Horns and the Buckhorn Hall of Feathers, each containing their respective mounted specimens of animal horns and Texas birds. Separate buildings house the Hall of Texas History Wax Museum, with figures that re-create Texas's early historic events, and the Buckhorn Hall of Fins, which includes specimens from the Gulf of Mexico and Texas rivers. Open daily. Fee. (210) 247–4000; www.buckhornmuseum.com.

Witte Museum of History and Science/H–E–B Science Treehouse. 3801 Broadway. This excellent museum focuses on natural history, especially as it relates to the state's Native American, Spanish, and Mexican heritage. Open daily. The museum is also home to the H–E–B Treehouse, a collection of hands-on exhibits illustrating scientific principles. Fee. (210) 357–1866; www.wittemuseum.org.

Marion Koogler McNay Art Museum. 6000 North New Braunfels Avenue. Located in a Spanish Mediterranean mansion that was once the home of art lover Marion Koogler McNay, the museum houses a nationally known collection of modern art as well as medieval and Gothic works. It also holds the largest collection of European and American graphic art in the Southwest. In the Tobin wing, visitors find one of the country's best theater arts research centers. Open Tuesday through Sunday. Free. (210) 824–5368; www .mcnayart.org.

San Antonio Museum of Art. 200 West Jones Avenue. This extensive art museum is housed in the former Lone Star Brewery. The collection ranges from ancient Egyptian artifacts to nineteenth-century art. The museum recently opened the Nelson A. Rockefeller Collection of Mexican Folk Art, one of the best in the nation. Open Tuesday through Sunday. Fee. (210) 978–8100; www.sa-museum.org.

far northwest

Beyond Loop 410, the city begins to give way to the Hill Country, the rolling, oak-covered land that's still largely rural. This is also the home of San Antonio's two theme parks.

where to go

SeaWorld of Texas. Ellison Drive and Westover Hills Boulevard, off Highway 151; 18 miles northwest of downtown, between Loop 410 and Loop 1604. This 250-acre, Texas-size park is the largest marine-life park in the world. It's the home of Shamu the killer whale, plus dolphins, penguins, sea otters, and more. Visitors can enjoy two fast-moving water rides as well as acres of quiet gardens dotted with statues of famous Texans. Entertainment includes twenty-five shows, featuring a waterskiing extravaganza and breathtaking cycling perform-ances. New interactive programs enable guests (for an additional fee) to don wet suits for up-close encounters with beluga whales or California sea lions, to dine with killer whales, or to go behind the scenes to watch the care of more than 11,000 animals.

The park also offers two roller coasters as well as plenty of water rides.

Other attractions include a beautiful coral reef, a petting pool with people-friendly dol-phins, and a Garden of Flags overlooking a map of the United States. Painted on concrete, the map is the size of a parking lot, and children are encouraged to race from "coast to coast." Open daily late May through November; weekends only during cooler months. Call for hours. Fee. (800) 700–7786 or (210) 523–3618; www.seaworld.com.

Six Flags Fiesta Texas. I–10 and Loop 1604, 15 miles northwest of downtown. This $100 million plus theme park focuses on the history, culture, and music of San Antonio and the Southwest. The main draw of this 200-acre spread is live entertainment. Seven theaters delight visitors with more than sixty performances daily, including the award-winning and always packed "Rockin' at Rockville High" *Grease*-style musical production. For thrill seek-ers, there are thirteen rides that range from whitewater rafting to the Rattler, one of the tallest wooden roller coasters in the world and a real white-knuckle ride.

The park's latest addition is the Superman Krypton Coaster, a mile-long thrill ride that takes riders through six inversions and a 114-foot vertical loop at 70 miles per hour.

The park is divided into four "villages," each featuring a different style of music and entertainment: Hispanic (Los Festivales), German (Spassburg), country-western (Crackaxle Canyon), and rock 'n' roll (Rockville). You'll also find the Boardwalk, a 1950s-themed area complete with a sand "beach," and a 90-foot Ferris wheel that provides an unbeatable view of the park and, just at the edge of the horizon, the city.

Open seasonally March through November; call for hours. Fee. (800) 473–4378 or (210) 697–5050; www.sixflags.com/sanantonio/.

where to stay

Hyatt Regency Hill Country Resort. 9800 Hyatt Resort Drive. This full-service resort offers the area's most luxurious getaway with an eighteen-hole golf course and a four-acre water park with a cascading waterfall and man-made Ramblin' River for inner-tube floaters. This 500-room resort nestles on 200 acres of a former cattle ranch, rolling land sprinkled with prickly pear cacti, wildflower meadows, and live oaks. With its limestone architecture and western decor, the four-story hotel captures the atmosphere of the Hill Country, from windmills to gingerbread trim featuring the Lone Star (which often decorated homes of the German pioneers who settled the area). For meetings, the resort built a traditional "Sunday" house, modeled after the small, two-story homes that distant farmers often owned in town so that they could spend Saturday afternoon at market, Saturday night in town, and Sunday morning at church. $$$. (800) 233–1234 or (210) 647–1234; www.hyatt.com.

especially for winter texans

Admiralty RV Resort Park. 1485 North Ellison Drive, off Loop 1604. This 240-pad RV park is located minutes from SeaWorld and Loop 1604. It includes a heated pool, brick patios at each site, cable TV hookups, and organized get-togethers during the winter (potluck dinners, card games, and dominoes). Winter residents can take advantage of special monthly rates. (800) 999–RVSA.

day trip 02

southwest

**gruene, new braunfels:
old-world fun**

gruene

Once a separate community but now part of New Braunfels, Gruene is a popular destination for shoppers and water-recreation lovers. Head south on Interstate 35 for 30 miles to San Marcos (see South Day Trip 3 for attractions in that city). Continue south for 17 miles to exit 191. Turn west and continue to the intersection with Hunter Road, then turn left and continue to this historic area.

Once a ghost town, Gruene has been transformed into a very popular shopping destination. A historic inn, river rafting, lots of good food, and Texas's oldest dance hall draw visitors from around the state.

Although it has the feel of a separate community, Gruene actually sits within the northern New Braunfels city limits. Exit I–35 on FM 306 and head west for 1½ miles to Hunter Road. Turn left and continue to Gruene. Like Waxahachie and Refugio, the pronunciation of Gruene is one of those things that sets a real Texan apart. To sound like a local, just say "Green" when referring to this weekend destination.

In the days when cotton was king, Gruene was a roaring town on the banks of the Guadalupe River. Started in the 1870s by H. D. Gruene, the community featured a swinging dance hall and a cotton gin. Prosperity reigned until the boll weevil came to Texas, with the Great Depression right on its heels. Gruene's foreman hanged himself from the water tower, and H. D.'s plans for the town withered like the cotton in the fields. Gruene became a ghost town.

One hundred years after its founding, investors began restoring Gruene's historic buildings and, little by little, businesses began moving into the once-deserted structures. Now Gruene is favored by antiques shoppers, barbecue and country music lovers, and those looking to step back into a simpler time. On weekdays you may find Gruene's streets quiet, but expect crowds every weekend.

There's free parking across from the Gruene Mansion Inn, former home of H. D. Gruene. Today the mansion is a private residence owned by the proprietors of an adjacent bed-and-breakfast.

Gruene is compact, with everything within easy walking distance. If you'd like more information on the community's history, pick up a free copy of "A Pedestrian Guide for Gruene Guests" at local shops.

More than one hundred arts and crafts vendors sell their wares during Market Days. This event is held February through November on the third Saturday and Sunday of the month, and a Christmas market takes place on the first weekend in December.

southwest day trip 02

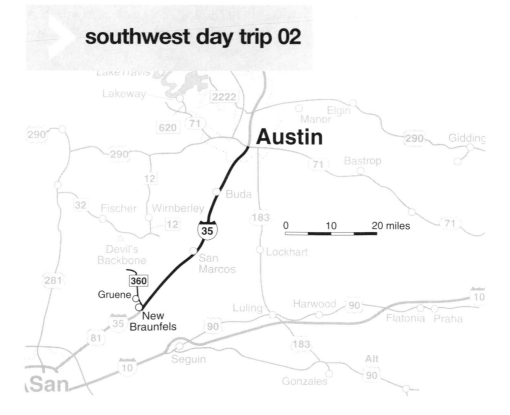

where to go

Gruene Hall. 1281 Gruene Road. The oldest dance hall in Texas is as lively today as it was a century ago. Dances and concerts are regularly held here (even though the hall has no air-conditioning), and it is also open to tour. Burlap bags draped from the ceiling dampen the sound, and 1930s advertisements decorate the walls. The hall opens at 11:00 A.M. most days. On weekdays, there's usually no cover charge for evening performances; weekend cover charges vary with the performer. Call for a schedule of events. (830) 606–1281; www.gruenehall.com.

where to shop

Gruene General Store. 1610 Hunter Road. This shop brings back memories of small-town life during Gruene's heyday as a cotton center. This was the first mercantile store, built in 1878 to serve the families that worked on the cotton farms. It also served as a stagecoach stop and a post office. Today instead of farm implements and dry goods, this 1990s general store sells cookbooks, fudge, and Texas-style clothing. Belly up for a soda at the old-fashioned fountain, and have a taste of homemade fudge. (830) 629–6021.

Gruene River Raft Company. 1404 Gruene Road. See the Guadalupe at your own pace—during a leisurely tube ride or on an exciting whitewater raft journey—with this outfitter. (888) 705–2800 or (830) 625–2800.

Lone Star Country Goods. 1613 Hunter Road. Bring the cowboy look to your home with the accessories in this shop. Lamps, dinnerware, and folk art are offered for sale. (830) 609–1613.

Texas Homegrown. 1641 Hunter Road. Like the name suggests, the merchandise is Texas-themed and features everything from bluebonnet earrings to coyote T-shirts. Open daily. (830) 629–3176.

Gruene Antique Company. 1607 Hunter Road. Built in 1904, this was once a mercantile store. Today it's divided into several vendor areas and filled with antiques. Open daily. (830) 629–7781.

Buck Pottery. 1296 Gruene Road. Here you can watch crafters make pottery in the back room. This shop sells dinnerware, gift items, and outdoor pots, all made with unleaded glazes. Open daily. (830) 629–7975.

Gruene Haus Country Store. 1297 Gruene Road. Built in the 1880s, this shop was the former home of H. D. Gruene's foreman. Linens, lace runners, silk bluebonnets, gifts for cat lovers, and decorative accessories are for sale. Open daily. (830) 620–7454.

where to eat

Guadalupe Smoked Meats. 1299 Gruene Road. Outstanding barbecue, potato salad, and beans are popular choices at this restaurant housed in the old Martin Brothers Store. The owners also operate a mail-order business for people who can't find barbecue like this at home. Open daily for lunch and dinner. $$. (830) 629–6121.

Gristmill River Restaurant and Bar. 1287 Gruene Road. Housed in the ruins of a 120-year-old cotton gin, this restaurant serves chicken, chicken-fried steak, catfish, burgers, and other Texas favorites. You can eat inside or outside on the deck overlooking the Guadalupe River. Open daily. $$. (830) 625–0684; www.gristmill restaurant.com.

where to stay

Gruene Mansion Inn. 1275 Gruene Road. Guests at this inn stay in restored 1870s cottages on a bluff overlooking the Guadalupe River. Eight lovely rooms are decorated with period antiques. A two-night rental is required on weekends. $$$. (830) 629–2641; www.gruenemansioninn.com.

new braunfels

Continue south on Gruene Road into New Braunfels. This city has just about everything to offer travelers, including historic buildings, German food, an enormous water-theme park, and enough antiques shops to merit the title "The Antique Capital of Texas."

If you're looking for a romantic getaway in a historic inn or a weekend of outdoor fun, New Braunfels is the place. Just a half hour south of Austin on I–35, this town of 36,500 offers something for every interest, from antiques and water sports to German culture.

In the 1840s, a group of German businessmen bought some land in Texas, planning to parcel off the acreage to German immigrants. Led by Prince Carl of Germany's Solms-Braunfels region, the group came to Texas to check on their new purchase. They discovered that it was more than 300 miles from the Texas coast, far from supplies in San Antonio, and located in the midst of Comanche Indian territory. Prince Carl sent a letter warning other settlers not to come, but it was too late—almost 400 already had set sail for Texas. The prince saved the day by buying another parcel of land, this in the central part of the state. Called "The Fountains" by the Native Americans, it offered plentiful springs and agricultural opportunities. The Germans soon divided the land into farms, irrigating with springwater. The settlement they founded was named New Braunfels in honor of their homeland.

New Braunfels has never forgotten these ties to the old country. Even today German is spoken in many local homes. Every November the town puts on its *lederhosen* for Wurstfest, one of the largest German celebrations in the country.

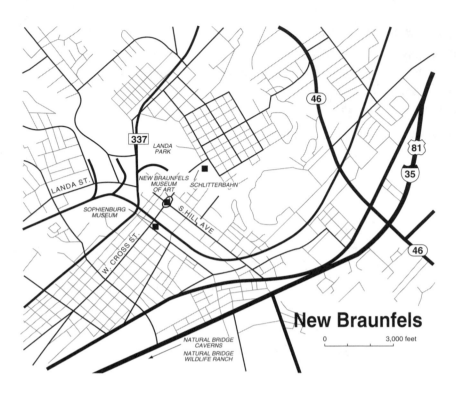

The German settlers were a practical lot, and they saved old items of every description. Everything from handmade cradles to used bottles and jars were kept and passed down through generations. Because of this, New Braunfels touts itself as "The Antique Capital of Texas."

The early settlers of New Braunfels also were attracted by the Comal and Guadalupe Rivers. Today swimmers, rafters, inner-tubers, and campers are drawn to these shady banks. The 2-mile-long Comal holds the distinction as the world's shortest river. Its crystal-clear waters begin with the springs in downtown Landa Park, eventually merging with the Guadalupe River, home to many local outfitters. Located on the scenic drive called River Road, the outfitters provide equipment and transportation for inner-tubers and rafters of all skill levels who like nothing better on a hot Texas day than to float down the cypress-shaded waters.

where to go

Chamber of Commerce. 390 South Seguin Avenue. Drop by for maps, brochures, shopping information, and friendly hometown advice about the area. Open daily. (800) 572–2626 or (830) 625–2385; www.nbcham.org.

Schlitterbahn. 305 West Austin Street. From I–35, take the Boerne exit (Loop 337) to Common Street, then turn left and continue to Liberty Street. This water park ranks first in Texas and is tops in the United States among seasonal water parks. This is the largest water-theme park in the state.

Schlitterbahn, which means "slippery road" in German, is also the largest tubing park in the world, with nine tube chutes, two uphill water coasters, seventeen water slides, five playgrounds, and more. The Comal River supplies 24,000 gallons a minute of cool spring-water and also provides the only natural river rapids found in a water-theme park.

Among the most colorful rides is the Soda Straws, made of huge Plexiglas-enclosed slides that take riders from the top of a 27-foot concrete soda to a pool below. In 1986 the cola glasses were filled with 2,000 gallons of soda and Blue Bell ice cream to create the world's largest Coke float. There's a steep 60-foot Schlittercoaster and the mile-long Raging River tube chute for daredevils, and a 50,000-gallon hot tub with a swim-up bar and the gentle wave pool for the less adventurous.

Two popular attractions here are the Boogie Bahn, a moving mountain of water for surf-ing, and the Dragon Blaster, the world's first uphill water coaster. The latter shoots inner-tube riders uphill for a roller-coaster-type ride through hills, dips, and curves. Plan to spend a whole day here, and bring a picnic if you like. Open May through September. Fee. (830) 625–2351; www.schlitterbahn.com.

New Braunfels Museum of Art and Music. 1259 Gruene Road. This 15,000-square-foot collection (formerly the Hummel Museum) houses changing art displays by local residents. Call for hours. (830) 625–5636; www.nbmuseum.org.

Sophienburg Museum. 401 West Coll Street. For a look at the hard-working people who settled this rugged area, spend an hour or two at the Sophienburg. Named for the wife of settlement leader Prince Carl, the museum's displays include a reproduction of an early New Braunfels home, a doctor's office (complete with medical tools), a blacksmith's shop, and carriages used by early residents. Open daily, but call for hours. Fee. (830) 629–1572.

Lindheimer Home. 491 Comal Avenue. Located on the banks of the Comal River, this home belonged to Ferdinand Lindheimer, a botanist who lent his name to more than thirty Texas plant species. Now restored, it contains early memorabilia from Lindheimer's career as both botanist and newspaper publisher. A backyard garden is filled with examples of his native flora discoveries. Hours are seasonal; call before you go. Fee. (830) 608–1512.

Museum of Texas Handmade Furniture. 1370 Church Hill Drive, in Conservation Plaza. This nineteenth-century home contains cedar, oak, and cypress furniture handcrafted by early German settlers. Open Tuesday through Sunday from Memorial Day through Labor Day, and on weekend afternoons the rest of the year. Fee. (830) 629–6504.

Natural Bridge Caverns. On RR 3009, southwest of New Braunfels. Named for the rock arch over the entrance, this cave is one of the most spectacular in the area. The guided tour is well lit; the slope of the trail may be taxing for some. Kids can "pan" for small pieces of amethyst, sapphire, obsidian, topaz, and more at the attraction's Natural Bridge Mining Company. And adventurous travelers can make reservations for the South Cave Tour, rappelling and crawling in spelunking gear to see remote cave regions. Open daily year-round; phone for tour times. Fee. (830) 651–6101; www.naturalbridgecaverns.com.

Natural Bridge Wildlife Ranch. Next to the caverns. From I–35 south of New Braunfels, take RR 3009 west. From Highway 46 west of town, you also can take a left on RR 1863 for a slightly longer but more scenic route.

For more than a century this property has operated as a family ranch, and since 1984 it has showcased exotic species, today holding the title as the oldest and most-visited safari park in the state. More than fifty native, exotic, and endangered species roam the grounds. The ranch offers a drive past zebras, gazelles, antelope, ostriches, and more. You'll be given animal feed when you arrive, so be prepared for the animals to come right up to the car for a treat. (Watch out or the ostrich will put his head inside the car in search of that food!) A large cat run gives jaguar and cougar plenty of room to stroll, and another area houses three species of primates, scarlet macaws, and other exotic birds. A walking area holds some species that require a little more attention, such as reticulated giraffes, Bennett wallabies, and Patagonian cavies. Children love the petting zoo for the chance to get face to face with pint-size, friendly animals. Open daily. Fee. (830) 438–7400; www.wildliferanchtx.com.

Landa Park. Landa and San Antonio Streets. Named for Joseph Landa, New Braunfels's first millionaire, this downtown park includes a miniature train, a glass-bottom boat cruise, a golf course, and a one-and-a-half-acre spring-fed swimming pool. This is the headwaters of the Comal River, where springs gush eight million gallons of pure water every hour. Picnicking is welcome in the park, but no camping. Free. (830) 608–2160.

Canyon Lake. FM 306, northwest of town. With 80 miles of protected shoreline, Canyon Lake is very popular with campers, bicyclists, scuba divers, and boaters. The lake has seven parks with boat ramps and picnic facilities. (800) 528–2104.

River Road. This winding drive stretches northwest of the city for 18 miles from Loop 337 at the city limits to the Canyon Lake Dam. It's lined with river outfitters and beautiful spots where you can pull over and look at the rapids, which delight rafters, canoeists, and innertubers.

Rockin' R River Rides. 1405 Gruene Road. You can take a river ride anytime between March and October. Excursions range from family tubing trips to whitewater thrillers. This company also operates a campground, Camp Hueco Springs, on River Road. (800) 55–FLOAT or (830) 629–9999; www.rockinr.com.

The Children's Museum. Off I–35 at exit 187. Bring the kids to enjoy hands-on fun at this interactive museum that features a television studio. Open daily. Fee. (830) 620–0939.

where to shop

New Braunfels Marketplace. Exits 187 and 189 off I–35. What started out as a single factory store has become a destination for busloads of shoppers from Houston and Dallas. Goods from sportswear to books to leather goods are featured in the many shops. Open daily. (830) 620–7475; www.nbmarketplace.com.

Palace Heights Antiques. One block west of I-35 at exit 189. This extensive store (which resembles a white castle outside) opened in 1972. The antiques mall features a wide variety of items from many vendors. Open Monday through Saturday 10:00 A.M. to 5:00 P.M., Sunday noon to 5:00 P.M. (830) 625–0612; www.papaceheights antiques.com.

where to eat

Oma's Haus. Take Seguin exit 1890 off I–35 and drive east to 541 Highway 46 South. This restaurant serves a wide selection of German dishes in a family atmosphere. The menu includes chicken and pork schnitzel, and a specialty of the house called Oma's Pride, a spinach-filled pastry shell. For the less adventurous, chicken-fried steak and chicken breast are also offered. Open for lunch and dinner daily. $$. (830) 625–3280.

Naegelin's Bakery. 129 South Seguin Avenue. Naegelin's has operated on the same spot since 1868. The original building is gone, replaced by the current structure in 1942. The store's specialty is apple strudel, a 2-foot-long creation that is certain to make any pastry-lover's mouth water. During the holidays, some of Naegelin's biggest sellers are springerle, a licorice cookie, and lebkucken, a frosted gingerbread cookie. $. Open Monday through Saturday. (830) 625–5722.

New Braunfels Smokehouse. Highway 46 and U.S. Highway 81. If you get the chance to attend Wurstfest, you'll undoubtedly sample the product of this smokehouse. For this fall event, New Braunfels Smokehouse produces between 40,000 and 60,000 pounds of sausage. That sausage is the specialty of the house, but the restaurant has a little of everything, including smoked ham and barbecue brisket. A large gift shop up front offers Texas specialty foods and cookbooks. The company's mail-order business ships more than 600,000 catalogs to sausage lovers around the country. Open daily. $–$$. (830) 625–2416; www.nbsmokehouse.com.

where to stay

New Braunfels has plenty of accommodations for everyone. Check with the Chamber of Commerce. (800) 572–2626.

Prince Solms Inn. 295 East San Antonio Street. Built in 1900, this quiet bed-and-breakfast has two suites and a guest parlor downstairs; upstairs there are eight guest rooms. All rooms are furnished with period antiques. $$$. (800) 625–9169 or (830) 625–9169; www.princesolmsinn.com.

Faust Hotel. 240 South Seguin Avenue. A New Braunfels tradition, this 1929 four-story, renovated hotel features a bar that's popular with locals and visitors. The lobby is appointed with beautiful antique furnishings. $$. (830) 625–7791; www.fausthotel.com.

John Newcombe's Tennis Ranch. 325 Mission Valley Road. This resort is especially noted for its tennis facilities, with covered clay and lighted courts. Professional instruction is available; during the summer, the resort offers children's learning programs. $$–$$$. (800) 444–6204; www.newktennis.com.

especially for winter texans

Heidelberg Lodges. 1020 North Houston Avenue. Located near the headwaters of the Comal River, this scenic family resort is popular in the summer with swimmers, snorkelers, and scuba divers. During off-season it's home to Winter Texans, who are welcomed with potluck dinners and get-togethers. Accommodations include A-frame cottages and motel units. Call for long-term winter rates. $$. (830) 625–9967.

day trip 03

southwest

**wimberley, devil's backbone
scenic drive, fischer, blanco:
kodak country**

wimberley

From Austin, follow U.S. Highway 290 west to the small community of Dripping Springs. Turn south on RR 12 and continue 15 miles to Wimberley, a favorite shopping destination from Thursday through Monday. Wimberley's also a great summer destination because of its location on the Blanco River and Cypress Creek.

Wimberley's history goes back to the 1850s when a resourceful Texas Revolution veteran named William Winters opened a mill here. As was tradition at the time, he named the new community Winters' Mill. When Winters died, John Cade bought the mill, and the town became Cade's Mill. Finally in 1870, a wealthy Llano man named Pleasant Wimberley rode into town. Tired of Indian raids on his horses in Llano, he moved in, bought the mill, and changed the town's name one last time.

The small town of Wimberley is one of those "shop 'til you drop" kinds of places. Even with only 3,700 residents, the town boasts dozens of specialty stores, art galleries and studios, and accommodations ranging from river resorts to historic bed-and-breakfasts.

Wimberley is a quiet place except when the shops open their doors on Monday, Thursday, Friday, and on weekends. The busiest time to visit is the first Saturday of the month, from April through December. This is Market Day, when more than 400 vendors set up to sell antiques, collectibles, and arts and crafts.

southwest day trip 03

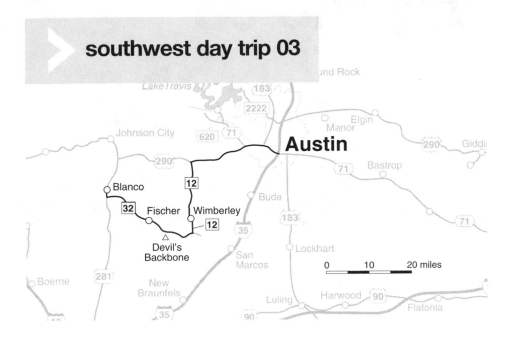

Many visitors come to enjoy the town's two water sources: the Blanco River and clear, chilly Cypress Creek. Both are filled with inner-tubers and swimmers during hot summer months. The waterways provide a temporary home for campers and vacationers who stay in resorts and cabins along the shady water's edge.

where to go

Wimberley Chamber of Commerce. Wimberley North Shopping Center, RR 12 past Cypress Creek. Stop by the Chamber offices on weekdays to load up on brochures, maps, and shopping tips. (512) 847–2201; www.wimberley.org.

Pioneertown. 7-A Ranch Resort, 1 mile west of RR 12 on County Road 178, at the intersection of County Road 179. See a medicine show, tour a general store museum, or spend some time at the town jail in this Wild West village. There's also a child-size train ride with a mile of tracks, an old log fort, cowboy shows, and a western cafe. Open weekends year-round for visits and daily during the summer months for rides and shops. Free. (512) 847–2517; www.7aranchresort.com.

where to shop

Like the nearby town of Blanco, Wimberley is home to many artists who've relocated to Texas's serene Hill Country. Specialty shops abound, selling everything from imports to sculpture and antiques. Arts and crafts are especially well represented. Plan to shop Thursday through Monday. Some stores are open all week, but most close midweek, especially during cooler months.

Rancho Deluxe. On the square, 14010 RR 12. Bring the cowboy look to your home with this shop's western merchandise. You'll find everything from spurs to Mexican sideboards, and from horns to handcrafted furniture. Open daily. (877) 847–9570 or (512) 847–9570; www.ranchodeluxe.net.

Wimberley Glass Works. 1.6 miles south of the square on RR 12. Watch demonstrations on the art of glass blowing and shop for one-of-a-kind creations. Open daily. (512) 847–9348; www.wgw.com.

Wimberley Stained Glass Shop. On the square. Highlighted by handcrafted Tiffany lamp reproductions, this shop also features custom-leaded doors, window panels, and sun catchers. Open daily (afternoons only on Sunday). (512) 847–3930.

where to stay

Wimberley is filled with bed-and-breakfast accommodations that range from historic homes in town to ranches in the surrounding Hill Country to camps along Cypress Creek. For information on these many accommodations, give one of the reservations services a call: Bed and Breakfast of Wimberley, (800) 827–1913; All Wimberley Lodging, (800) 460–3909, www.texhillcntry.com/wimberley; Texas Hill Country Retreats, (800) 236–9411, www.texas hillco.com; Hill Country Accommodations, (800) 926–5028. For brochures on Wimberley's other accommodations, call the Chamber of Commerce at (512) 847–2201.

devil's backbone scenic drive

From Wimberley, continue south on RR 12 to RR 32. Turn west and sit back for this slow, scenic drive. There aren't any steep climbs or stomach-churning lookouts; a high ridge of hills provides a gentle drive with excellent views along the way. There's very little traffic, and there's a beautiful picnic spot on the left, just a few miles before Fischer. This stretch of road is often cited as one of the most scenic drives in Texas and is well known for its fall color.

fischer

Continue on RR 32 to the tiny hamlet of Fischer. Retrace your drive south on U.S. Highway 281 for a couple of miles to the intersection of RR 32. Take a left and enjoy a quiet ride through miles of ranch land and rolling hills.

Fischer is on the left side of the road. Today not much remains of this community, just a post office, complete with an old-fashioned postmaster's cage and tiny brass mailboxes. Inside, enormous counters span the length of the dark and musty building.

blanco

After passing through Devil's Backbone, continue on RR 32 to US 281. Turn right and head north to Blanco, the home of a beautiful state park.

Formerly a "Wild West" kind of town, the community was originally the seat of Blanco County. Although the county seat eventually moved to nearby Johnson City, where it remains today, local residents have restored Blanco's old limestone courthouse as a visitor center, gift shop, and community center. The former courthouse is located at the intersection of US 281 and Highway 165. Stop by for brochures and shopping.

Around the courthouse square are several art galleries and antiques shops aimed at weekend visitors, many of whom stop to camp at the Blanco River State Recreation Area south of town.

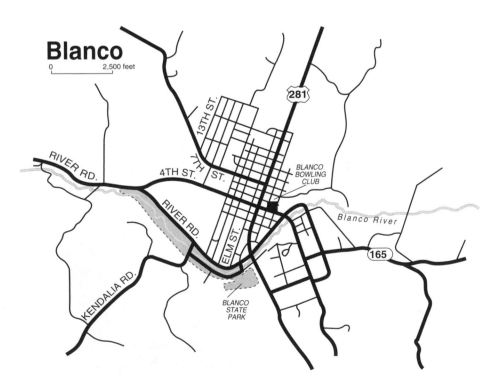

musical chairs with the county seat

Built in 1888, the former Blanco County Courthouse has been one of the most used buildings in the county—for everything except as a courthouse, that is. The year after its construction, an election moved the county seat to Johnson City. The courthouse was used a total of four years for its original purpose, then it went into a long career of different uses. For two different periods, the building served as a schoolhouse; it also became a bank. Later it served the community as a town hall, library, opera house, and even the office of the local newspaper. From 1937 to 1961 the building served as a hospital but later became a Wild West museum and then a barbecue restaurant. Today the building houses the visitor center and is used for community events.

where to go

Blanco State Park. South of Blanco on US 281. During the Depression, the Civilian Conservation Corps built two stone dams, a group pavilion, stone picnic tables, and an arched bridge in this 104-acre riverside park. Today the park is popular with swimmers, anglers, and campers. Fee. (830) 833–4333; www.tpwd.state.tx.us/park/blanco.

Blanco Bowling Club. East of the square on Fourth Street. Housed in 1940s buildings, the bowling club and the adjacent cafe have changed little with the passing years. The nine-pin game is still set up by hand as it has been for generations. The bowling club opens at 7:30 P.M., Monday through Friday (except during football season, when everyone's at the Friday night high school game). To bowl you must be a league member. Fee. (830) 833–4416.

where to eat

Blanco Bowling Club Cafe. East of the square on Fourth Street. This is a traditional Texas diner, with linoleum floor and Formica tables, and chairs filled with locals who come here at the same time every day. Chicken-fried steak is the specialty; on Friday nights there's a catfish plate as well. Stop by in the morning for huge glazed twists and doughnuts made from scratch. Open daily for breakfast, lunch, and dinner (no dinner on Sundays). $. (830) 833–4416.

day trip 04

southwest

comfort, sisterdale, boerne: that's history

This is a cultural journey from Austin, a trip through three small towns that share a strong German heritage. It includes some curving farm-to-market roads that are very susceptible to flooding. If it's raining heavily, save this trip for another day!

comfort

From Austin, head west on U.S. Highway 290 to Johnson City and Fredericksburg (see West Day Trip 2 for attractions in this city). In Fredericksburg, turn south on U.S. Highway 87 and continue for 23 miles. This small community is big in history and attractions. The downtown area is a National Historic District, filled with homes and businesses built by early settlers.

Comfort was founded by German pioneers in 1854 who wanted to name the town Gemütlichkeit, meaning peace, serenity, comfort, and happiness. After some deliberation, though, they decided on the easier to pronounce "Comfort" instead.

Today Comfort offers tourists numerous historic buildings to explore, filled with antiques shops and restaurants. Visitors also find a historic inn and the oldest general store in Texas. Weekends are the busiest time to visit, but even then the atmosphere is relaxing, unhurried, and, well, comfortable.

where to go

"Treue der Union" (True to the Union) Monument. High Street, between Third and Fourth Streets. During the Civil War, German residents of Comfort who did not approve of slavery and openly swore their loyalty to the Union were burned out of their farms. The Confederates responsible also lynched locals who refused to pledge their allegiance to the movement. Several German farmers decided to defect to Mexico but were caught by Confederate soldiers and killed on the banks of the Nueces River, their bodies left unburied.

Finally retrieved in 1865, the remains were returned to Comfort and buried in a mass grave. A white obelisk, the oldest monument in Texas and the only monument to the Union located south of the Mason-Dixon line, was dedicated here in 1866. One of only six such sites in the country, the shrine recently received Congressional approval to keep the flag at half mast. The flag that waves here has thirty-six stars, the same number it had when the marker was dedicated in 1866. Free. (830) 995-3131.

Ingenhuett Store. 830 High Street. Built in 1880 by Peter Ingenhuett, this general store is now operated by fourth- and fifth-generation family members. One of the oldest continuously operating general stores in Texas, the shop includes an Ingenhuett history display, complete with photos of the Ingenhuett ancestors and Comfort's early days. Closed Sunday. Free. (830) 995-2149.

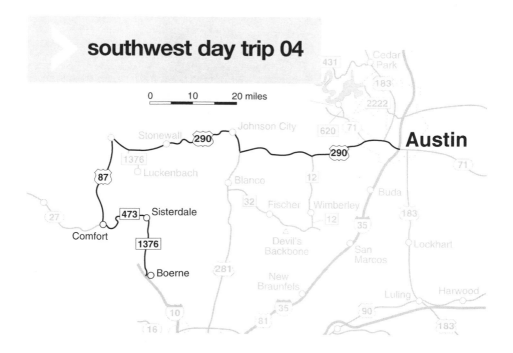

southwest day trip 04

Bat Roost. FM 473, on private land. As you leave Comfort for Sisterdale, this historic structure sits 1 mile from town on the right side of the road behind private gates. While it's generally known now that bats feed on disease-spreading mosquitoes, the folks here were aware of the importance of these furry mammals since 1918, when Albert Steves constructed hygieostatic bat roosts in an experimental attempt to control malaria. The roosts were intended to encourage the area's large bat population to remain in the region. Only sixteen such roosts were built in the country, and this is the oldest of three known still to exist. Free, but view only from the road. (830) 995–3131.

Bat Tunnel. Fifteen miles northeast of Comfort off Highway 473 on old Highway 9. View the evening flight of 1.2 million Mexican free-tailed bats from this abandoned railroad tunnel now managed by the Texas Parks and Wildlife Department. Closed October to May. Free. (830) 995–3131.

where to shop

The Comfort Common. 818 High Street. This combination bed-and-breakfast inn and indoor shopping area is located within the historic Ingenhuett-Faust Hotel. Several buildings behind the hotel display antique primitives and furniture. Open daily. (830) 995–3030.

Bygone Days. Highway 87. This year-round Christmas store features handmade Santa Claus figures as well as numerous antiques, all in a historic building with original counters and fixtures. Open daily. (830) 995–3003.

where to eat

Cypress Creek Cafe. 408 West Highway 27. Order up Texas fare such as chicken-fried steak, T-bone, or lighter dishes of seafood or sandwiches at this casual restaurant. Open daily for lunch; open for dinner Wednesday through Saturday. $–$$. (830) 995–3977.

where to stay

The Comfort Common. 818 High Street. This bed-and-breakfast operates within the 1880 Ingenhuett-Faust Hotel. The five suites are decorated in English country, American country, and Victorian decor. All rooms include private baths and period furnishings. The backyard cottage has a fireplace and complete kitchen. All rates include breakfast. As rooms book quickly for weekends, consider a midweek stay. $$. (830) 995–3030.

sisterdale

From Comfort, head out on FM 473 to nearby Sisterdale, best known as the home of a small winery. The burg, like nearby Boerne, was settled by a group of intellectuals. Today the population has dwindled to a handful of residents, and you have to look carefully to keep from passing right through town.

where to go

Sister Creek Vineyards. FM 1376, off FM 473. These vineyards thrive in "downtown" Sisterdale, located between the East and West Sister Creeks. The winery, a restored cotton gin, produces traditional French wines. Open daily for self-guided tours. Free. (830) 324–6704; www.sistercreekvineyards.com.

Sisterdale General Store. FM 473. This historic general store and adjoining bar have served generations of customers. The bar sells Sister Creek Wine. Closed Monday. (830) 324–6767.

boerne

From Sisterdale, head south on FM 1376 to Boerne (pronounced "Bernie"). Boerne is located on the banks of Cibolo Creek in the rolling Texas Hill Country. The community was founded in 1849 by German immigrants, members of the same group who settled nearby New Braunfels. They named the town for author Ludwig Börne, whose writings inspired many people to leave Germany for the New World.

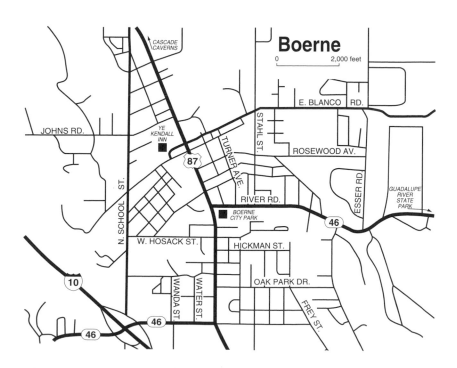

During the 1880s, Boerne became known as a health spot, and vacationers came by railroad to soak in mineral-water spas and enjoy the clean country air. Although no mineral spas remain today, Boerne still offers a quiet country atmosphere and dozens of antiques shops in which to browse.

Summer also brings seasonal fun to Boerne. A favorite activity on Main Plaza is *Abendkonzerte,* summer concerts performed by the Boerne Village Band. For nearly 140 years this German band (the oldest continuously active German band in the country and the oldest in the world outside of Munich) has entertained residents and visitors with its Old World sound. Abendkonzerte takes place on selected Tuesday nights throughout the summer.

where to go

Chamber of Commerce. One Main Plaza, beside Ye Kendall Inn. Stop here for brochures and maps to Boerne attractions and shopping areas. Open daily Monday through Friday, and Saturday morning. (888) 842–8080 or (830) 755–8080.

Agricultural Heritage Center. Highway 46 East, 1 mile from Main Street. This museum features farm and ranch tools used by pioneers in the late nineteenth and early twentieth centuries, including a working steam-operated blacksmith shop. Six acres surrounding the museum are covered with hand-drawn plows, wagons, early tractors, and woodworking tools. Open Saturday mornings and Sunday afternoons. Free. (830) 249–6007.

Cascade Caverns. From Interstate 10 take exit 543 and follow signs on Cascade Caverns Road. This family-owned cavern, located in a 105-acre park, maintains a year-round temperature of 68°F so this attraction is popular on both cold winter days and sweltering summer days. The cave has a 100-foot waterfall, an unusual underground sight. Guided tours take forty-five minutes. Open daily. Fee. (830) 755–8080; www.cascadecaverns.com.

main street

Boerne's Main Street serves as a focal point for shoppers. Antiques shops and unique boutiques fill this area. "There are a lot of special retail shops," says Michael Giddens of the Boerne Merchants Association. "We've really come a long way in the last eight years. We have about thirty to forty different shops now." Giddens himself operates The Christmas Shoppe, where it's always the holiday season. The store's especially known for its pickle ornament. Why a pickle, you might ask? The pickle is a German symbol of good luck.

Cibolo Wilderness Trail. Boerne City Park, Highway 46 at Cibolo Creek. Enjoy grassland, marshland, and woodland in this park that offers a slice of the Hill Country. Visitors can also view dinosaur tracks. The wilderness area includes both reclaimed prairie and reclaimed marsh, with walking trails that range from 1/4 to 1 mile in length. Free. (830) 249–4616.

Kuhlmann-King Historical House and Graham Building and Museum Store. Main Street and Blanco Road. The Kuhlmann-King house was built by a local businessman for his German bride in 1885. Today the two-story stone home is staffed by volunteers. The Graham Building, located next door, is home to the Boerne Area Historical Preservation Society with exhibits on local history. Open Sunday afternoons. Free. (830) 249–2030.

Guadalupe River State Park. Thirteen miles east of Boerne off Highway 46 on Park Road 31. The star of this park is the clear, cold Guadalupe River. Camp, swim, hike, or just picnic on its scenic banks, or on Saturday mornings, take an interpretive tour of the Honey Creek State Natural Area to learn more about the plants and animals of the region. Fee. (830) 438–2656; www.tpwd.state.tx.us.

Cave Without a Name. 325 Kreutzberg Road. Guided tours take groups through six rooms of this family-owned cavern. A subterranean river and numerous cave formations fill the tour. Open daily. Fee. (830) 537–4212; www.cavewithoutaname.com.

Honey Creek State Natural Area. Spring Branch, 13 miles east of Boerne off Highway 46 on Park Road 31. Use of this park is limited to those on guided tours. A two-hour guided look at the park's history and ecology is offered every Saturday morning at 9:00 A.M.; reservations aren't necessary, but call to confirm that a tour will be offered. Access into the park is through the Guadalupe River State Park. Fee. (830) 438–2656; www.tpwd.state.tx.us.

where to eat

Ye Kendall Inn. 128 West Blanco Street, Main Plaza. In 1859 the owners of this two-story structure began renting rooms to stagecoach travelers, eventually developing the property into an inn. Over the years, its famous guests have included Confederate President Jefferson Davis and President Dwight D. Eisenhower. Along with thirteen bed-and-breakfast rooms furnished with period antiques, the inn includes a restaurant with adjoining bar. Open daily for lunch, dinner Tuesday through Saturday. $$. (800) 364–2138.

Family Korner. 1234 Main Street. This family restaurant serves up Southern dishes ranging from fried chicken to chicken-fried steak. Open for breakfast and lunch daily. $$. (830) 249–3054.

Peach Tree Kountry Kitchen. 448 South Main Street. This casual eatery serves up good, old-fashioned family fare such as meatloaf and chicken-fried steak. Open for lunch Tuesday through Saturday. $$. (830) 249–8583.

Po Po Family Restaurant. 435 Northeast I-10 West Access Road. Once a stagecoach stop, this site now houses a locally popular restaurant. Along with its home-cooked meals, the restaurant is also known for its plates themselves—over 1,300 of them decorate the walls! Open daily for lunch and dinner. $$. (830) 537–4194.

day trip 05

southwest

**bandera, medina, vanderpool:
cowboy country**

bandera

Take Interstate 35 south from Austin through San Marcos and New Braunfels (see South Day Trip 3 and Southwest Day Trip 2 for information). In New Braunfels, take Highway 46 west to Boerne (see Southwest Day Trip 4). Continue on Highway 46 for 11 miles until it adjoins Highway 16. Continue west 12 miles to Bandera, "The Cowboy Capital of the World." This town is well known for its plentiful dude ranches, country-western music, rodeos, and horse racing.

Once part of the Wild West, Bandera Pass, located 12 miles north of town on Highway 173, was the site of many battles between Spanish *conquistadors* and both Apache and Comanche Indians. Legend has it that following a battle with the Apaches in 1732, a flag (or *bandera* in Spanish) was hung at the pass to mark the boundary between the two opposing forces.

Bandera has open rodeos weekly from Memorial Day to Labor Day. Typically rodeos are held Tuesday night at Mansfield Park and Friday night at Twin Elm Guest Ranch, and, during the summer, several rodeos at Mansfield Park. For schedules, call the Bandera Convention and Visitors Bureau at (800) 364–3833 or see www.banderacowboy capital.com.

Today the wildest action in town occurs in the dance halls every night except Monday and Tuesday. Put on your boots, crease your best jeans, and get ready to two-step with locals and vacationers alike.

where to go

Frontier Times Museum. Thirteenth Street, 1 block north of the courthouse. Established in 1927, this museum is a good place to learn more about Bandera's early days. The stone building is filled with cowboy paraphernalia, Native American arrowheads, and prehistoric artifacts. Its most unusual exhibit is a shrunken head from Ecuador, part of a private collection donated to the museum. Open daily. Fee. (830) 796–3864; www.frontiertimesmuseum.com.

Historical Walking Tours. Have a look at the buildings that witnessed Bandera's evolution from a frontier town to a vacation destination with a self-guided tour. Thirty-two sites along the route lead visitors to the county courthouse, the old jail, Bandera's first theater, and many homes that date back to the community's earliest days. Pick up your walking-tour brochure at the Bandera County Visitors Center, 1808 Highway 16 South. Free. (800) 364–3833.

Hill Country State Natural Area. South on Highway 173 to FM 1077, then right for 12 miles. This rugged park preserves 5,400 acres of Hill Country land. Only primitive camping is available; you must bring your own water, and pick up and remove your own trash. This park was originally open primarily for horseback riding, but today it has become popular with hikers and bicyclists. There are 34 miles of quiet trails and camp areas for backpackers and equestrians. Cool off with a dip in West Verde Creek or fish for catfish, perch, and large-mouth bass. Horse rentals are available off-site. Open daily February through October; open Friday through Sunday the rest of the year. Fee. (830) 796–4413; www.tpwd.state.tx.us.

Medina River. Highway 16, east of town. The cypress-lined Medina River is a popular spot during the summer months, when swimmers, canoeists, and inner-tubers enjoy the cool water. The Medina can be hazardous during high water, however, with rocky rapids and submerged trees. There is public access to the river from the Highway 16 bridge in town.

Running-R Ranch Trail Rides. Located 11 miles from Bandera off FM 1077. Enjoy one-, two-, or three-hour rides with an experienced wrangler. The ranch also offers all-day rides with a picnic and cowboy cookout. Children six and older are accepted. Fee. (830) 796–3984; www.rrranch.com.

The Silver Dollar Bar. 308 Main Street. Pick up a longneck, grab a partner, and start boot-scootin' at this Texas honky-tonk. Owner and singer Arkey Blue performs country-and-western hits here as crowds fill the sawdust-covered dance floor. (830) 796–8826.

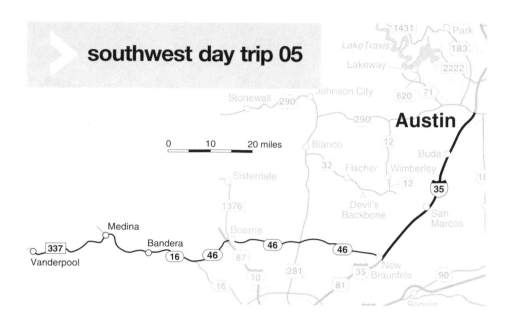

southwest day trip 05

where to shop

Love's Antiques Mall. 310 Main Street. Located in the historic Carmichael and Hay Store, this antiques mall features custom-crafted western furniture, wrought iron, sculpture, and collectibles. (830) 796–3838.

where to stay

The country around Bandera is dotted with dude ranches. Rates usually include three meals daily as well as family-style entertainment and supervised children's programs. Horseback riding is often part of the weeklong package. A minimum stay of two or three days is required at most ranches during peak summer season.

For a complete listing of Bandera's dude ranches, as well as other accommodations and campgrounds, call the Bandera Convention and Visitors Bureau. (800) 364–3833.

Mayan Ranch. Highway 16, 2 miles west of Bandera. For more than forty years this sixty-room ranch has entertained vacationers with cowboy breakfasts, cookouts, horseback riding, angling, and hayrides. Summer also brings organized children's programs. Rooms are appointed with western-style furniture. Call for rates. (830) 796–3312; www.mayan ranch.com.

Dixie Dude Ranch. South on Highway 173 1½ miles to FM 1077, then southwest for 9 more miles. Five generations of the Whitley family have welcomed guests to this nineteen-room ranch since 1937.

For more than sixty years the Dixie Dude Ranch has offered potential cowpokes the opportunity to enjoy a taste of ranch life. Start your morning with a leisurely trail ride followed by a genuine cowboy breakfast, then enjoy a day filled with hiking trails, hunting for Native American arrowheads, taking country-and-western dance lessons, fishing, or tossing horseshoes. The ranch includes nineteen units made up of individual cottages, duplex cabins, and lodge rooms featuring early Texas architecture. Rates include meals and two horseback rides daily. Call for rates. (800) 375–YALL; www.dixieduderanch.com.

Flying L Guest Ranch. From Highway 16, turn south on Highway 173 for 1½ miles, then left on Wharton Dock Road. This 542-acre ranch has thirty-eight guest houses, each with two rooms, refrigerator, microwave, coffee pot, and TV. You can choose many different packages offering horseback riding, hayrides, and even golf at the ranch's eighteen-hole course. During the summer there's a supervised children's program. Nightly entertainment ranges from western shows to "branding" parties. (800) 292–5134; www.flyingl.com.

The Silver Spur Dude Ranch. Located 10 miles south of Bandera on FM 1077. Pull on your boots and grab your Stetson before heading to this 275-acre ranch near the Hill Country State Natural Area. You'll stay busy out of the saddle with nearby angling, tubing, canoeing, golfing, plus swimming in the ranch pool. (830) 796–3037; www.ssranch.com.

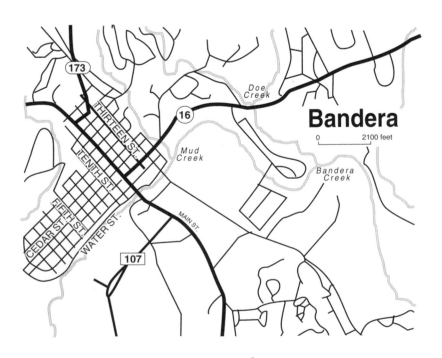

Twin Elm Guest Ranch. Just ½ mile off FM 470 from Highway 16 (4 miles from Bandera). This 200-acre dude ranch is on the Medina River. All the usual cowboy activities are available, from angling to horseback riding and horseshoe pitching. From May through September, the ranch hosts a weekly rodeo every Friday. (888) 567–3049 or (830) 796–3628; www.twinelmranch.com.

LH7 Ranch Resort. FM 3240 (5 miles from Bandera). This 1,200-acre ranch, which raises longhorn cattle, has cottages with kitchenettes, plus RV hookups. There's plenty to keep any cowpoke busy, including angling in a fifty-acre lake. Or take a hayride, trail ride, or nature walk. (830) 796–4314.

Bandera Lodge. 700 Highway 16 South. This forty-four-room lodge offers trail rides as well as a restaurant and bar, a pool, and cable TV. $. (830) 796–3093.

especially for winter texans

Besides the dude ranches, Bandera has excellent RV parks. Many weekly activities are of special interest to the Winter Texans who call Bandera home. Country-and-western dances are held Wednesday through Saturday, and there's bingo on Friday and Sunday. For a complete listing, contact the Bandera Convention and Visitors Bureau. (800) 364–3833.

medina

From Bandera, continue west on Highway 16 to the tiny community of Medina, best known for its dwarf apple trees that produce full-size fruit in varieties from Crispin to Jonagold.

where to go

Love Creek Orchards. RR 337 west of Medina. From May through October, these beautiful orchards are open to the public by guided tour only; call to set up a tour time. Free. (800) 449–0882 or (830) 589–2588; www.lovecreekorchards.com.

where to shop

The Cider Mill and Country Store. Main Street (Highway 16), downtown. This shop sells Love Creek apples from June through November. Butter, sauces, vinegars, jellies, syrups, pies, breads, and even apple ice cream are sold here year-round. If you're ready to start your own orchard but you're short on room, you can buy "the patio apple orchard," a dwarf tree grown on a trellis in a wooden planter. Open daily. (830) 589–2202.

> ## taking a shine to medina

*If there's any truth to the saying that "an apple a day keeps the doctor away,"
then the physicians of Medina, Texas better just close up shop. This Hill Country
community is the core of the Texas apple industry, a business that's growing by
the bushel.*

*Today Medina is recognized as the capital of the Texas apple industry, a busi-
ness that took root in 1981 when Baxter Adams and wife Carol moved to Love
Creek Ranch outside of Medina. Baxter spent thirty years as an exploration geolo-
gist for the oil industry before moving to this region. It's a land of rocky, rugged
hills, with fertile valleys irrigated by the cool waters of Love Creek, a spring-fed
creek that originates on the ranch.*

*These valleys gave Adams the idea for an orchard, an orchard which would
not take a great deal of land. "I don't have much tillable land," Adams explained to
us, pointing to the steep hills where goats once grazed. "I've got to really make it
count. It's a matter of trying to squeeze the most possible dollars out of the smallest possible area."*

And that's just what Baxter Adams has done.

*This Texas version of Johnny Appleseed specializes in dwarf apple trees,
plants which reach a height of only five or six feet. The lilliputians boast full-size
apples, however, up to fifty pounds per tree, in varieties from the common Red
Delicious to the unusual Gala and Crispin.*

*Baxter and Carol started with just 1,000 trees in 1981, and they were soon in
the apple business. Unlike the full-sized trees that take seven years to produce a
crop, the dwarfs yield fruit in just a year and a half. Another advantage Adams has
over the northern producers is his growing season. Texas apples ripen weeks
before their Northern cousins.*

vanderpool

Vanderpool is a quiet getaway during all but the fall months. Tucked into the hills surrounding the Sabinal River, this small town is a center for sheep and goat ranching.

where to go

Lost Maples State Natural Area. West on RR 337 to the intersection of RR 187; turn
north and continue 5 miles. This state park is one of the most heavily visited sites in Texas

during October and November when the bigtooth maples provide some of the best color in the state. Weekend visits at this time can be very crowded, so note that the parking is limited to 250 cars. The best time to visit is midweek, when you can enjoy a walk in the natural area without crowds. (800) 792–1112; www.tpwd.state.tx.us.

There are 10 miles of hiking trails to enjoy all year along the Sabinal River Canyon. In the summer visitors can swim and fish in the river. Camping includes primitive areas on the hiking trails and a thirty-site campground with rest rooms and showers as well as a trailer dump station. Open daily. Fee. (830) 966–3413.

leaf peeping

Are you starting to dream about the feel of a cool autumn breeze? To hear the crackle of leaves beneath your feet? To smell the smoke of an evening campfire?

Central Texas may not have the blazing colors of New England, but with a little looking, you will find a brilliant quilt of fall colors.

The top destination for many leaf peepers is Lost Maples State Natural Area in Vanderpool. The maples, located so far from other specimens of the beautiful tree, may seem lost, but there's no doubt that the park itself has been found. This state park is one of the most heavily visited sites in Texas during October and November when the bigtooth maples provide some of the best color in Texas. Weekend visits during this time can be very crowded and note that the parking here is limited to only 250 cars. The best time to visit is during mid-week when you can enjoy a walk into the park without crowds.

Fall colors generated by blazing sumacs, sycamores, chinaberries, and cottonwoods can be seen along the scenic drive along RR 1050 from Utopia to US 83. RR 337 from Camp Wood to Leakey is another favorite of ours, as is the Devil's Backbone Scenic Drive, a stretch of RR 32 from Wimberley to Blanco.

To find out the status of fall colors, call the Texas Travel Information Center at (800) 452–9292 or the Texas Parks and Wildlife hotline at (800) 792–1112. The brilliant colors require cold night temperatures, an occurrence that can reach the Hill Country valleys long before the warmer city locations.

Every July, the Hill Country celebrates this blooming industry with the International Apple Festival. What began as an orchard party has become a Texas-sized festival. The party begins the night before with a street dance and continues the next day with activities for the whole family. Activities include contests for the best apple, best apple pie, and best apple anything. There is also a quilt contest, volleyball championship, and, for the really energetic, a "triapple-on."

Scenic Drive. Utopia to U.S. Highway 83. West of Utopia, RR 1050 winds its way through the Hill Country, crossing the Frio River before eventually intersecting with US 83 north of Concan. During late fall, the drive is dotted with blazing sumacs, sycamores, chinaberries, and cottonwoods. Free.

Scenic Drive. RR 337. This drive from Camp Wood to Leakey (pronounced LA-key) is often termed the most scenic in Texas and is an excellent spot for fall color. The road climbs to some of the highest elevations in the Hill Country at more than 2,300 feet, and roadside lookouts offer great vistas of reds, greens, and golds. Free.

day trip 06

southwest

**castroville, uvalde, concan:
alsatian escape**

castroville

Castroville is located 20 miles west of San Antonio on U.S. Highway 90 and can be enjoyed as an extension of a San Antonio day trip (see Southwest Day Trip 1). This small town serves up a mixture of many cultures: French, German, English, Alsatian, and Spanish. It's best known for its Alsatian roots and sometimes is called "The Little Alsace of Texas."

The community was founded by Frenchman Henri Castro, who contracted with the Republic of Texas to bring settlers from Europe. These pioneers came from the French province of Alsace in 1844, bringing with them the Alsatian language, a Germanic dialect. Today only the older residents of Castroville carry on this mother tongue.

Although the language has dropped out of everyday use, many other Alsatian customs and traditions have survived. The city still sports European-style homes with nonsymmetrical, sloping roofs. The Alsatian Dancers of Texas perform folk dancing at many festivals, including San Antonio's Texas Folklife Festival in June and during the town's St. Louis Day celebration. (See "Festivals and Celebrations" at the back of this book.)

Castroville is usually busy on weekends, as San Antonio residents come to shop the town's numerous antiques stores, dine in the Alsatian restaurants, and tour the historical sites.

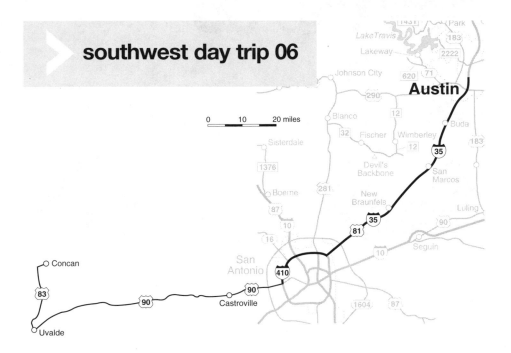

where to go

Landmark Inn State Historical Park. 402 East Florence Street. The Texas Parks and Wildlife Department operates the historic Landmark Inn and Museum. The inn was first a home and general store before becoming the Vance Hotel. Robert E. Lee and Bigfoot Wallace, a famous Texas Ranger, were said to have stayed here on the banks of the Medina River.

During World War II the hotel was renamed the Landmark Inn. Aside from accommodations (see Where to Stay), the inn contains displays illustrating Henri Castro's early efforts to recruit settlers, as well as exhibits covering early Castroville life. Also recommended is a self-guided tour of the beautifully manicured inn grounds. Open daily. Free. (830) 931–2133; www.tpwd.tx.us.

Castroville Walking Tour. Pick up a map from the Chamber of Commerce to see sixty-five points of interest, from Civil War–era homes to an 1845 church. Free. (800) 778–6775 or (830) 538–3142; www.castroville.com.

Castroville Regional Park. South off US 90. Camp along the banks of the Medina River or enjoy swimming, picnicking, and walking in this park. Fee for camping hookup and picnic table. (830) 931–0033.

where to eat

Alsatian Restaurant. 403 Angelo Street. Housed in a historic nineteenth-century cottage typical of the provincial homes of Castroville, this restaurant specializes in Alsatian and German food, including spicy Alsatian sausage, crusty French bread, homemade noodles, and red sauerkraut. Steaks and seafood also are served. If it's a nice day, don't miss the chance to dine outside in the open-air biergarten. Open daily for lunch; dinner Thursday through Sunday. $$. (830) 931–3260.

Haby's Alsatian Bakery. 207 U.S. Highway 290 East. With Castroville's rich Alsatian and German heritage, you know the town has to have a great bakery. Well, here it is. Try to choose from among apple strudel, molasses cookies, and fresh baked breads. Open Monday through Saturday. $. (830) 931–2118.

where to stay

Landmark Inn State Historical Park. 402 Florence Street. Guests at this historic inn can stay in one of eight beautifully appointed rooms as well as in a separate cottage that may have once served as the only bathhouse between San Antonio and Eagle Pass. Most rooms

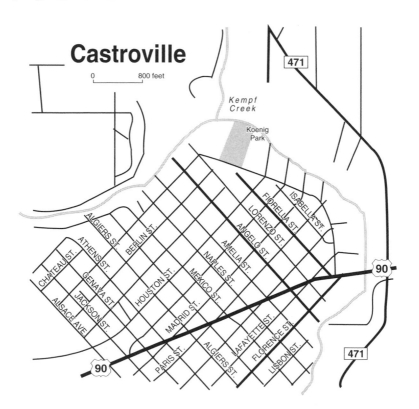

come with private baths; none have telephones or televisions. All rooms now have air-conditioning. Make your reservations early, especially for weekends. $. (830) 931–2133 or (512) 389–8900; www.tpwd.state.tx.us.

uvalde

Continue west on US 90 to Uvalde, which is located on the Leona River in the last out-reaches of the Hill Country.

Spanish settlers came to this area in 1674. A century later they attempted to construct missions to convert the Lipan-Apache Indians, the foremost of the Apache groups in Texas. This plan was soon abandoned because of repeated Indian attacks on the mission. The Apaches were defeated in 1709 by Spanish military leader Juan del Uvalde in what's now known as Uvalde Canyon.

For years Uvalde was famous as the onetime home of Dale Evans Rogers, Vice President John Nance Garner, and Texas's Governor Dolph Briscoe. Today it's best known as the hometown of actor Matthew McConaughey.

where to go

John Nance Garner Home and Museum. 333 North Park Street. This was once the home of Uvalde's most famous citizen, John Nance Garner, vice president of the United States during Franklin Roosevelt's first and second presidential terms. The museum is filled with reminders of Garner's political career. Open Monday through Saturday; extended hours during summer months. Fee. (830) 278–5018.

Uvalde Grand Opera House. 100 West North Austin Street. Even if a performance isn't scheduled, this 1891 opera house deserves a peek. Open daily 9:00 A.M. to 5:00 P.M. Free. (830) 278–4184.

Fort Inge County Park. Located 1½ miles south of Uvalde on FM 140. This park is the site of Fort Inge, a Cavalry post that dates back to 1849. Travelers find picnic sites as well as hiking trails and camping here along with good bird-watching. The park is located on the Leona River. Open daily. Free.

Briscoe Art and Antique Collection. 200 East Nopal Street. On display at the First State Bank, this multimillion-dollar art collection was developed by the former Texas governor Dolph Briscoe and his wife. Pieces from artists ranging from Rembrandt to Salinas are on display. Tours are available. Open weekdays. Free. (830) 278–6231.

National Fish Hatchery. FM 481, 1 mile south of Uvalde. This hatchery specializes in endangered fish species, but visitors will also find good bird-watching here as well as hiking and picnicking. Open weekdays. Free. (830) 278–2419.

where to eat

Casa Mortell. 705 N. Getty Avenue. Located next to the opera house, this coffee shop is a local favorite. Its specialties include frozen mocha cappuccino and foccaccia sandwiches. Open Monday through Saturday. $. (830) 591–1353.

Evett's Barbecue. 301 East Main Street. This casual eatery serves up traditional Texas barbecue fare—brisket, sausage, and chicken—on picnic tables. Open Tuesday through Saturday. $–$$. (830) 278–6204.

Rexall Drug and Soda Fountain. 201 North Getty Street. Step back to the days of old-time soda fountains at this favorite eatery. Sandwiches, burgers, and Blue Bell ice cream top the menu. Open Monday through Saturday for lunch. $. (830) 278–2589.

Town House Restaurant. 2105 East Main Street. The menu at this casual restaurant offers a taste of several Texas favorites: Tex-Mex, seafood, and, of course, chicken-fried steak. Open daily for breakfast, lunch, and dinner. $$. (830) 278–2428.

Where to Shop

Market Square Antiques. 103 North West Street. This downtown antiques dealer houses wares supplied by many dealers. Look for antique furniture, collectibles, jewelry, and gift items. Open daily. (830) 278–1294.

Opera House Antiques. 100 West North Street. Housed on the first floor of the Uvalde Grand Opera House, this shop contains antiques and collectibles. Open Monday through Saturday. (830) 278–9380.

Joe Pena Saddle Shop. 2521 East Main Street. This longtime shop has produced leather items for actors Nick Nolte and John Wayne, as well as the Texas Rangers. The shop is located inside Uvalco Supply. (830) 278–6531.

South Texas Fine Woods. 4326 US 90 East. Handcarved mesquite furniture is showcased in this retail shop. Tours of the workshop are also available. Open Monday through Saturday; hours vary. (830) 278–1832.

where to stay

Holiday Inn. 920 East Main Street. This 150-room hotel includes a restaurant, a pool, a laundry, and room service. $$. (830) 278–4511.

concan

Word has it that this town is named for "coon can," a Mexican gambling game. Today it's a safe gamble for outdoor recreation from swimming to camping.

where to go

Garner State Park. Located 31 miles north of Uvalde on U.S. Highway 83 or 8 miles north of Concan on the Frio River. From US 83, turn east on FM 1050 for ½ mile to Park Road 29.

Named for John Nance Garner, this beautiful state park is located on the chilly, spring-fed waters of the Frio River (*frio* means "cold" in Spanish). There are campsites, screened shelters, cabins with double beds, an eighteen-hole miniature golf course, and a 1-mile hiking trail blazed by the Civilian Conservation Corps during the 1930s. The highlight of the park is the river, filled with swimmers, inner-tubers, and paddleboaters during the warmer months.

Other activities include bicycling along a surfaced trail, hiking on 5½ miles of trails, miniature golfing in season, and paddleboating. Campers can bring their own gear or rent a screened shelter or cabin. (The park is so popular that travelers who rent a cabin on either Friday or Saturday night must take both nights.) Open daily. Fee. (830) 232–6132; www.twpd.state.tx.us.

west

day trip 01

west

**bee cave, south lake travis:
willie nelson country**

bee cave

This small community is quickly growing as Austin expands westward toward the Hill Country.

where to go

Hamilton Pool Preserve. Highway 71 west through the town of Bee Cave and turn left onto FM 3238 (Hamilton Pool Road). Travel 13 miles to the preserve entrance, on your right. This beautiful swimming hole is formed by a grotto fed by a 50-foot waterfall. After a dip, enjoy a picnic or hike along the canyon, which is home to several rare plant species. Guided tours are available. (512) 264–2740. It is also a good idea to call before a swimming trip to this site as bacteria levels occasionally cause the closing of the pool.

where to stay

Barton Creek Resort and Spa. 8212 Barton Club Drive. This expansive resort is known for its four golf courses; guests can also sign up for the golf school. The spa features a variety of treatments incorporating local elements such as the Texas mountain laurel body wrap and the Texas margarita salt glow. $$$. (800) 336–6158 or (512) 329–4000; www.barton creek.com.

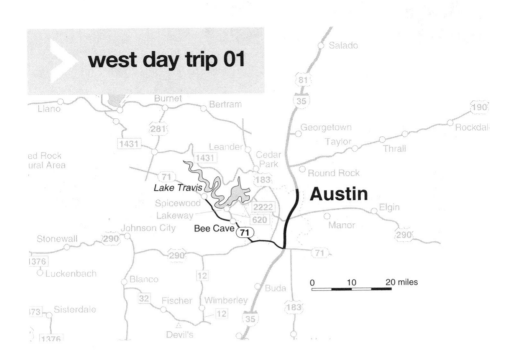

west day trip 01

where to eat

County Line on the Hill. 6500 West Bee Caves Road. Like its sister restaurant, County Line on the Lake, this eatery serves traditional Texas barbecue ranging from brisket to ribs. Open daily for lunch and dinner. $$–$$$. (512) 327–1742.

south lake travis

This day trip takes anglers, swimmers, and boaters to the numerous parks found on the southern reaches of Lake Travis.

where to go

Narrows Recreation Area. Upper south side of Lake Travis near the community of Spicewood. From Austin, to the southeast, take Highway 71 and turn north onto Spur 191; proceed approximately 1 mile to Spicewood. Continue traveling north 1.1 miles on Burnet County Road 410 to the intersection of Burnet County Road 411, which is a gravel road. Once on County Road 411, travel approximately 1½ miles north to the entrance for the Narrows Resource Area. This free recreation area is used by boaters looking for a launching site onto the upper south side of Lake Travis. The ramp, however, should be used with caution during low water periods. Only minimal facilities (no rest rooms or drinking water) are available here with a few camping sites and metal fire rings. This recreation area should be avoided during heavy rains; the access road traverses a low water crossing that may become impassable. Free. (800) 776–5272; www.lcra.org.

Grelle Recreation Area. Upper south side of Lake Travis near the community of Spicewood. From Austin, to the southwest, take Highway 71 and turn north onto Spur 191; proceed approximately 1 mile to Spicewood. Take a right onto Burnet County Road 404 and travel approximately 1 mile to the intersection of Burnet County Road 412, a gravel road. Turn left and travel approximately .6 mile to the entrance for the Grelle Resource Area.

Grelle is often visited for its 2-mile hiking trail, which leads visitors along a steep path to a plateau with views of Lake Travis. The site is also popular for its shoreline. Visitors here will find only primitive facilities: a composting toilet, metal fire rings, and a small parking area. (800) 776–5272; www.lcra.org.

Muleshoe Recreation Area. Upper south side of Lake Travis near the Ridge Harbor sub-division. From Austin, to the southeast, take Highway 71. Turn right onto Burnet County Road 404 and proceed about 4½ miles to Burnet County Road 414. Turn right and travel about 1½ miles, then turn right before the entrance to Ridge Harbor. The pavement ends, but continue for .3 mile on the gravel road to the entrance. Muleshoe Bend is appropriately named: a 2-mile looped trail is a favorite with those looking to take a four-legged ride through undeveloped hill country. Horseback riders and hikers enjoy the trail located on the upper area of the park. With its 1,000 acres, this is the largest property in the Lower Colorado River Authority (LCRA) system, but it offers only primitive facilities: composting toilets, metal fire rings, and a parking area. (800) 776–5272; www.lcra.org.

Krause Springs. Highway 71 to Spur 191, 7 miles after the Pedernales River Bridge. Turn right on to Spur 191 to a gravel road. Krause Springs is one of Central Texas's hidden wonders. As its name suggests, the highlight of this private park is the natural springs. Clear, cool waters and waterfalls draw swimmers and snorkelers during warm-weather months. Camping also is available. Fee. (830) 693–4181.

willie's town

Willie Nelson, one of Austin's most famous residents, doesn't actually call the city home but owns an 800-acre spread near Spicewood. This is far more than just a place to kick off his boots, though; the private complex includes a recording studio, golf course, and even a miniature Western "town" named Luck that's used for movie shoots.

Spicewood Vineyard. Off Highway 71, turn on to County Road 408 south for .7 mile then right onto County Road 409 for 1½ miles. This vineyard offers tours and tastings. Free. (830) 693–5328; www.spicewoodvineyards.com.

where to eat

Poodie's Hilltop Bar and Grill. 22308 Highway 71 West. Willie Nelson is almost an unofficial symbol of Austin, but the musician is all too often on the road again, playing Austin fewer days than he did in his early days. But now there's Poodie's Hilltop Bar and Grill. You might not see Willie during your visit but keep an eye out for other stars; everyone from Billy Bob Thornton to Merle Haggard has popped in at one time or another. Serving up burgers and Texas food, the roadhouse is really known for its live music, enjoyed almost every night. $-$$. (512) 264–0318.

day trip 02

west

>>> pedernales falls state park, johnson city,
stonewall, luckenbach, fredericksburg,
enchanted rock state natural area:
lbj country

pedernales falls state park

For the stair-stepped Pedernales Falls, head 32 miles west of Austin on U.S. Highway 290 then north on FM 3232 for 6 miles. A favorite summer getaway, this 4,800-acre state park is highlighted with gently cascading waterfalls. The falls draw swimmers and also anglers in search of catfish. The falls are spectacular, but visitors should note that this park can experience dangerous flash floods. With even a slight rise in the river, visitors should get to higher ground immediately. Swimming, angling, hiking, and camping available. Open daily. Fee. (830) 868–7304.

johnson city

Head west of Austin on US 290 for 42 miles to the intersection of U.S. Highway 281. Turn north and continue for 6 miles to LBJ country. President Johnson's boyhood home is open to visitors, along with the Johnson Settlement where LBJ's grandfather organized cattle drives over a century ago.

The Lyndon B. Johnson National Historic Park takes in two areas: Johnson City and the LBJ Ranch, located in Stonewall.

LBJ brought the attention of the world to his hometown, located 14 miles north from Blanco on US 281. The most popular stop here is the LBJ Boyhood Home, managed by

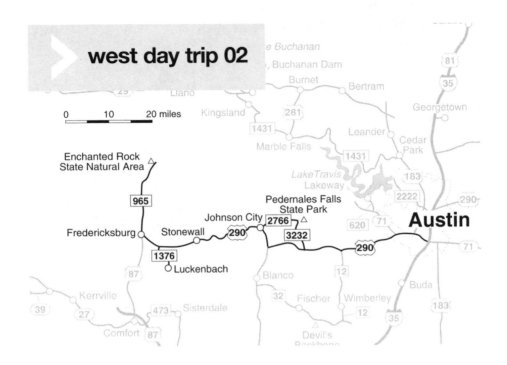

> **west day trip 02**

0   10   20 miles

Enchanted Rock
State Natural Area

965

Fredericksburg   Stonewall

1376

87   Luckenbach

the National Park Service. LBJ was five years old in 1913 when his family moved from their country home near the Pedernales River to this simple frame house. The visitor center provides information on this location, nearby Johnson Settlement, and other LBJ attractions. Park admission is free, a stipulation of the late president.

Johnson City hosts Historic Nugent Street Market Days on the third weekend of every month from April through October, with antiques, crafts, collectibles, and food booths.

where to go

LBJ National Historic Park. South of US 290 at Ninth Street. Park at the visitor center and go inside for brochures and a look at exhibits. From the center you can walk to two historic areas: Johnson Settlement and the LBJ Boyhood Home.

Johnson Settlement. The settlement gives visitors a look at the beginnings of the Johnson legacy. These rustic cabins and outbuildings once belonged to LBJ's grandfather, Sam Ealy Johnson, and his brother Tom. The two cattle drivers lived a rugged life in the Hill Country during the 1860s and 1870s. An exhibit center tells this story in pictures and artifacts. You also can tour the brothers' cabins and see costumed docents carrying out nineteenth-century chores. Open daily. Free. www.nps.gov.

LBJ Boyhood Home. Next to the Johnson Settlement. LBJ was a schoolboy when his family moved here in 1913. The home is still furnished with the Johnsons' belongings. Guided tours run every half hour. Open daily. Free.

Captain Perry Texas Ranger Museum. 404 West Main Street. Learn more about the life of a Texas Ranger in the 1830s with a visit to this one-room cabin. The self-guided look at the furnished cabin, the former home of Texas Ranger Cicero Rufus Perry, includes a video about the famous lawkeepers. Open when adjacent Johnson City visitor center is open. Free. (830) 868–7684; www.johnsoncity-texas.com.

Texas Hills Vineyard. RR 2766, 1 mile east of Johnson City. Texas wines produced with an Italian influence are the specialty of this vineyard. Open Monday through Saturday 10:00 A.M. to 5:00 P.M., and Sunday noon to 5:00 P.M. for tastings. (830) 868–2321; www.texas hillsvineyard.com.

Whittington's Jerky. 604 US 281 South. This factory produces true Texas jerky; stop by for free samples or to shop for jerky and other food items. (877) 868–5501 or (830) 868–5500; whittingtonsjerky.com.

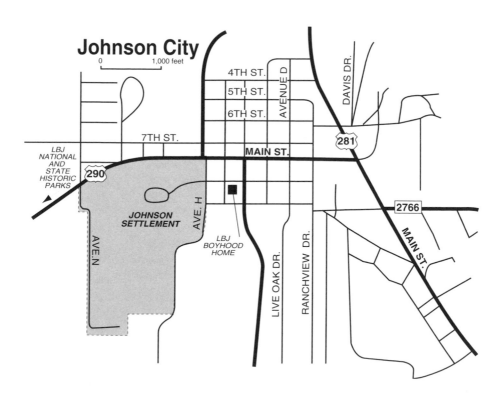

The Exotic Resort Zoo. Four miles north of Johnson City on US 281. Unusual species (including many endangered animals) roam the 137 acres of wooded Hill Country. In this park, leave the driving to someone else and enjoy a guided ride aboard a safari truck. Professional guides conduct tours of the ranch and provide visitors with information such as animal behavior as you feed the friendly park residents. After the tour, you can see some wildlife up close at the petting zoo. Kids enjoy petting child-size miniature donkeys, baby deer, llama, baby elk, and even a kangaroo at this special area. Open daily. Fee. (830) 868–4357; www.zooexotics.com.

where to eat

Uncle Kunkel's Bar B Q. 208 US 281 South. For years the Kunkels did the catering for the LBJ Ranch, and today they prepare their award-winning pork ribs, brisket, and sausage for the public. Have a plate of smoked meats with side dishes of potato salad, coleslaw, or pinto beans, followed by a slice of homemade pie. $. (830) 868–0251.

where to stay

Bed and Breakfast of Johnson City. Choose from seven properties that range from a stone cottage to an antiques-filled home. Some properties come with wood-burning stoves, kitchens, and porch swings; all feature air-conditioning and sleep at least four guests. $$. (830) 868–4548.

stonewall

Continue west on US 290 to the tiny community of Stonewall, the capital of the Texas peach industry. The road passes through miles of peach orchards, and during early summer, farm-fresh fruit is sold at roadside stands throughout the area. Stonewall is also the home of the LBJ National and State Historic Parks, encompassing the LBJ Ranch. This is a great opportunity to visit a working cattle ranch.

where to go

LBJ National and State Historic Parks. Located 14 miles west of Johnson City on US 290, these two combined parks together span approximately 700 acres. The area is composed of three main sections: the visitor center, the LBJ Ranch and tour, and the Sauer-Beckmann Farm. The most scenic route to the LBJ park falls along RR 1, paralleling the wide, shallow Pedernales River. (Exit US 290 a few miles east of Stonewall.)

During Johnson's life, the ranch was closed to all but official visitors. In hopes of catching a glimpse of the president, travelers often stopped along RR 1, located across the river from the Texas White House, the nickname of the Johnsons' home. Today the parks draw

peach fun

Stonewall's called the "Peach Capital of Texas," and every June Stonewall is ripe with fun and festivities. The third weekend of June is set aside for a celebration of the Hill Country's sweetest product at the annual Peach JAMboree. The festivities are genuine Texas fun, from a rodeo with bareback riding, calf roping, team roping, and bull riding, to a parade and a baking contest at the fire station. Other activities include a fiddlers' contest (open to competitors), a washer pitching tournament, and, of course, the Gillespie County Peach Queen Pageant. The sweetest event is the Peach Show and Auction, with plenty of prize-winning examples of Stonewall's fuzzy treasure.

Gillespie County, including Stonewall and nearby Fredericksburg, is filled with orchards where you can pick your own peaches. These shady groves yield their fruit until late July and offer a dozen varieties. The earliest to ripen are the cling peaches, ones whose fruit clings to the pit. As the summer progresses, varieties such as Red Skin, Loring, and Harvest Gold begin to mature.

visitors from around the world, who come for a look at the history behind the Hill Country, the presidency of LBJ, and a working Texas ranch.

Make your first stop the visitor center for a look at displays on LBJ's life, which include mementos of President Johnson's boyhood years. Attached to the visitor center is the Behrens Cabin, a dogtrot-style structure built by a German immigrant in the 1870s. Inside, the home is furnished with household items from more than a century ago.

While you're in the visitor center, sign up for a ninety-minute guided tour of the LBJ Ranch, operated by the National Park Service. Tour buses run from 10:00 A.M. to 4:00 P.M. daily and travel across the president's ranch, making a stop at the one-room Junction School where Johnson began his education. The bus slows down for a photo of the Texas White House, then continues past the president's airstrip and cattle barns. Other stops include a look at the reconstructed birthplace home as well as the family cemetery where the former president is buried.

Near the end of the tour, the bus makes an optional stop at the Sauer-Beckmann Living Historical Farm. The two 1918 farm homes are furnished in period style. Children can have a great time petting the farm animals. From here, it's just a short walk back to the visitor center.

Although the park does not have overnight facilities, there are two picnic areas and hiking trails for day use. Open daily. Free; fee for bus tour. (830) 644–2252; www.nps.gov and www.tpwd.state.tx.us.

Grape Creek Vineyards. Four miles west of Stonewall on US 290. The fertile land of the Pedernales Valley is a natural for vineyards, and you'll find acres of beautiful grapevines at this winery that produces cabernet sauvignon and chardonnay varieties. The winery is open daily. Call for tour times. Free. (830) 664–2710; www.grapecreek.com.

where to shop and eat

Grape Creek Country Market. US 290 west of Stonewall. This expansive market puts crafts market, country market, barbecue eatery, antique rose garden and nursery under one roof. Open daily. (830) 990–4021.

where to eat

Austin's Restaurant at Rose Hill Manor. 2614 Upper Albert Road. The window-lined dining room of this elegant eatery overlooks the scenic countryside. Specialties like New Zealand venison medallions with German potatoes are accompanied by an extensive wine list showcasing Hill Country vintages—the perfect end to a day of wine country touring. Open for dinner Wednesday through Sunday. $$$. (877) ROSEHIL; www.rose-hill.com.

luckenbach

Waylon Jennings's popular country-and-western song made this community a Texas institution. The town consists of a shop or two and a small general store serving as a post office, dance hall, beer joint, and general gathering place.

To reach Luckenbach, leave Stonewall on US 290. Turn left on FM 1376 and continue for about 4¼ miles. Don't expect to see signs pointing to the turnoff for Luckenbach Road; they are often stolen as fast as the highway department can get them in the ground. After the turn for Grapetown, take the next right down a narrow country road. Luckenbach is just around the bend.

This town was founded in 1852 by Jacob, William, and August Luckenbach. The brothers opened a post office at the site and called it South Grape Creek. In 1886 a man named August Engel reopened the post office and renamed it Luckenbach in honor of the early founders.

The most happening place in town is the dance hall, an expansive traditional Texas dance hall. Dances are held monthly, usually on Saturday nights.

The old post office is still there, the walls covered with scrawled names penned by Luckenbach fans. The store sells souvenirs of the town. Open daily. (888) 311–8990; www.luckenbachtexas.com.

fredericksburg

Retrace your steps from Luckenbach and continue west on US 290 to Fredericksburg, once the edge of the frontier and home to brave German pioneers. These first inhabitants faced many hardships, including hostile Comanche Indians. Now the town is a favorite with antiques shoppers, history buffs, and fans of good German food.

US 290 runs through the heart of the downtown district, becoming Main Street within the city limits. Originally the street was designed to be large enough to allow a wagon and team of mules to turn around in the center of town. Today, Main Street is filled with shoppers who come to explore the stores and restaurants of downtown Fredericksburg.

Fredericksburg welcomes all visitors—just look at the street signs for proof. Starting at the Adams Street intersection, head east on Main Street and take the first letter of every intersecting street name: they spell "all welcome." Drive west on Main Street starting after the Adams Street intersection, and the first letter of the intersecting streets spell "come back."

where to go

Fredericksburg Convention and Visitors Bureau. 106 North Adams. Stop by the Chamber of Commerce at 302 East Austin for brochures, maps, and information on a self-guided walking tour of historic downtown buildings, many of which now house shops and restaurants. The staff here also can direct you to bed-and-breakfast facilities in the area. Open daily. Free. (888) 997–3600 or (830) 997–6523; www.fredericksburg-texas.com.

National Museum of the Pacific War. 340 East Main Street. This historic park (formerly the Admiral Nimitz State Historical Park) is composed of numerous sections: the former Nimitz Steamboat Hotel, the Japanese Garden of Peace, the George Bush Gallery, the Pacific Combat Zone, the Plaza of the Presidents, and the Memorial Wall.

The complex was first named for Admiral Chester Nimitz, World War II Commander-in-Chief of the Pacific (CinCPac), Fredericksburg's most famous resident. He commanded 2.5 million troops from the time he assumed command eighteen days after the attack on Pearl Harbor until the Japanese surrendered.

The Nimitz name was well known here even years earlier. Having spent time in the merchant marines, Captain Charles H. Nimitz, the admiral's grandfather, decided to build a hotel here, adding a structure much like a ship's bridge to the front of his establishment. Built in 1852, the Nimitz Steamboat Hotel catered to guests who enjoyed a room, a meal, and the use of an outdoor bathhouse.

Today the former hotel houses a three-story museum honoring Admiral Nimitz and Fredericksburg's early residents. Many exhibits are devoted to World War II, including several that illustrate the Pacific campaign. In addition to displays that record the building's past, several early hotel rooms, the hotel kitchen, and the bathhouse have been restored.

Behind the museum lies the Garden of Peace, a gift from the people of Japan. This classic Japanese garden includes a flowing stream, a raked bed of pebbles and stones representing the sea and the Pacific islands, and a replica of the study used by Admiral Togo, Nimitz's counterpart in the Japanese forces.

Follow the signs from the Garden of Peace for one block to the Pacific History Walk. This takes you past a collection of military artifacts including a "fat man" Nagasaki-type atomic bomb case, a Japanese tank, and a restored barge like the one used by Nimitz. Open daily. Fee. (830) 997–4379; www.nimitz-museum.org.

Pioneer Museum Complex. 309 West Main Street. This collection of historic old homes includes an 1849 pioneer log home and store, the old First Methodist Church, and a smokehouse and log cabin. Also on the premises you'll see a typical nineteenth-century Sunday house. Built in Fredericksburg, Sunday houses catered to farmers who would travel long distances to do business in town, often staying the weekend. With the advent of the automobile, such accommodations became obsolete. Today the old Sunday houses scattered throughout the town are used as bed-and-breakfasts, shops, and even private residences. They are easy to identify by their small size and the fact that most have half-story outside staircases. Open Monday through Saturday 10:00 A.M. to 5:00 P.M., Sunday noon to 5:00 P.M. Fee. (830) 997–2835.

Fort Martin Scott Frontier Army Post. 1606 East Main Street, 2 miles east of Fredericksburg on US 290. Established in 1848, this was the first frontier military fort in Texas. Today the original stockade, a guardhouse, and visitor center with displays on local Native Americans are open to tour, and historic reenactments keep the history lesson lively. Ongoing archaeological research conducted here offers a glimpse into the fort's past. Reenactments involving costumed Native Americans, infantrymen, and civilians are scheduled at least once a month. Open Tuesday through Sunday 10:00 A.M. to 5:00 P.M. for self-guided tours. Free. (830) 997–9895; www.fortmartinscott.com.

Vereins Kirche Museum. Market Square on Main Street across from the courthouse. You can't miss this attraction: It's housed in an exact replica of an octagonal structure erected in 1847. Back then the edifice was used as a church, as well as a school, fort, meeting hall, and storehouse. The museum is sometimes called the Coffee Mill (or Die Kaffe-Muehle) Church because of its unusual shape. Exhibits here display Fredericksburg's German heritage, plus Native American artifacts from archaeological digs. Open daily (afternoon only on Sunday). Free. (830) 997–7832 or (830) 997–2835.

fredericksburg's wine industry

Dawn breaks over a dew-crystallized vineyard. Nearby, the vintner arrives for an early start to the day. In the distance, pickup trucks meander down the ranch-to-market road, greeted by the calls of onlooking cattle and goats.

It's another day in Texas wine country.

Much of the Lone Star State's fast-growing wine industry is centered in the Hill Country near Fredericksburg, founded by German settlers who planted the Vitis vinifera grapes that thrived in the Mediterranean climate of their new home. It would be a century before production would begin on a serious scale, but the roots of the Texas wine industry had been planted.

This community remembers its Old-World heritage with German-style buildings, shops, and restaurants. Those roots are also evident at the downtown Fredericksburg Winery (247 West Main Street, 830–990–8747, www.fbgwinery .com), where signature labels like the Texas Chardonnay "Adelsverein" (named for the Society of Noblemen formed by German princes to help emigrants to the newly-formed Republic of Texas) feature artwork and a little history.

Like many local wineries, this is a family-run operation, headed by no-nonsense Cord Switzer (look for the man in the gimme cap), along with his wife Sandy, brothers Jene and Burt, and mother "Oma," charged with labeling each bottle by hand.

Fourteen miles north of Fredericksburg, you'll find Bell Mountain Vineyards (463 Bell Mountain Road, 830–685–3297, www.bellmountainwine.com), located in Texas's first designated winegrowing area, or head east where "bouquet" describes not only wine but wildflowers.

Further east stands Stonewall, home to Lyndon Baines Johnson's "Texas White House," and also home to Grape Creek Vineyards (4 miles west of Stonewall on US 290, 830–644–2710, www.grapecreek.com), where acres of climbing vines yield the prize-winning Cabernet Trois.

Nearby, Becker Vineyards (10 miles east of Fredericksburg off US 290, 830–644–2681, www.beckervineyards.com), with forty-six acres of French Vinifera vines, boasts Texas's largest underground wine cellar. It's filled with specialties such as the 2002 Viognier, an elegant wine with a hint of violets and peach, served at a dinner for Australia's Prime Minister at President Bush's Prairie Chapel Ranch, and the 2002 Cabernet Sauvignon Reserve, poured at a White House dinner.

Bell Mountain Vineyards. Highway 16 North, 14 miles from Fredericksburg. Tour the chateau-type winery that produces chardonnay, Riesling, pinot noir, and several private reserve estate varieties. Guided tours and tastings are offered every Saturday from February through December. Free. (830) 685–3297; www.bellmountainwine.com.

Fredericksburg Herb Farm. 402 Whitney Street. These gardens produce the herbs for everything from teas to potpourris. Tour the grounds, then visit the shop for a look at the final product. A bed-and-breakfast also is located on-site. Open daily (afternoon only on Sunday). Free. (800) 259–HERB or (830) 997–8615; www.fredericksburgherbfarm.com.

where to shop

Fredericksburg's many specialty shops offer antiques, linens, Texana, art, and collectibles. Most stores are in historic buildings along Main Street.

Charles Beckendorf Gallery. 105 North Adams Street. This enormous gallery showcases the locally known work of artist Charles Beckendorf and is a good place to pick up a print of regional scenes, from one-room schoolhouses to brilliant fall scenics. Open daily. (800) 369–9004; www.beckendorf.com.

Whistle Pik Galleries. 425 East Main Street. This fine-arts gallery features bronzes, limited-edition prints, and original artwork. Special events throughout the year showcase artists in a variety of media. Open Monday through Saturday 10:00 A.M. to 5:30 P.M. (800) 999–0820 or (830) 990–8151; www.whistlepik.com.

where to eat

Hill Top Cafe. U.S. Highway 87, 10 miles north of Fredericksburg. This local favorite is known not only for its food (especially Sunday brunch), but also for its live music on Friday and Saturday nights. Open Wednesday through Sunday for lunch and dinner. (830) 997–8922; www.hilltopcafe.com.

Fredericksburg Brewing. 245 East Main Street. This downtown brewery is known for its ales and lagers but is equally notable for its casual restaurant. The restaurant, housed in an 1890 building, also includes a *biergarten.* Next door, a "bed and brew" offers twelve accommodations. $–$$. (830) 997–1646.

Altdorf German Biergarten and Restaurant. 301 West Main Street. Take a break from shopping and enjoy some good German food in a pleasant outdoor setting. Sandwiches, steaks, burgers, and Mexican food are served here as well. There's also dining in an adjacent stone building erected by the city's pioneers. The restaurant is open daily for lunch and dinner; closed January. $–$$. (830) 997–7865.

Peach Tree Tea Room. 210 South Adams Street. Enjoy a lunch of quiche, soup, and salad in this tearoom whose name is synonymous with Fredericksburg. Open for lunch Monday through Saturday. $. (830) 997–9527; www.peach-tree.com.

where to stay

Fredericksburg is the capital city of Texas bed-and-breakfast inns, with accommodations in everything from Sunday houses to local farmhouses to residences just off Main Street. Several reservation services provide information on properties throughout the area.

Gastehaus Schmidt. 231 West Main Street. This service represents one hundred bed-and-breakfast accommodations, including cottages, log cabins, and a 125-year-old rock barn. All price ranges. (830) 997–5612; www.fbglodging.com.

Be My Guest. 110 North Milam. More than twenty-five properties in Fredericksburg and nearby Lost Maples are handled by this service, with choices ranging from log cabins to historic homes. All price ranges. (830) 997–7227 or (866) 997–7227; www.bemyguest fredericksburgtexas.com.

First-Class Bed-and-Breakfast Reservation Service. 909 East Main Street. This service represents a wide variety of Fredericksburg area bed-and-breakfast properties and guest houses. (888) 991–6749; www.fredericksburg-lodging.com.

especially for winter texans

If you're traveling by RV or trailer, spend some time at the 113-site Lady Bird Johnson Municipal Park, just southwest of Fredericksburg on Highway 16. Campsites have electrical, water, sewer, and cable TV hookups. There's a fourteen-day limit on camping from April through September. The park recently opened a self-guided nature trail.

The park also sports an eighteen-hole golf course, six tennis courts, and badminton and volleyball courts. There's also a seventeen-acre lake for fishing. Pick up a checklist of birds or insects found in the region. (830) 997–4202.

enchanted rock state natural area

Whether you're a climber or just looking for a good picnic spot, drive out to Enchanted Rock State Natural Area. Located 18 miles north of Fredericksburg on RR 965, this state park features the largest stone formation in the West. Nationally this 640-acre granite outcropping takes second only to Georgia's Stone Mountain. According to Native American legend, the rock is haunted. Sometimes as the rock cools at night, it makes a creaking sound, which probably accounts for the story.

People of all ages in reasonably good physical condition can enjoy a climb up Enchanted Rock. The walk takes about an hour, and hikers are rewarded with a magnificent view of the Hill Country. In warm weather (from April through October), start your ascent early in the morning before the relentless sun turns the rock into a griddle.

Experienced climbers can scale the smaller formations located adjacent to the main dome. These bare rocks are steep and dotted with boulders and crevices, and their ascent requires special equipment.

Picnic facilities and a sixty-site primitive campground at the base of the rocks round out the offerings. No vehicular camping is permitted. Buy all your supplies in Fredericksburg; there are no concessions. To prevent overcrowding, a limited number of visitors are allowed in the park during peak periods. Arrive early. Open daily. Fee. (325) 247–3903; www.tpwd .state.tx.us.

day trip 03

west

kerrville, ingram, hunt, y. o. ranch: hill country escape

kerrville

To reach Kerrville from Austin, follow U.S. Highway 290 west through Johnson City and Fredericksburg (see West Day Trip 2 for attractions in those cities). Turn south on Highway 16 to Kerrville.

Kerrville is popular with retirees, hunters, Winter Texans, and campers. The town of 20,000 residents is home to a 500-acre state park and many privately owned camps catering to youth and church groups. Started in the 1840s, the town was named for James Kerr, a supporter of Texas independence. With its unpolluted environment and low humidity, Kerrville later became known as a health center, attracting tuberculosis patients from around the country. The town is still considered one of the most healthful places to live in the nation because of its clean air and moderate climate.

Throughout Kerrville the Schreiner name appears on everything from Schreiner College to Schreiner's Department Store. Charles Schreiner, who became a Texas Ranger at the tender age of fifteen, came to Kerrville as a young man in the 1850s. Following the Civil War, he began a dry goods store and started acquiring land and raising sheep and goats. The Charles Schreiner Company soon expanded to include banking, ranching, and marketing wool and mohair. This was the first business in America to recognize the value of mohair, the product of Angora goats. Before long, Schreiner made Kerrville the mohair capital of the world.

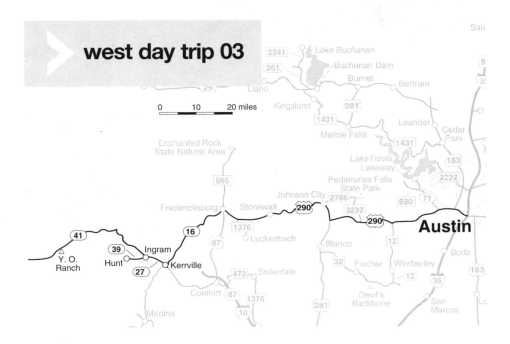

> west day trip 03

In 1880 Schreiner acquired the Y. O. Ranch, which grew over the next twenty years to more than 600,000 acres, covering a distance of 80 miles. Today the Schreiner family still owns this well-known ranch, located in nearby Mountain Home.

Whether you're looking for cowboys or for culture, you'll find it in the city that many consider the capital of the Hill Country. Kerrville offers visitors plenty of fun with attractions ranging from fine art to outdoor activities to some of the top festivals in the state.

Start your visit with a look at Kerrville's recently revitalized downtown, where antiques shops and art galleries offer excellent shopping. Under the Texas Main Street program, the city has been revitalized in the form of $9.5 million in renovations. Today travelers can "shop 'til they drop" in one-of-a-kind boutiques and galleries and enjoy the special atmosphere of this 37-block revitalized area.

The high quality of the artwork available in Kerrville attests to the community's status as a magnet for artists from across the Southwest. For a look at more western art, make a visit to the Museum of Western Art. This hilltop museum features western-themed paintings and sculpture.

Both fine art and performance art headline Kerrville's well-known festivals. Memorial Day weekend brings artists from around the state to Kerrville to participate in the official Texas State Arts and Crafts Fair, an event that showcases only the one-of-a-kind work by Texas artists. From late May to mid-June, tap your feet to the tunes of the Kerrville Folk Festival. One of Texas's best-loved music gatherings, this extravaganza of song features more than 150 singer-songwriters. The eighteen-day festival is held 9 miles south of Kerrville at the Quiet Valley Ranch.

where to go

The Museum of Western Art. 1550 Bandera Highway (Highway 173). This museum (formerly the Cowboy Artists of America Museum) features work by members of the Cowboy Artists of America. The building is constructed of eighteen *boveda* brick domes, an old construction method used in Mexico. Western-themed paintings and sculpture fill the museum. Visitors also can take in special programs on the folklore, music, and history of the Old West. Open Tuesday to Saturday 9:00 A.M. to 5:00 P.M., Sunday 1:00 to 5:00 P.M. Fee. (830) 896–2553; www.caamuseum.com.

The Hill Country Museum. 226 Earl Garrett Street. This local history museum traces the development of Kerrville. Housed in Charles Schreiner's former mansion built in 1879, the building has granite porch columns, wooden parquet floors, and a bronze fountain imported from France. Open Monday through Saturday. Fee. (830) 896–8633.

Kerrville-Schreiner State Park. 2385 Bandera Highway, 1 mile southwest on Highway 173. This park offers 7 miles of hiking trails, as well as angling and swimming in the Guadalupe River. During summer months, tubes and canoes are for rent for an afternoon excursion on the river. Mountain bikers will find 6 miles of beginner/intermediate trails. Campsites include water, electricity, sewage hookups, and screened shelters. Fee. (830) 257–5392; www.tpwd.state.tx.us.

Louise Hays City Park. Off Highway 16 at Thompson Drive. Bring your picnic lunch to this beautiful spot on the Guadalupe River. Ducks and cypress trees abound. Open daily. Free. (830) 792–8386.

Mooney Aircraft Tours. Highway 27 East. Take a one-hour plant tour to see single-engine aircraft on the manufacturing line. No cameras are allowed on the tour, and it is not recommended for children younger than eight. This tour passes through a plant with no air-conditioning, so expect to be warm during the summer months, and bring comfortable walking shoes. Open for guided tours Tuesday at 10:00 A.M.; reservations required. Free. (830) 896–6000.

where to shop

Artisan Accents. 826 Water Street. Both regional and nationally recognized artists are showcased at this gallery. Housed in a building that a century ago served as a bakery, the gallery features decorative arts, wearable art, furnishings, and fine art. Open Monday through Friday. (830) 896–4220.

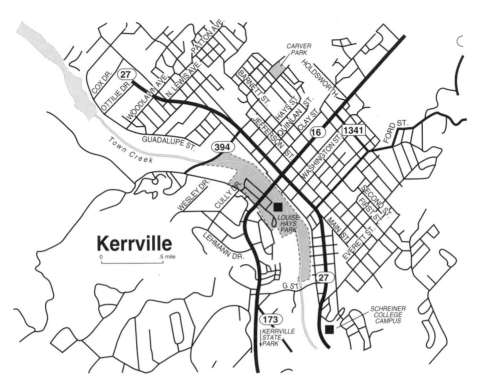

James Avery, Craftsman. Located 3½ miles north of Kerrville on Harper Road. Since 1954 James Avery has been one of Texas's premier silversmiths. He began crafting silver crosses and religious symbols, but today his work includes gold and silver renditions of many subjects, from prickly pears to dolphins. Shop open Monday through Saturday; visitor center open weekdays. (830) 895–1122.

Sunrise Antiques Mall. 820 Water Street. Kerrville's largest antiques shop is housed in a century-old building that once served as a furniture store. Today the mall features everything from antique furniture to antiques and artwork. Open Monday through Saturday. (830) 257–5044.

where to eat

Bill's Barbecue. 1909 Junction Highway. This barbecue eatery serves up Texas favorites, such as brisket, sausage, and chicken, with the usual side dishes. Open Tuesday through Saturday for lunch. $$. (830) 895–5733.

Del Norte Restaurant. 710 Junction Highway. This cafe offers Texas favorites including Tex-Mex, barbecue, and chicken-fried steak. Open for breakfast and lunch Monday through Saturday. $$. (830) 257–3337.

Hill Country Cafe. 806 Main Street. This diner is a favorite with local citizens as well as travelers looking for a small-town atmosphere. The day starts out with traditional American breakfast as well as specialties such as huevos rancheros; for lunch look for burgers as well as chicken-fried steak. Open for breakfast and lunch weekdays; breakfast only Saturday. $$. (830) 257–6665.

Joe's Jefferson Street Cafe. 1001 Jefferson Street. This elegant eatery, housed in a Victorian mansion, serves up Texas and southern favorites, such as shrimp, catfish, and steak. Open for lunch weekdays, dinner Monday through Saturday. $$–$$$. (830) 257–2929.

Kathy's on the River. 417 Water Street. This restaurant is an excellent spot for those looking for outdoor dining with a view of the river. The menu offers a little bit of everything, from traditional chicken-fried steak to dishes with an Asian flair. $$–$$$. Open Tuesday through Saturday. (830) 257–7811.

where to stay

Y. O. Ranch Resort Hotel and Conference Center. 2033 Sidney Baker, at Highway 16 and Interstate 10. This 200-room hotel salutes the famous Y. O. Ranch in Mountain Home, located 30 miles from Kerrville. The lobby is filled with reminders of the area's major industries—cattle and hunting. Twelve hotel suites include amenities such as fireplaces, furniture covered in longhorn hide, and wet bars. In keeping with the Wild West spirit, the hotel has a bar called the Elm Water Hole Saloon and a swim-up bar dubbed the Jersey Lilly. $$. (830) 257–4440; www.yoresort.com.

art walk

Many Hill Country communities offer monthly markets featuring arts and crafts, but Kerrville takes their special event one step further. The "Second Saturday Art Trail" offers visitors not only the chance to shop for art but to visit the city's growing number of galleries. From 10:00 A.M. to 6:00 P.M. on the second Saturday of every month, the city's galleries (now over two dozen strong) open their doors, provide special demonstrations, serve refreshments, and help introduce all the members of the family to various types of artwork. For more information, see www.artinthehills.com.

especially for winter texans

Kerrville is home to over a dozen RV parks, some of which are designated "adults only." For a listing, contact the Kerrville Convention and Visitors Center. (800) 221–7958; www .kerrrvilletx.com. The Kerrville Chamber of Commerce can provide a listing of condominium and apartment properties with short-term leases. A welcoming committee greets Winter Texans as well as the many retirees who relocate to the area. (830) 896–1155.

ingram

To reach Ingram, leave Kerrville on Highway 27 and continue northwest for 7 miles. This small community on the banks of the Guadalupe River was started in 1879 by Reverend J. C. W. Ingram, who built a general store and post office in what is now called Old Ingram.

Old Ingram, located off Highway 27 on Old Ingram Loop, is home to many art galleries and antiques shops. Ingram proper lies along Highway 27, and it features stores and outfitters catering to white-tailed deer, turkey, and quail hunters. The town is particularly busy during deer season, from November to early January. Hunting licenses are required and are sold at local sporting-goods stores. For more information, call the Texas Parks and Wildlife Department at (512) 389–4800 in Texas or (800) 792–1112 elsewhere, or write: 4200 Smith School Road, Austin, TX 78744.

where to go

Kerr County Historical Murals. At Highway 27 and Highway 39. Sixteen murals decorate the T. J. Moore Lumber Company building, the work of local artist Jack Feagan. The scenes portray historical events in Kerr County, starting with the establishment of shingle camps (where wooden roofing shingles were produced in 1846). Other paintings highlight cattle drives, the birth of the mohair industry, and the last Indian raid.

Hill Country Arts Foundation. Highway 39, west of the Ingram Loop. The foundation, located 6 miles west of Kerrville in Ingram, is one of the oldest multidiscipline arts centers in the nation. For more than thirty-five years, this fifteen-acre center on the banks of the Guadalupe River has encouraged students in the fields of art, theater, photography, printmaking, and even quiltmaking. American musicals and plays are performed during the summer months at the open-air Point Theatre; indoor shows entertain audiences at other times throughout the year. A gallery exhibits the work of many artists and is open daily. The Gazebo Gift Shop is a sales outlet for local artists, open Monday through Friday afternoons. Call for a schedule of play times or special events. (800) 459–HCAF or (830) 367–5121; www.hcaf.com.

where to shop

Guadalupe Forge. Highway 27, just off Highway 39. You can have your own brand made in this blacksmith shop, the walls of which are decorated with cattle brands ranging from simple initials to more elaborate renderings of stars or the rising sun. Call for times. (830) 367–4433; www.guadalupeforge.com.

Southwestern Elegance. Old Ingram Loop. This unique store specializes in Mexican collectibles and antiques (especially primitives), Mennonite furniture, and Tarahumara Indian collectibles. Open daily; call for hours. (830) 367–4749.

hunt

Continue west on Highway 39 for 7 miles to Hunt, a small community best known for its year-round outdoor recreational camps catering to Scouts as well as youth and church groups.

where to go

Kerr Wildlife Management Area. RR 1340, 12 miles northwest of Hunt. Enjoy a driving tour over this 6,493-acre research ranch owned by the Texas Fish and Game Commission. Purchased to study the relationship between wildlife and livestock, the ranch is home to white-tailed deer, javelinas, wild turkeys, bobcats, gray foxes, and ringtails. Pick up a booklet at the entrance or write: Kerr Wildlife Management Area, Route 1, Box 180, Hunt, TX 78024. Open daily, but call during hunting season when the area may be closed for a hunt. Free. (830) 238–4483.

Stonehenge II. FM 1340, just out of Hunt. Located on private land, this replica of England's Stonehenge may be viewed from a roadside parking area. A sign provides information on the original Stonehenge and its smaller Texas cousin. Open daily. Free. (No phone.)

y. o. ranch

From Hunt, head west on FM 1340 to Highway 41. Turn left and the Y. O. Ranch will soon appear on your right. This ranch dates back to 1880, a part of the 550,000 acres purchased by Captain Charles Schreiner, former Texas Ranger and longhorn cattle owner.

The Y. O. spans 60 square miles and supports over 1,000 registered longhorns, the largest such herd in the nation. Charlie Schreiner III, the original owner's grandson, brought the breed back from near extinction in the late 1950s, founding the Texas Longhorn Breeders Association. The Y. O. hosts a longhorn trail drive at the ranch each spring.

After the devastating Texas drought in the 1950s, the Schreiners began to diversify the use of their ranch, stocking the land with the largest collection of natural roaming exotics in the country, including many rare and endangered species. More than 10,000 animals range the hills, including zebra, ostrich, giraffe, emu, and ibex.

You may visit the Y. O. Ranch only by reservation. Both day and overnight programs are offered. Day-trippers can enjoy the spread on a lunch tour or photo safari. The ranch also hosts an Outdoor Awareness Program, an environmental education camp that teaches horseback riding, rappelling, gun handling, and wildlife study. Overnight accommodations are available in the 1800s-era cabins; meals are included. For general information, call (800) YO–RANCH or (830) 967–2624.

northwest

day trip 01

northwest

mount bonnell, lake travis, lakeway: lakeside luxury

This is a popular hot-weather day trip. Bring your swimsuit from April through October, along with an old pair of sneakers to navigate the rocky Lake Travis beaches.

mount bonnell

A beautiful lookout is located within the Austin city limits. Turn left off RR 2222 onto Mount Bonnell Road, which will take you to the highest point in town with a panoramic view of the city and the surrounding hills. Visitors must park and walk up some steep steps to the lookout, but the view is well worth the climb. Free.

where to go

Loop 360 Boat Ramp. From the intersection of Loop 360 and FM 2222, travel south on Loop 360 across the Loop 360 Bridge over Lake Austin. The entrance to the boat ramp is on the east side of Loop 360, directly below the bridge. As its name suggests, this park is primarily used by boaters as a launch onto Lake Austin. It is located under the south side of Pennybacker Bridge. You'll also find areas for fishing and picnicking. Open daily. (512) 854–7275.

Mary Quinlan Park. From the intersection of RR 620 and FM 2222, take RR 620 south 2.1 miles to Quinlan Park Road. Turn left onto Quinlan Park Road and travel 5½ miles to the park

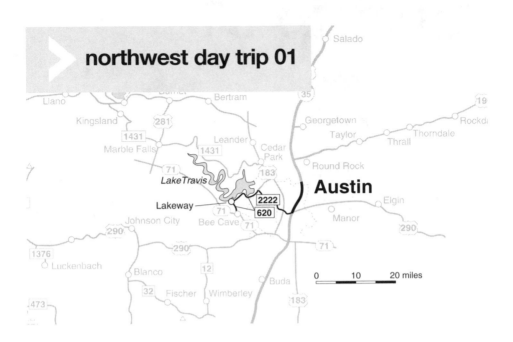

entrance. This quiet park has the only public boat ramp for miles along Lake Austin. It is a beautiful place to enjoy the quiet of one of Lake Austin's narrow passages and to view the bluffs against the water's emerald depths. Open daily. (512) 854–7275.

where to eat

County Line on the Lake. 5204 FM 2222. This is one of the few barbecue restaurants in Texas where you could wear a coat and tie and not look like a "city slicker." Enjoy full table service at this excellent restaurant on Lake Austin, ordering from a menu that features brisket, sausage, and ribs. Located right on the shores of Lake Austin with an excellent view, this eatery is a popular summer stop. Open for lunch every day but Saturday; dinner daily. $$–$$$. (512) 346–3664.

lake travis

Continue northwest on FM 2222. This winding road is filled with treacherous curves, so take it *slow.* At the intersection of RR 620, you have two choices: turn west onto RR 620 and continue to Mansfield Dam and the remainder of this trip, or turn east to some county parks and Austin's best-known outdoor dining spot. This side excursion affords a beautiful drive past some of Austin's most expensive homes.

where to go

McGregor/Hippie Hollow Park. From RR 620, turn right onto Comanche Trail. This is a clothing-optional park, the only one in the Austin area. On summer weekends, it is packed with nudists, curious onlookers, and swimmers who want to enjoy a beautiful swimming hole. The parking area is located away from the bathing area. (Nudity is not permitted in the parking lot.)

Onlookers outnumber nudists many weekends, but to see the beach (and the swimmers) you must leave your car and walk down the trail to the water's edge. The swimming area is protected from curious boaters, who are kept at a distance by patrolling Parks Department boats. No children allowed. Fee. Day use only. (512) 854–7275.

Bob Wentz at Windy Point. Comanche Trail, 1 mile past Hippie Hollow. Open for camping. Mention Windy Point and Austinites think of windsurfing, sailing, or scuba diving. A top spot on Lake Travis for water sports, this Lower Colorado River Authority (LCRA) park recently completed a $2.5 million renovation of its facilities. It offers a hiking and biking trail, sand volleyball courts, and a boat ramp for sailboats. Open daily. Fee. (800) 776–5272; www.lcra.org.

Sandy Creek Park. From the intersection of RR 620 and FM 2222, take Bullock Hollow Road west 2½ miles to FM 2769. Turn left onto FM 2769 and travel 4 miles to Lime Creek Road, through the town of Volente. Entrance is on the left. This quiet park is far less visited than many other north Lake Travis sites and is popular with swimmers and nature lovers. Open daily. (800) 776–5272; www.lcra.org.

Cypress Creek Park. From the intersection of RR 620 and FM 2222, take Bullock Hollow Road west 2 miles. The park entrance is on your left, just before the intersection of Bullock Hollow Road and FM 2769 (Old Anderson Mill Road). A favorite for lake lovers, this day-use LCRA park includes a boat ramp. It is frequented by many campers, boaters, picnickers, and anglers. Open daily. (800) 776–5272; www.lcra.org.

Volente Beach Club. 16107 Wharf Cove, FM 2769 in Volente. This favorite summer hangout offers a pool, giant water slides, sand beach, motorized water sports, volleyball, and more. There's also a casual restaurant on-site. Hours vary with season. Fee. (512) 258–5109; www.volentebeach.com.

Pace Bend Park. From the intersection of RR 620 and Highway 71, take Highway 71 west 11 miles to RR 2322 (Pace Bend Park Road). Turn right on RR 2322 and travel 4.6 miles to the park entrance. Pace Bend is one of the top parks, not only of the LCRA sites, but also in the entire region. Nine miles of shoreline appeal to swimmers and boaters; horseback riders and hikers also find diversions with a large natural area. Part of the park is managed as a wildlife preserve and can be reached by rugged trails; an excellent destination for wildlife-viewing and bird-watching. Open daily. (800) 776–5272.

Selma Hughes Park. From the intersection of RR 620 and FM 2222, take RR 620 south 2.1 miles to Quinlan Park Road. Turn right on Quinlan Park Road and travel 4.6 miles to Selma Hughes Road. Turn left on Selma Hughes Road and proceed to park entrance. Along with Fritz Hughes and Mary Quinlan Parks, Selma Hughes Park is one of the few public-access sites along this part of Lake Austin. Here the lake is narrow and quiet, and in the park, visitors are usually local residents. Visitors will find picnicking, swimming, and fishing areas.

Tom Hughes Park. From the intersection of RR 620 and FM 2222, take RR 620 south 2.3 miles to Marshall Ford Drive. Turn right onto Marshall Ford Drive and travel .2 mile to Park Drive. Turn right and travel 2.8 miles to park entrance. Scuba divers call this park a favorite. The walk to the water's edge is steep and brushy.

Fritz Hughes Park. From the intersection of RR 620 and FM 2222, take RR 620 south 3.7 miles to Low Water Crossing Road (just before Mansfield Dam). Turn left on Low Water Crossing Road and travel .2 mile to Fritz Hughes Park Road. Turn left to park entrance. Along with Mary Quinlan and Selma Hughes Parks, this is one of only three access points along the north side of Lake Austin. The small LCRA park is usually frequented by local residents. The park offers picnicking, swimming, and fishing. Open daily. (800) 776–5272; www.lcra.org.

Mansfield Dam Park. From the intersection of RR 620 and FM 2222, travel south 4.9 miles. Turn right onto Mansfield Dam Road, just south of Mansfield Dam. The park entrance is on the left. One of the most visited LCRA parks along Lake Travis, Mansfield Dam Park is one of the top boat-launching sites on the lake. The park also appeals to campers and picnickers; a primitive area is located nearby. Open daily. (800) 776–5272; www.lcra.org.

where to eat

The Oasis. 6550 Comanche Trail. Known as "The Sunset Capital of Texas," this restaurant is famous for its open decks overlooking Lake Travis. On weekends this becomes a popular stop after a day of boating or swimming. The lake views and the surrounding hills provide a lovely backdrop for a sunset meal, the highlight of the day at this unusual restaurant. Open daily for lunch and dinner. $–$$. (512) 266–2441; www.oasis-austin.com.

where to stay

Lake Austin Spa Resort. 1705 Quinlan Park Road. Located on the shores of Lake Austin, this well-known resort caters to guests with special menus, dietary consultations, and European spa services. $$$. (800) 847–5637 or (512) 372–7300; www.lakeaustin.com.

lakeway

Continue west on RR 620 across Mansfield Dam to the village of Lakeway and the Lakeway Resort and Conference Center. This 1,200-person resort community boasts recreational facilities and accommodations for golf and tennis buffs. You can't miss it; just look for the water tower shaped and painted like a golf ball.

Lakeway offers thirty-two tennis courts, three championship golf courses, a golf academy, a full-service marina, party boats, horseback riding, hayrides, two swimming pools, a fitness center, and a conference center. The World of Tennis, one of the finest tennis facilities in the country, is also located here. Guests can stay at the Lakeway Inn, purchasing various packages that include the use of these facilities.

what to do

Golf. The Live Oak and the Yaupon eighteen-hole courses are open to the public. Golf packages in conjunction with the Lakeway Inn also are available. (512) 261–7173; www.clubsoflakeway.com.

Students of the Academy of Golf hone their skills on three full-length holes, a driving range, and a putting green. The academy is located in The Hills of Lakeway, a private eighteen-hole course designed by Jack Nicklaus. Call for class information; reservations required. Closed Monday. (800) 879–2008.

Tennis. 1 World of Tennis Square. The World of Tennis has twenty-six world-class indoor courts, including a stadium court. Tennis packages in conjunction with the Lakeway Inn are available. Open daily. (512) 261–7222 or 261–7257.

where to stay

Lakeway Inn. 101 Lakeway Drive. Adjacent to the marina, this large hotel has recently renovated rooms featuring Southwest decor and a lake view. Some accommodations include fireplaces and kitchens. A lobby bar serves evening cocktails, and an attractive restaurant offers breakfast, lunch, and dinner. $$$. (800) LAKEWAY or (512) 261–6600; www.lakewayinn.com.

day trip 02

northwest

north lake travis, marble falls,
kingsland:
granite world

The Highland Lakes region is comprised of a series of seven lakes that form back-to-back "stair steps" along the Colorado River. Built in the 1930s by the Lower Colorado River Authority (LCRA) to bring electricity to rural Texas and to control flooding along the river, the lakes now provide 150 miles of water recreation.

north lake travis

This sprawling lake offers anglers, boaters, and swimmers innumerable coves and quiet stretches. LCRA operates many public parks in this region. To reach the northern shores of Lake Travis, take U.S. Highway 183 north of Austin. In Cedar Park, turn west on FM 1431.

where to go

Shaffer Bend Recreation Area. Seventeen miles west of Lago Vista or 9 miles east of Marble Falls near the Smithwick Community. Take FM 1431 to County Road 343A and continue about 1 mile. This park is one of the largest on Lake Travis, with 523 acres, and one of the top LCRA parks. Shaffer is a favorite with day-trippers and campers looking for an undeveloped site that offers good lake views, plenty of wildlife, and various kinds of vegetation. The recreation area, located between Marble Falls and Lago Vista on the lake's north shore, is dotted with hills of dense cedar. From these peaks, you can enjoy good lake views at several points along the park road.

The hills gradually give way to savannah shaded by oaks and pecan trees. Here you can also see the guayacan, a plant not usually seen east of Del Rio. A mile-long swimming area offers a chance to cool off after hiking. Open daily. Free. (800) 776–5272; www.lcra.org.

Camp Creek Recreation Area. North side of Lake Travis about 18 miles west of Lago Vista or 8 miles east of Marble Falls near the Smithwick community. Take FM 1431 to County Road 343 and continue about a ½ mile on this road to the site entrance. Camp Creek Area offers a loop hiking trail and, in early mornings and late evenings, visitors can see local wildlife. The park is shaded by large pecan trees and is especially good for those looking for a quiet, undeveloped site. This area should, however, be avoided during heavy rains. The access to Camp Creek is a steep gravel road with two low-water crossings that are often covered after rainstorms.

The park is adjacent to Burnet County Park, a five-acre site on the waterfront. Here campers will find sites as well as tables, grills, trash cans, and a boat ramp. (Skip this boat ramp when the lake level is low, however. The ramp makes a sharp drop at the end.) Open daily. Free. (800) 776–5272; www.lcra.org.

Gloster Bend Recreation Area. North side of Lake Travis approximately 6 miles west of Lago Vista near the Travis Peak community. Take FM 1431 to Singleton Road and continue 3.3 miles to the site entrance. This large day-use park, divided into woodlands on the south and grasslands on the north, boasts the highest visitation of all the Lake Travis recreation

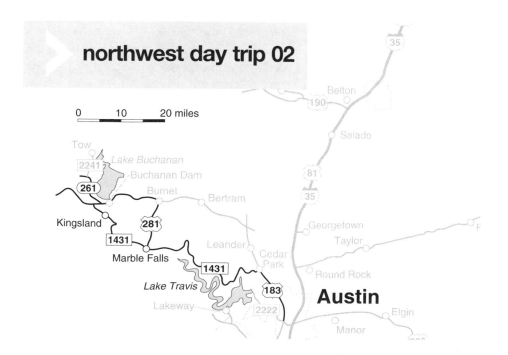

northwest day trip 02

areas. The site has only minimal facilities including composting toilets, fire rings, and trash cans. More than 1 mile of shoreline can be easily accessed. Open daily. (800) 776–5272; www.lcra.org.

Arkansas Bend Park. FM 1431 south to Lohmans Crossing Road. Turn left on Lohmans Crossing Road and travel 4½ miles to Sylvester Ford Road. Turn left on Sylvester Ford Road and travel 1½ miles to the park entrance. This is one of the quieter parks along Lake Travis, thanks to its remote location. The park offers camping, picnicking, fishing, and a boat ramp. Open daily. (800) 776–5272; www.lcra.org.

Turkey Bend Recreation Area. North side of Lake Travis approximately 9½ miles west of Lago Vista. Take FM 1431 to Shaw Drive and continue 1.8 miles to the site entrance. This 400-acre park winds along 2 miles of Lake Travis's northern shoreline. The recreation area is popular with those looking for a real back-to-nature getaway. The site has been left mostly undeveloped, with no rest rooms, drinking water, or trash collection. Some primitive camp-sites are marked with fire rings.

Horseback riders and hikers frequent the park for its loop trail with good views of the lake. One warning: During hunting season there is hunting on adjacent private land so be wary when approaching fence lines. Open daily. (800) 776–5272; www.lcra.org.

marble falls

Continue west on FM 1431 to Marble Falls. Drive south on U.S. Highway 281 to the over-look at the edge of town for a terrific view of the 780-acre Lake Marble Falls. It's said that this sight inspired local songwriter Oscar J. Fox (who penned "Home on the Range" and "Get Along Little Dogie") to write his popular tune "Hills of Home." Today a marker com-memorates this local hero.

Normally the falls that gave this town its name are beneath the lake, but occasionally the falls are visible when the LCRA does repair work on the dam.

While the town may be named for marble, granite is king here. Granite Mountain at the edge of town is the home of a huge quarry that sells pink granite to places around the coun-try. This quarry supplied the granite used in building the State Capitol and also many of the jetties along the Texas coast. Visitors are not allowed in the quarry but can observe the oper-ation from the rest stop on the side of FM 1431.

where to go

Marble Falls/Lake LBJ Chamber of Commerce. 801 US 281. Stop by this one-hundred-year-old railroad depot station to get brochures and maps on area shopping, dining, and park recreation. Open Monday through Friday 8:00 a.m. to 5:00 p.m. (800) 759–8178 or (830) 693–4449; www.marblefalls.org.

Highland Arts Guild Gallery. 318 Main Street. Have a look here at the work of more than fifty local artists who call the Highland Lakes their home. The gallery sells original arts and crafts, including many bluebonnet paintings. Open Monday through Saturday. (830) 693–7324.

Cottonwood Recreation Area, Lake LBJ. On south side of Lake LBJ next to Wirtz Dam. Access road is off FM 2147, 5 miles west of Marble Falls. FM 2147 can be reached from the east via US 281 or from the west by Highway 71. This day-use park is primarily frequented by boaters and offers seventeen acres. Open daily. Free. (800) 776–5272; www .lcra.org.

Hills of Home Memorial. US 281 south of the Colorado River. The memorial remembers Oscar J. Fox, the composer of "Home on the Range," "Get Along Little Dogie," and "Hills of Home," said to be inspired by the view from this spot.

where to eat

Inman's Ranch House Barbecue and Turkey Sausage. US 281 and Sixth Street. This little restaurant uses Texas's favorite cooking method—barbecue—on turkey to produce a spicy sausage that's mighty tasty and not as greasy as its pork cousin. Beef brisket and sides of coleslaw and beans also appear on the menu. $. (830) 693–2711.

Blue Bonnet Cafe. US 281 near the bridge. This is an example of a good old-fashioned Texas diner at its best. For more than sixty years, the Blue Bonnet Cafe has served locals and visitors plenty of country cooking, including chicken-fried steak, fried chicken, and burgers. $–$$. (830) 693–2344.

where to stay

Horseshoe Bay Resort Marriott. FM 2147, west of Marble Falls. Horseshoe Bay, located on Lake LBJ, is one of the premier resorts in Central Texas. Golfers have their choice of three courses, including Robert Trent Jones's Applerock. Other features include Oriental gardens, a yacht club, horseback trails, and tennis courts. $$$. (800) 452–5330 or (888) 236–2427; www.horseshoebaymarriott.com.

Liberty Hall. 119 Avenue G. This historic guest house was originally the home of General Adam Rankin Johnson, founder of Marble Falls. In later years, the two-story home was the residence of "Birdie" Harwood, a woman elected mayor—by an all-male voting population. Today the bed-and-breakfast includes cozy bedrooms with brass beds, antique furnishings, and a homey atmosphere. $$. (800) 232–4469.

kingsland

Continue west on FM 1431 from Marblehead Falls to the fishing community of Kingsland.

Once named Granite Shoals, Lake LBJ was renamed for President Lyndon Baines Johnson who, as a young senator, brought the lakes project to Central Texas. Today the narrow, winding lake is popular with both anglers and skiers. Edged by steep hills, its clear and calm waters are protected from the winds that often buffet the larger lakes.

Kingsland is a sleepy community catering to those who come to enjoy a few days of bass fishing. Several lodges lie near the junction of the Llano and Colorado Rivers, where quiet coves afford a catch of black bass, white bass, crappie, catfish, and perch. Be sure to stop at the scenic overlook on FM 1431 just past the edge of town for a grand view of the lake and its shoreline homes.

where to go

Kingsland Archaeological Center. Nine miles north of Marble Falls on Lake LBJ. From Marble Falls, follow FM 1431 to Burnet County Road 126 (at the Twin Isles and Hidden Oaks subdivision), turn left and follow the signs. Discovered in 1988, this archaeological site has yielded artifacts dating from the Paleo-Indian (more than 10,000 years ago) to the late prehistoric periods (700 years ago). A small visitor center and museum house artifacts from the site. Open for tours on Sunday afternoons and by appointment. Free. (800) 776–5272.

where to stay

Longhorn Resort. RR 2900, at Llano River Bridge. This fishing resort has air-conditioned units with kitchenettes, a covered fishing marina, boat stalls, and launch ramp. It also provides camper hookups. $$. (325) 388–4343; www.longhornresort.com.

day trip 03

northwest

cedar park, leander, bertram, burnet, buchanan dam, tow: ranch road rambling

This day trip is filled with winding roads, historic attractions, and natural wonders.

Visitors to this Hill Country vicinity must travel over some dirt and gravel roads, especially in rock-hunting areas. Near Mason are numerous low water crossings, and on some back roads you must drive across dry creek beds. Flash flooding is a very real hazard in the Hill Country, especially during the spring and fall months. Be aware of weather conditions when you make these trips, and never cross swiftly flowing water.

cedar park

Cedar Park is a thirty-minute drive north from Austin via U.S. Highway 183, a congested highway that leads to the Texas Hill Country. Now primarily a suburb, once this was called "cedar chopper" country. Cedar choppers were independent people who worked the hilly land to the west, cutting juniper trees to provide fence posts for area ranchers. This generations-old trade is still plied by some Hill Country families. The town celebrates its heritage with an annual Cedar Chopper Festival in June.

where to go

Austin Steam Train. US 183 and FM 1431. Take a ride on the *Hill Country Flyer,* running from Cedar Park to Burnet (where visitors stop to eat lunch and shop). Each of the 1930s–era cars is restored to original splendor. The locomotive, donated to the city of Austin by the Southern Pacific Railroad in 1956, resided for many years in a downtown park as playground equipment. After a complete restoration in 1991, she's once again whistling through Central Texas. Reservations required. Fee. (512) 477–8468; www.austinsteamtrain.org.

where to shop

Callahan's General Store. US 183 North, in Cedar Park. This classy general store stocks everything Texan, from western wear to blue-speckled dinnerware to gourmet gift items, not to mention agricultural supplies. (512) 335–8585.

Lakeline Mall. US 183 and RR 620. Shop this Texas-size mall, with a decor that's complete with a free-standing replica of the state capitol dome and the Austin skyline. Open daily. (512) 257–7467.

where to eat

La Fiesta. 200 Buttercup Boulevard. Bring a big appetite to this top Tex-Mex spot. Try the regular dinner, with a cheese enchilada and a tamale plus sides of rice and beans, or order the La Fiesta Salad—a taco, guacamole salad, and a dollop of *chile con queso*. $–$$. (512) 331–0055.

northwest day trip 03

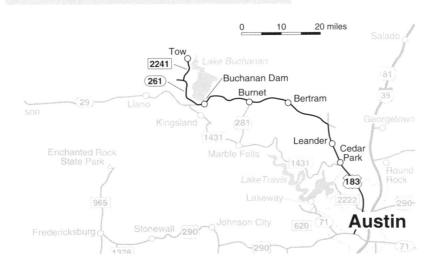

leander

Continue north on US 183 to neighboring Leander, a small town that boasts many historic markers. To the right as you approach town, you'll see a marker for the Blockhouse Creek subdivision, named for a blockhouse used as an interim prison by the Texas Rangers a century ago.

Another historic marker stands just east of US 183 on FM 2243. The Davis Cemetery, as the marker recounts, is the site of a mass grave, a reminder of an Indian attack that ended with the deaths of many pioneers.

where to go

Dinosaur Tracks. South San Gabriel River, just north of town. Park your car at the bridge and walk upstream for a half mile to see these three-toed dinosaur tracks. Free. (512) 259–1907.

bertram

From Leander, continue north on US 183 to the intersection of Highway 29. Drive west then on Highway 29 for 12 miles to Bertram. This is a sleepy little town most of the year, but on Labor Day weekend the streets throng with travelers from around the state who come for the annual Oatmeal Festival. Visitors attend the celebration to witness an oatmeal cook-off, take part in a fun run, or see a parade. The festival is named for the hamlet of Oatmeal, located 6 miles south of Bertram on RR 243.

where to shop

Jimmy's Antiques. Highway 29. If you're looking for Texas antiques, this is a good place to start. Jimmy's has the usual glassware, china, and jewelry, but it also handles many local treasures such as Texas Ranger saddlebags, western saddles, Native American artifacts, and arrowheads. Open daily. (512) 355–2985.

burnet

Continue west on Highway 29 from Bertram to Burnet. This is the closest town of any size to Lake Buchanan (pronounced "BUCK-an-an"). It's a good place to stop for picnic supplies and sunscreen products during summer visits (there are few facilities once you leave the city limits). Outdoor activities popular throughout the year include spelunking and bird-watching.

burnet treasure

Longhorn Caverns, outside Burnet, is said to be the home of more than one treasure trove. One tale involves who else but Sam Bass, who allegedly used the cavern as a hide-out following nearby robberies. Today the main opening of the cave is called the Sam Bass entrance. No Bass treasure has been found, but even today, parts of the 11-mile cavern are still being explored.

Another Longhorn Cavern tale involves the search for a treasure supposedly buried on Woods Ranch near Burnet. After years of searching, one of the treasure hunters went to seek the advice of a palmist, whose cryptic recommendation was to dig "under the footprint." There was speculation that this "footprint" might be a foot-shaped impression on the ceiling of one of the Longhorn Cavern rooms. The crew dug below this formation—only to find a container-shaped hole below the surface. Where there had once been a metal container—and possibly a treasure—there was only a rust-lined hole.

The Sam Bass legends are not the only treasure-filled stories flying around the region. One treasure story dates back to an ancient Spanish document regarding an old Spanish mine, located somewhere near Burnet. According to an Austin American *story in the early 1920s, a "pack train of burros carrying forty jackloads of silver was pursued by a band of Comanche Indians and . . . the men in charge of the pack train buried the silver near where the town of Leander is now located."*

No one's found the Spanish silver cache, but some treasure seekers in this area have struck gold—or gemstones, as the case may be. In 1925, W. E. Snavely of Taylor, who had hunted treasure for sixty years, found a ruby arrowhead weighing fifteen karats, along with many other gemstones.

where to go

Fort Croghan Museum. Highway 29 on the western edge of town. Fort Croghan was constructed here in the 1840s, one of eight forts built from the Rio Grande to the Trinity Rivers to protect the region from Indian attacks. The museum and the adjacent fort sit on the left side of the road. Exhibits include household items used by residents over one hundred years ago. You can take a walking tour of the fort, the blacksmith shop, the powder house, and a two-room cabin where one family raised ten children. Open Thursday through Saturday during peak season; by appointment only during winter months. Free. (512) 756–8281; www.fortcroghan.org.

Vanishing Texas River Cruise. A few miles past Fort Croghan on Highway 29, turn right on FM 2341 and follow the signs 14 miles to the cruise entrance. This excellent bird-watching cruise is popular with travelers who come to see American bald eagles from November through March. The rest of the year, you might see javelinas, wild goats, and white-tailed deer. The route takes in 50-foot Fall Creek Falls and a narrow, cliff-lined passage on the Colorado River. Cruises also travel past Fall Creek Vineyards on the lake's shore. Dinner cruises May through October; reservations required. Closed Tuesday. $$. Fee. (800) 4RIVER4 or (512) 756–6986; www.vtrc.com.

Inks Lake State Park. From Highway 29, turn left onto Park Road 4. This 1,200-acre park offers camping, lakeside picnicking, swimming, and even a golf course. White-tailed deer are a common sight during evening hours. Open daily. Fee. (512) 793–2223 for park information; (512) 389–8900 for reservations; www.tpwd.state.tx.us.

Inks Dam National Fish Hatchery. Park Road 4 off US 281. This facility raises fish to be shipped throughout the country. Guided tours can be arranged (call in advance) for a look at the hatching process. Open weekdays. Free. (512) 793–2474.

Highland Lakes Squadron of the Commemorative Air Force. At the Burnet Municipal Airport off US 281, 1.5 miles south of Burnet. Here you can have a look at World War II airplanes as well as memorabilia from the men who fought the battles. Operated by the Highland Lakes Squadron of the Commemorative Air Force. Open weekends. Fee. (512) 756–2226; www.highlandlakessquadron.com.

Longhorn Cavern State Park. From Highway 29, turn left onto Park Road 4. This cavern has few formations but a long and interesting history. In one story, Comanches raided San Antonio, kidnapped a young woman named Mariel King, and brought her back to the cavern, unknowingly followed by three Texas Rangers. A hand-to-hand battle ensued, and Mariel King was rescued. Ending the story with a fairy-tale flourish, Miss King later married one of her rescuers, and the couple lived on in Burnet. The guided tour is nonstrenuous, with wide, well-lit trails through the huge limestone rooms. Open daily. Fee. (877) 441–CAVE or (830) 598–CAVE; www.tpwd.state.tx.us.

From the cavern, return to Burnet by retracing your steps on Park Road 4.

where to eat

Burnet County BBQ. Highway 29. This casual restaurant serves up all the main ingredients of a Texas barbeque: brisket, ribs, and sausage. The atmosphere here is casual and families are welcome. Open Wednesday through Sunday. $. (512) 756–6468.

buchanan dam

Continue driving west on Highway 29 to the village of Buchanan Dam, a fishing and retirement community. Lake Buchanan, the jewel of the Highland Lakes with more than 23,000 surface acres of water, is formed by Buchanan Dam, the largest multiarch dam in the world.

Lake Buchanan's own gem is the freshwater pearl. Created by freshwater mussels in the Colorado River, some pearls found here have been valued at several thousand dollars.

Many anglers are familiar with one of the most popular sites along Lake Buchanan: Black Rock Park. This location underwent a major renovation with improvements that include new campsites and rest rooms. Anglers can try their luck with either bank or boat fishing. Boats can launch without charge from the ramp at neighboring Llano County Park.

Birders also find this park a favorite destination. The northeast side of the lake offers one of the best opportunities to spot the American bald eagle from November through March. Other species often sighted include great blue herons, kingfishers, double-crested cormorants, roadrunners, ospreys, red-breasted mergansers, common loons, horned grebes, and Bonaparte's gulls.

If you'd like to extend your stay at Black Rock, spend the night at one of the park's thirty campsites, each with a table and grill. Campsites can fill up on busy weekends and they are offered on a first-come, first-served basis.

where to go

Buchanan Dam Visitors Center and Museum. Highway 29, at the dam. Here you can find brochures on area campgrounds and activities as well as maps of the Highland Lakes. A museum adjacent to the center provides a look at how the mighty Colorado was tamed. Photographs recount the backbreaking labor involved in the massive project. During spring and summer months, tour the dam on Saturday and Sunday afternoons; call for times. Hours vary seasonally. Free. (512) 793–2803.

Black Rock Park. Lake Buchanan. From Burnet, travel west on Highway 29 and turn right on Highway 261. Drive about four miles to the park. This newly renovated park offers something for everyone. The northeast side of the lake offers some of the area's best birding; the park has also been a longtime favorite with anglers. If you'd like to extend your visit to Black Rock, stay at one of the park's numerous campsites. Sites can fill up on busy weekends, and they are offered on a first-come, first-served basis. (800) 776–5272; www.lcra.org.

Buchanan Dam Art Gallery. Highway 29, 1 mile past the dam. This is the oldest continuously operating artists' cooperative in the country, and it's a great place to buy a bluebonnet painting at a reasonable price. The April arts and crafts show is held here, with booths set up outdoors. During the show local artists sell bluebonnets painted on everything from saw blades to mussel shells. Open daily. Free. (512) 793–2858.

where to eat

Big John's Bar-B-Q. Highway 29 and FM 1431, 2 miles west of Buchanan Dam. There's nothing fancy about this old-fashioned barbecue joint, serving sliced beef, ribs, and sausage. Dine indoors or out on big picnic tables. Open Thursday through Sunday for lunch and dinner. $$. (512) 793–2261.

where to stay

Canyon of the Eagles Lodge and Nature Park. RR 2341. This 900-acre park serves as an ecotourism destination for all types of travelers, whether they are seeking a hotel, campground, or RV park. Along with a 64-room lodge, the park includes bird and butterfly trails, nature trails, a fishing pier, kayaking, cruises, and an observatory. $–$$$. (800) 977–0081; www.canyonoftheeagles.com.

tow

If you're interested in wine, take a drive up to the community of Tow (rhymes with "cow") on the edge of Lake Buchanan. From Highway 29, head north 8 miles on Highway 261, then 6 miles on FM 2241.

where to go

Fall Creek Vineyards. 2.2 miles northeast of the Tow Post Office on FM 2241. Since opening in 1975, Fall Creek has been known as one of the top wineries in Central Texas, winning numerous awards. Located right on the shores of Lake Buchanan, the vineyards here span sixty-five acres. You can take a tour of the entire operation and sample the wine made on the premises. Tours run Monday through Friday 11:00 A.M. to 4:00 P.M., Saturday noon to 5:00 P.M., Sunday noon to 4:00 P.M. Free. (512) 476–4477 (Austin sales office) or (325) 379–5361 (winery); www.fcv.com.

day trip 04

northwest

llano, mason:
rock hound's delight

This trip is a favorite with rock hounds and outdoor lovers. To reach Llano, travel U.S. Highway 183 north from Austin through Cedar Park and Leander. Take Highway 29 West to Burnet and continue through Buchanan Dam (see Northwest Day Trip 3 for local attractions).

llano

Continuing west on Highway 29 from Buchanan Dam, you'll see more and more granite outcroppings—huge boulders protruding from the rugged land. This entire region is called the Llano Uplift, a geological formation caused by igneous rocks from 40 miles below ground being pushed up to the surface.

As a result of the formation, the rich minerals found here turned Llano into a boomtown in the 1880s. Huge deposits of iron ore were found in the area, and some industrialists had dreams of making Llano the "Pittsburgh of the West." Tent cities were erected, mining went full swing, and downtown Llano was spruced up with the money that came pouring into town. All too soon, though, one hard fact came to light: To make steel you have to have coal as well as iron, and there was no coal in the area. To bring coal in was far too costly. As quickly as it began, the iron ore business came to a halt.

But Llano was by then well known for another mineral: granite. During its heyday, the city boasted ten granite quarries and five finishing plants and shipped several varieties of granite around the country. When rail prices increased, Llano's granite business also came to a stop, although vast quantities of granite still remain.

Granite brought many prominent people to the area. Sculptor Frank Teich, a nationally famous German artist, owned a monument company (as well as the town of Teichville). His World War I monument stands on the courthouse lawn here. Teich came to Llano for its healthy climate when doctors told him that he had only six months to live. Either the doctors were wrong in their diagnosis or Llano's healthy atmosphere really worked, because Teich lived in the town for another thirty-eight years! Even today, Llano is listed by the U.S. Census as one of the healthiest places to live in the country.

Another prominent Llano citizen was Professor N. J. Badu, a mineralogist who came to town to operate a manganese mine and tried to focus the attention of the mineralogy world on Llano's many minerals. Today his elegant home is a busy bed-and-breakfast inn.

The Llano area is still a collector's paradise, with more than 240 different rocks and minerals discovered in the region. The area's granite, feldspar, graphite, and talc have commercial value, while the more precious yields, such as garnet, amethyst, tourmaline, and quartz—even gold and silver—are sought by visiting rock hounds.

Public rock hunting is allowed on the Llano River in town. Stop by the park on the south bank of the river just across from the public library and try your luck. The riverbanks are dotted with rocks of all varieties and offer some pretty picnic spots as well.

> # northwest day trip 04

buried treasure

Following the robber from Round Rock to Burnet and finally to Llano, we're once again on the trail of Sam Bass. Allegedly, the robber hid canvas sacks marked "U.S." and filled with gold in a cave on Packsaddle Mountain. Some say the treasure was found by a Mexican laborer, hired by a local rancher to cut fence posts on Packsaddle Mountain. According the one version of the story, the rancher went to look for the laborer when he failed to return to the ranch. All the rancher found was a cave, and a piece of canvas sack with "U.S." imprinted on it. Another version of the story says the gold still lies hidden somewhere in the mountain.

Packsaddle Mountain is also the home of the Blanco Mine, named for a Spaniard who found the location long ago. According to J. Frank Dobie's book Coronado's Children, the mine was rediscovered in the 1800s by a Llano settler named Larimore. While hunting, Larimore discovered the old mine—with its contents of lead and a high percentage of silver.

In 1860 Larimore took a last trip to the mine with a man named Jim Rowland. The two men hauled out several hundred pounds of the metal, shaping it into bullets. Larimore, who was leaving the country, declared that he would hide the mine so well no other person would ever find it. Supposedly, he diverted a gully directly into the mine, filling it with silt. Rowland carved his initials on a large stone marking the entrance to the mine, then covered it with earth . . . where it remains today.

Llano County is home to other buried treasure sites, including $60,000 in gold and silver coins buried by Sam Bass near the community of Castell in the western part of the county. Bass buried the loot on a creek bed, marking the spot with a rock in a fork of a tree.

where to go

Llano County Historical Museum. 310 Bessemer Avenue, Highway 16. This museum, housed in the old Bruhl Drugstore, has displays on the area's early Native American history and Llano's boomtown days. An exhibit contains samples of Llano's many rocks and minerals. Open Wednesday through Saturday 11:00 a.m. to 5:00 p.m., Sunday afternoons. Free. (325) 247–3026.

Walking Tour of Llano. Stop by the Chamber of Commerce at 700 Bessemer Avenue for a brochure outlining twenty-six historic stops in town. Open Monday through Friday. Free. (325) 247–5354.

Hill Country Wildlife Museum. 326 Ford Street. This museum is home to the Campbell Collection, considered the world's third-largest taxidermy collection. Open Thursday through Saturday. Fee. (325) 247–2568.

Robinson City Park. Llano River banks. This park includes RV camping, golf, swimming pool, fishing, picnicking, and it has a playground. Open daily. Free.

where to shop

Llano Fine Arts Guild Gallery. 503 Bessemer Avenue. Located across from the Llano County Historical Museum, this art gallery features the works of many local residents. Works range from fine arts to ceramics, photographs, and stained glass. Open Wednesday through Sunday. (325) 247–4839; www.llanofineartsgallery.com.

where to eat

Inman's Kitchen and Catering Service. 809 West Young (Highway 29 West). Barbecue is king here, including beef brisket, chicken, pork, and the restaurant's specialty: turkey sausage. This spot is more elegant than many barbecue restaurants, with a carpeted, air-conditioned dining area. Lunch and dinner served Monday through Saturday; Sunday during deer season. $. (325) 247–5257.

Cooper's Old Time Pit Barbecue and Catering. 506 West Young (Highway 29 West). Step up to the smoker and pick out your meat—brisket, sausage, pork ribs, beef ribs, chicken, sirloin steak, pork chops, and even goat. The pit master slices off the amount you want, then you go inside and help yourself to white bread, beans, and sauce in the cinder block dining room. $. (325) 247–5713.

where to stay

The Badu House. 601 Bessemer Avenue, Highway 16. This two-story stone and brick inn, circa 1891, was the former home of mineralogist N. J. Badu, who put Llano on the map by discovering the mineral llanite here at the turn of the century. The building has been elegantly renovated, and all eight bedrooms feature private baths, ceiling fans, air-conditioning, and period furnishings. Late afternoon cocktails are served in a club adjacent to the restaurant that offers everything from filet mignon to oven-roasted quail. $$–$$$. (325) 247–1207; www.baduhouse.com.

Dabbs Hotel. 112 East Burnet Street, behind the Llano Museum. At the turn of the century, this railroad hotel was the last outpost of civilization for frontiersmen heading west. Today's guests stay in one of twelve quiet rooms with period furnishings, double beds, a breezy screened porch, and a peaceful atmosphere overlooking the Llano River. Saturday nights feature western cookouts. Dinner reservations required. $. (325) 247–7905.

mason

From Llano, continue west on Highway 29 for 34 miles to Mason, once the home of the late Fred Gipson, author of *Old Yeller.* Like neighboring Llano, the land around Mason is rocky and dotted with granite.

Mason was settled by cattle ranchers and German families who came from nearby Fredericksburg. In 1851 Fort Mason was built on a hilltop to afford a better look at oncoming Comanches. (The post's best-known soldier was Lieutenant Colonel Robert E. Lee.) Constructed of sandstone, in 1869 the fort was dismantled and the salvaged stone was used to build local businesses and homes.

Even after the fort was no longer necessary, frontier justice was still a part of Mason. In 1875 the Mason County War, also known as the Hoodoo War, broke out. It all started when the sheriff arrested a group of men who were taking cattle to Llano, allegedly without the owner's permission. The men were set free on bond and ordered to remain in town, an order they promptly forgot. The sheriff re-arrested as many of the rustlers as he could find. A few nights later, a group freed the prisoners, sparking a round of shootings and lynchings that left a dozen men dead. The feud continued until January 1877, when the Mason County Courthouse was set on fire, destroying any evidence against the cattle rustlers.

Rock hounds come to Mason County today in search of topaz, the Texas state gem, which develops in colors ranging from clear to sky blue. Most local topaz turns up near the small communities of Streeter, Grit, and Katemcy, all north and northeast of Mason. Searchers usually find the stones in streambeds and ravines by using picks and shovels to loosen rocks and a wire screen to sift the debris.

where to go

Fort Mason. Follow Post Hill Street south from the courthouse to Post Hill. These reconstructed officers' quarters are furnished with typical 1850s' belongings as well as photographs from Mason's early days. The back porch has an unbeatable view of the town below and miles of Hill Country beyond. Open daily. Free. (325) 347–5758.

Gene Zesch Woodcarving Display at the Commercial Bank. 100 Moody Street, on the square. Gene Zesch is one of Mason's most famous citizens, known for his humorous woodcarvings of modern cowboys. His work was collected by President Johnson and is sold in galleries nationally. This exhibit features woodcarvings and bronzes made by the artist. Open Monday through Friday. Free. (325) 347–6324.

Mason County Museum. 300 Moody Street, south of the square. This local-history museum is housed in an old elementary school built in 1887. The contents include typical items used by area ranchers and housewives a century ago, from toys to needlework to farm equipment. There is also a display of local rocks and minerals. Call for hours. Free. (325) 347–5758.

Eckert James River Bat Cave. Write or call the Mason Chamber of Commerce (P.O. Box 156, Mason, TX 76856; 325–347–5758) for directions and a map to this bat cave, located about 13 miles south of Mason. The cavern is home to about 6 million Mexican free-tail bats. This is a "maternity cave," used during the spring and summer months by female bats to bear and rear their young. You can view the evening flight out of the cave, a sight heralded by high-pitched sounds. Open Thursday through Sunday 6:00 to 9:00 p.m., May through October. Free.

White-tailed Deer Hunting. Mason County claims to have more white-tailed deer per acre than any other county in Texas. Hunters flock here from around the Southwest to stalk deer during the winter months. For information on hunting licenses, call the Mason Chamber of Commerce (325) 347–5758 well before deer season begins.

Topaz Hunting. Two private areas charge a daily fee of $10 per person for topaz hunting. Visitors must bring their own equipment (including water during warm summer months) and may keep whatever they find. The following ranches offer topaz hunting from mid-January through September.

> **Wayne Hofmann Ranch,** c/o Wesley Loeffler, Menard Route, Mason, TX 76856; (325) 347–6415.

> **Garner Seaquist Ranch,** P.O. Box 35, Mason, TX 76856. This ranch also offers camping facilities, with both tent sites and camper hookups, with water, electricity, and showers. (325) 347–5713.

where to shop

Country Collectibles. U.S. Highway 87 North. If your search for topaz is futile, stop by this antiques store, which sells topaz and other stones indigenous to the area along with arrowheads, willow furniture, and collectibles of every description. (325) 347–5249.

where to stay

Mason County is filled with bed-and-breakfast accommodations, RV campsites, and guest ranches located outside of town. For a free copy of their "Bed and Breakfast and RV Sites" brochure, write or call the Mason County Chamber of Commerce, P.O. Box 156, Mason, TX 76856; (325) 347–5758; www.masontxcoc.com.

regional information

north from austin
day trip 01

Round Rock Chamber of Commerce
212 East Main Street
Round Rock, TX 78664
(800) 747–3479 or (512) 255–5805
www.roundrockchamber.org

Georgetown Convention and
Visitors Bureau
P.O. Box 409
Georgetown, TX 78627
(800) GEO–TOWN or (512) 930–3545
www.visitgeorgetown.org

Salado Chamber of Commerce
P.O. Box 1161
601 North Main Street
Salado, TX 76571
(254) 947–5040
www.salado.com

day trip 02

Belton Area Chamber of Commerce
P.O. Box 659
412 East Central
Belton, TX 76513
(254) 933–5836
www.seebelton.com

Killeen Civic and Conference Center
and Visitors Bureau
P.O. Box 1329
Killeen, TX 76540
(800) 869–8265 or (254) 501–3888
http://killeen-cvb.com

Temple Chamber of Commerce
P.O. Box 158
Temple, TX 76503
(800) 374–9123 or (254) 773–2105
www.temple-tx.org

day trip 03

Lorena City Hall
114 East Center Street
Lorena, TX 76655
(254) 857–4641

Waco Tourist Information Center
P.O. Box 2570
Waco, TX 76702
(800) WACO–FUN
www.wacocvb.com

northeast from austin
day trip 01

Taylor Chamber of Commerce
P.O. Box 231
1519 North Main Street
Taylor, TX 76574
(512) 352–6364
www.taylorchamber.org

Rockdale Chamber of Commerce
1203 West Cameron Avenue
Rockdale, TX 76567
(512) 446–2030
www.rockdalechamber.com

Calvert Chamber of Commerce
P.O. Box 506
300 South Main Street
Calvert, TX 77837
(979) 364–2559

day trip 02

Bryan–College Station Convention
and Visitors Bureau
715 University Drive East
College Station, TX 77840
(800) 777–8292 or (979) 260–9898
www.bryan-collegestation.org

east from austin

day trip 01

Elgin Chamber of Commerce
15 North Main Street
P.O. Box 408
Elgin, TX 78621
(512) 285–4515
www.elgintx.com

Giddings Chamber of Commerce
171 East Hempstead
Giddings, TX 78942
(979) 542–3455
www.giddingstx.com

day trip 02

Burton Chamber of Commerce
P.O. Box 670
Burton, TX 77835
(979) 289–3402 (City Hall)

Brenham–Washington County
Convention and Visitors Bureau
314 South Austin Street
Brenham, TX 77833
(888) BRENHAM or (979) 836–3695
www.brenhamtx.org

southeast from austin

day trip 01

Bastrop Chamber of Commerce
927 Main Street
Bastrop, TX 78602
(512) 303–0558
www.bastropchamber.com

Smithville Chamber of Commerce
P.O. Box 716
Smithville, TX 78957
(512) 237–2313
www.smithvilletx.org

La Grange Chamber of Commerce
171 South Main Street
La Grange, TX 78945
(800) LAGRANGE or (974) 968–5756
www.lagrangetx.org

day trip 02

Round Top Chamber of Commerce
P.O. Box 216
Round Top, TX 78954
(979) 249–4042
www.roundtop.org

south from austin

day trip 01

Lockhart Chamber of Commerce
P.O. Box 840
Lockhart, TX 78644
(512) 398–2818
www.lockhart-tx.org

Luling Area Chamber of Commerce
P.O. Box 710
421 East Davis Street
Luling, TX 78648
(830) 875–3214
www.lulingcc.org

Schulenburg Chamber of Commerce
618 North Main Street
Schulenburg, TX 78956
(866) 504–5294
www.schulenburgchamber.org

day trip 02

Gonzales Chamber of Commerce
P.O. Box 134
Gonzales, TX 78629
(830) 672–6532
www.gonzalestexas.com

Yoakum Chamber of Commerce
P.O. Box 591
105 Huck Street
Yoakum, TX 77995
(361) 293–2309
www.yoakumareachamber.com

day trip 03

San Marcos Convention and
Visitors Bureau
P.O. Box 2310
San Marcos, TX 78667
(888) 200–5620 or (512) 393–5900
www.toursanmarcos.com

day trip 04

Seguin–Guadalupe County Chamber
of Commerce
427 North Austin Street
Seguin, TX 78155
(800) 580–7322 or (830) 379–6382
www.seguintx.org

southwest from austin

day trip 01

San Antonio Convention and
Visitors Bureau
203 South St. Mary's Street
P.O. Box 2277
San Antonio, TX 78298
(800) 447–3372 or (210) 270–6700
www.sanantoniocvb.com

day trip 02

Gruene Tourist Information
1601 Hunter Road
New Braunfels, TX 78130
(830) 629–5077
www.gruene.net

New Braunfels Convention and
Visitors Bureau
P.O. Box 311417
New Braunfels, TX 78131
(800) 572–2626 or (830) 625–2385
www.nbcham.org

day trip 03

Wimberley Chamber of Commerce
P.O. Box 12
Wimberley, TX 78676
(512) 847–2201
www.wimberley.org

Blanco Chamber of Commerce
312 Pecan Street
P.O. Box 626
Blanco, TX 78606
(830) 833–5101
www.blancotex.com

day trip 04

Comfort Chamber of Commerce
P.O. Box 777
Seventh and High Streets
Comfort, TX 78013
(830) 995–3131
www.comfort-texas.com

Boerne Chamber of Commerce
126 Rosewood Avenue
Boerne, TX 78006
(888) 842–8080 or (830) 249–8000
www.boerne.org

day trip 05

Bandera County Convention and
Visitors Bureau
P.O. Box 171
Bandera, TX 78003
(800) 364–3833 or (830) 796–3045
www.banderacowboycapital.com

day trip 06

Castroville Chamber of Commerce
P.O. Box 572
802 London Street
Castroville, TX 78009
(800) 778–6775 or (830) 538–3142
www.castroville.com

Uvalde Convention and Visitors Bureau
300 East Main Avenue
Uvalde, TX 78801
(830) 278–3361
www.uvalde.org

west from austin
day trip 02

Johnson City Convention and
Visitors Bureau
P.O. Box 485
Johnson City, TX 78636
(830) 868–7684
www.johnsoncity-texas.com

Fredericksburg Convention and
Visitors Bureau
302 East Austin
Fredericksburg, TX 78624
(888) 997–3600 or (830) 997–6523
www.fredericksburg-texas.com

day trip 03

Kerrville Convention and Visitors Bureau
1700 Sidney Baker, Suite 100
Kerrville, TX 78028
(830) 896–1155
www.kerrvilletx.com

northwest
from austin

day trip 01

Lakeway City Hall
104 Cross Creek Drive
Lakeway, TX 78734
(512) 261–6090

day trip 02

Marble Falls/Lake LBJ Chamber
of Commerce
916 Second Street
Marble Falls, TX 78654
(800) 759–8178 or (830) 693–2815
www.marblefalls.org

Kingsland Chamber of Commerce
P.O. Box 465
Kingsland, TX 78639
(325) 388–6211

day trip 03

Cedar Park Chamber of Commerce
1490 East Whitestone Boulevard
Building 2, Suite 180
Cedar Park, TX 78630
(512) 260–7800
www.cedarparkchamber.org

Leander Chamber of Commerce
103 North Brushy
P.O. Box 556
Leander, TX 78646
(512) 259–1907
www.leandercc.org

Burnet Chamber of Commerce
703 Buchanan
Burnet, TX 78611
(512) 756–4297
www.burnetchamber.org

Lake Buchanan Chamber of Commerce
P.O. Box 282
Buchanan Dam, TX 78609
(512) 793–2803

day trip 04

Llano Chamber of Commerce
700 Bessemer Avenue
Llano, TX 78643
(325) 247–5354
www.llanochamber.org

Mason County Chamber of Commerce
P.O. Box 156
Mason, TX 76856
(325) 347–5758
www.masontxcoc.com

festivals and celebrations

Texas undoubtedly has more festivals than any other state. Regardless of the weekend, you'll find some town whooping it up with parades, music, and lots of food. There are festivals for every interest, whether yours is pioneer heritage, German food, or watermelon.

You can receive a free annual events calendar from the Texas Festivals and Events Association at P.O. Box 1025, Fredericksburg, TX 78624, (830) 997–0741 or see www.tour texas.com/tfea.

february

Williamson County Gem and Mineral Show, Georgetown. Dealers from around the United States showcase and sell the latest gems and minerals on the market. Demonstrations, exhibits, and lectures are given throughout the day. (800) GEO–TOWN or (512) 930–3545; www.visitgeorgetown.org.

Wine Lovers Trail, Fredericksburg. Over a dozen Hill Country wineries participate in this event. Sample the products of these vineyards and enjoy special events. (888) 997–3600 or (830) 868–2321; www.fredericksburg-texas.com.

march

National Rattlesnake Sacking Championship and Roundup, Taylor. This controversial festival is one of the most unusual events in Texas, held on the first weekend of the month. Two-person teams compete in this national event to see who can sack ten rattlers in the shortest amount of time. (512) 352–6364; www.taylorchamber.org.

SXSW (South by Southwest), Austin. This music conference, held in mid-March, attracts more than 3,500 people from the music and film industries to the capital city for music conferences and nighttime entertainment. During the festival, more than 400 acts perform at clubs throughout town. Wristbands permit music lovers to take in show after show, from rock to blues to Cajun music. (512) 467–7979; www.sxsw.com.

april

Easter Fires, Fredericksburg. Relive the Easter fires of 1847, when Comanches sat in the hills over Fredericksburg while women and children awaited the results of a peace talk. Mothers calmed their children's fears by explaining that the campfires belonged to the

Easter bunny. This story is recreated in a pageant on the Saturday eve before Easter. Advance tickets are suggested. Fredericksburg Easter Fires, P.O. Box 506, Fredericksburg, TX 78624; (830) 997–6523.

Eeyore's Birthday Party, Austin. Held the last Saturday of April, this is one of Austin's wackiest festivals, paying tribute to Eeyore of Winnie-the-Pooh fame. Outrageous costumes, live entertainment, food, drink, and games. A unique celebration of springtime. (800) 926–2282.

Highland Lakes Bluebonnet Trail, Burnet, Buchanan Dam, Llano, and area communities. The fragrant bluebonnet is the state flower of Texas. For two weekends in early April, a self-guided driving tour will take you past the area's prettiest bluebonnet fields. Each town on the trail, from Burnet to Llano, celebrates with art shows and a festival atmosphere. (512) 793–2803.

River Rendezvous, La Grange. This event draws canoeists from around the state. Visitors paddle down the Colorado River and enjoy camping, canoeing, fun, food, and old-fashioned storytelling. (800) LA–GRANGE; www.lagrangetx.org.

Round Top Antiques Fair, Round Top. Held the first weekend of April, this show features dealers from across the nation. It has been called the best antiques show in the state. (281) 493–5501; http://roundtopantiquesfair.com.

Smithville Jamboree, Smithville. This longtime event includes parades, a livestock show, softball, volleyball and horseshoe tournaments, nightly dances, an antique car show, carnival, and canoe races. (512) 237–2313; www.smithvilletx.org.

Texas Ladies' State Chili Cookoff, Seguin. Women from around the state test their skills at this chili cookoff. Along with taste testings, visitors enjoy live entertainment. (800) 580–PECAN; www.seguintx.org.

may

Chisholm Trail Roundup, Lockhart. Relive the Battle of Plum Creek, where the Texas militia joined forces with Tonkawa Indians to defeat a band of Comanches. You can also enjoy a dance, a parade, and a carnival. (512) 398–2818; www.lockhart-tx.org.

Cinco de Mayo and State Menudo Cook-off, San Marcos. This festival is held on the weekend closest to "Cinco de Mayo" (May 5), the celebration of the Mexican victory over the French. Besides a carnival and musical performances, there's plenty of Mexican food, including *menudo* (a dish made from tripe, hominy, and spices). (888) 200–5620; www.tour sanmarcos.com.

Fiesta Laguna Gloria, Austin. This festival combines art with the spirit of a Mexican party, complete with mariachis and Mexican folk dancers. More than 200 artists and crafters bring their work to this mid-May celebration. (800) 926–2282 or (512) 474–5171.

Folkfest, New Braunfels. This event, held at the Conservation Plaza and Texas Museum of Handmade Furniture, showcases the work of New Braunfels craftspeople and furniture makers through demonstrations, food, and live entertainment. Guided tours of local historic buildings are also available. (800) 572–2626; www.nbcham.org.

Funteer Days, Bandera. If they had festivals back in the Wild West days, they must have looked like this one. Professional Rodeo Cowboys Association (PRCA) rodeo, arts and crafts, country-and-western dances, fiddlin' contests, and an Old West parade draw crowds for this weekend late in May. (800) 364–3833; www.banderacowboycapital.com.

Kerrville Folk Festival, Kerrville. This is one of the biggest outdoor music festivals in the state. For eighteen days starting on the Friday of Memorial Day weekend, Quiet Valley Ranch is filled with music lovers who come to hear both local and nationally known performers. (830) 257–3600; www.kerrville-music.com.

May Fair, Air Show, and Art Walk on the Square, Georgetown. The first weekend in May hosts May Fair with more than one hundred vendors on hand selling arts and craft items, antiques, jewelry, and furniture in San Gabriel Park under the shady oak trees. The air show located at the municipal airport is the largest acrobatic air show in Central Texas, displaying war birds, fighter planes, and World War II planes. Art Walk on the Square showcases local artists' work, from sculptures to paintings; there is something for everyone. (800) GEO–TOWN; www.visitgeorgetown.org.

SpringFest, Marble Falls. Celebrate spring with live music on Friday and Saturday evening, a colorful carnival, 5K run, pageants, tournaments, parade, children's activities, and arts and crafts. (800) 759–8178; www.marblefalls.org.

Texas State Arts and Crafts Fair, Kerrville. Every Memorial Day weekend this festival opens its gates on the grounds of Schreiner College. Originally founded by the state of Texas, this enormous show features the paintings, sculptures, jewelry, and other artwork of over 200 Texas artists, all available to answer questions about their work. A special children's area includes crafts instruction. Musical entertainment rounds out the day. (830) 896–5711; www.kerrvilletx.com.

june

Boerne Berges Fest, Boerne. This festival, scheduled for Father's Day weekend, includes arts and crafts, live music, and a celebration of summer. (888) 842–8080; www.boerne.org.

Indian Hobbyists Meeting, Llano. More than 300 people come here in mid-June from around the state, setting up tepees and keeping alive Indian traditions. There's trading of Indian artifacts and products and a relaxed atmosphere. (325) 247–5354.

Peach Jamboree, Stonewall. The peach capital of Texas shows off its crop on the third Friday and Saturday of June. The local peach pit–spitting record is over 28 feet. (830) 644–2735.

Watermelon Thump, Luling. On the last Thursday, Friday, and Saturday of June, you can enjoy seed-spitting contests, watermelon-eating contests, and champion melon judging. There's also an arts and crafts show, carnivals, live entertainment, and street dances. A Guinness World Record was set here in 1989 for spitting a watermelon seed almost 69 feet. (830) 875–3214; www.lulingcc.org.

july

Fourth of July Celebration, Round Top. One of the oldest celebrations in the country of Independence Day winds through Round Top. Round Top Chamber of Commerce, Round Top, TX 78954. (979) 249–4042; www.roundtop.org.

Half Moon Holidays, Shiner. On the first Sunday in July, Shiner celebrates summer with a brisket cook-off, barbecue dinner, fireworks, carnival, horseshoe-pitching tournament, dance, and lots of music. (361) 594–4180.

Frontier Days, Round Rock. Come to Round Rock on the Friday and Saturday after Fourth of July to watch a reenactment of the infamous shoot-out between outlaw Sam Bass and the Texas Rangers. There's also plenty of food, games, and the atmosphere of a summer festival. (800) 747–3479; www.roundrockchamber.org.

July Fourth Parade, Seguin. In July get ready for a red, white, and blue party known as the biggest small-town Fourth of July parade in Texas. The annual Freedom Fiesta has been drawing onlookers and participants since the early 1900s. This year's activities start at 10:00 A.M. with a patriotic parade, followed by food booths, arts and crafts, family entertainment, and kiddie rides, for an old-fashioned street fair atmosphere. That evening, a street dance from 8:00 P.M. to midnight will keep the mood festive, as will the grand fireworks display in Max Starcke Park starting at 9:00 P.M. (800) 580–PECAN; www.sequintx.org.

Night in Old Fredericksburg, Fredericksburg. This annual event, held on Market Square, showcases a different local culture every night through arts and crafts, food, dances, and more. (888) 997–3600; www.fredericksburg-texas.com.

august

Gillespie County Fair, Fredericksburg. This event holds the record as the longest-running county fair in the state. The festivities include old-fashioned family fun from carnival rides to food booths. (888) 997–3600; www.fredericksburg-texas.com.

Grape Stomping Harvest Celebration, Tow. Jump in a bin of red grapes and start stomping during this late-August festival. Other activities include Cork Toss, Grape Walk, hayrides, and music. (325) 379–5361.

Hill Country Heritage Day, Johnson City. Stop back to the pioneer days at a chuckwagon camp with music and cowboy poetry. Held at the Johnson Settlement. (830) 868–7128; www.johnsoncity-texas.com.

LBJ Birthday Celebration, Johnson City. The legacy of this Hill Country president is rememebered with a wreath laying at the President's grave and free ranch tours. Held on the anniversary of LBJ's birth: August 27. (830) 868–7128; www.johnsoncity-texas.com.

International Barbeque Cook-off, Taylor. Barbeque beef, chicken, and sausage reign supreme at most Texas barbeque joints, but this mid-August cook-off also features seafood, lamb, goat, and even wild game. Over one hundred teams compete in catagories ranging from theatrics to most elaborate cooking equipment. (512) 352–6364 or (512) 365–8485; www.taylorchamber.org.

Salado Art Fair, Salado. More than 200 artists set up booths on the shady banks of Salado Creek in Pace Park. This weekend festival in early August is one of the most popular art shows in the state. (254) 947–5040; www.salado.com.

september

Comal County Fair, New Braunfels. This long-running fair ranks as one of the largest (and one of the oldest) in the state. The event includes everything from a rodeo to carnival rides to children's play areas. (800) 572–2626; www.nbcham.org.

Kerrville Wine and Music Festival, Kerrville. The Hill Country town celebrates fall with performances by Texas musicians and tasting of Texas wines. Held at Quiet Valley Ranch, the site of the June Music Festival. (830) 296–1155; www.kerrvilletx.com.

Oatmeal Festival, Bertram. This Labor Day weekend festival is named for the nearby community of Oatmeal, and all the events, from the street parade to the midway, continue the theme. (512) 355–2197.

october

Czhilispiel, Flatonia. When tiny Flatonia needed a doctor years ago, local citizens decided to send a hometown girl to medical school. To fund her education, they began this chili cook-off (now the second largest in Texas) and festival held in late October. There's lots of music, a quilt show, "the world's largest tented *biergarten,*" and a barbecue cook-off as well. (361) 865–3920.

Halloween on Sixth Street, Austin. In the capital city, October 31 is not just for kids. The treat is the sight of thousands of revelers in wild costumes parading through the Sixth Street entertainment district. After the late-night bacchanalian outing, the trick may be getting up the next morning. (866) GO–AUSTIN.

Heart O' Texas Fair and Rodeo, Waco. This ten-day fair draws over 200,000 visitors for a look at a championship rodeo, livestock shows, an art show, and nationally known entertainment. (800) WACO–FUN; www.wacocub.com.

Llano Heritage Day, Llano. This Hill Country town remembers its historic roots with Wild West shoot-outs, living history exhibits, wagon rides, and antiques shows on the third Saturday in October. (325) 247–5354; www.llanochamber.org.

Oktoberfest, Fredericksburg. On the first weekend in October, head to the "Old Country" by visiting this German Hill Country town. You'll find polka dancing and sausage galore, as well as arts and crafts, a street dance, and rides for the kids. Friday through Sunday. (888) 997–3600; www.fredericksburg-texas.com.

Oktoberfest, Round Top. Unlike other Oktoberfest celebrations, this one does it in the pioneer spirit, with demonstrations on everything from soap making to spinning. (979) 278–3530; www.roundtop.org.

Round Top Antiques Fair, Round Top. Called by some the best such show in the state, this extravaganza features antiques dealers from across the United States. Held the first weekend of the month, it attracts shoppers from around the country. (979) 493–5501; www.roundtop.org.

november

Highland Lakes Fall Arts Trail, Buchanan Dam, Kingsland, Burnet, Llano, and Marble Falls. The Highland Lakes Arts Council sponsors this early November arts-and-crafts trail along the same route as the spring bluebonnet festival. Each community has an art show, including Buchanan Dam's Arts and Crafts Gallery, the oldest artists' cooperative in the United States. (512) 756–4297.

Fredericksburg Food and Wine Fest, Fredericksburg. In late October the Fredericksburg Food and Wine Fest highlights the top wineries of Texas. Along with award-winning vineyards, the event showcases more than forty vendors who offer a taste of Texas through spices, salsas, cheeses, and more. Two stages offer plenty of musical entertainment, and the whole family finds plenty of just-for-fun activities such as grape-stomping and cork-tossing. (888) 997–3600; www.fredericksburg-texas.com.

Gathering of the Scottish Clans, Salado. Put on your tartans and grab your bagpipes for the oldest Scottish gathering in the Southwest. If there are Gaels and Celts in your ancestry, you can learn more about your family genealogy. Even if you're not a lass or laddie, enjoy traditional folk dances, Highland games, lots of bagpipe music, and Scottish foods like meat pies and scones. (254) 947–5040; www.salado.com.

Gospel Brunch, Gruene. Holiday visitors won't want to miss Gospel Brunch with a Texas Twist, a special event that takes place in Gruene Hall. Put your hands together and enjoy the sounds of gospel in this New Orleans–inspired event that includes brunch and, for extra charge, plenty of libations. The brunch is held the second Sunday of the month. The event runs from 10:45 A.M. to 1:00 P.M., and seating is very limited. (830) 629–5077; www.gruene.net.

Glowfest, New Braunfels. Hot-air balloons illuminate the darkness with their kaleidoscope of colors like giant Christmas ornaments in the night sky. This event calls itself Texas's only winter holiday balloon festival and includes daytime balloon races. Balloons launch from Comal County Fairgrounds, and the nightly "glow" takes place at Prince Solms Park. (800) 572–2626; www.nbcham.org.

Mesquite Art Festival, Fredericksburg. Visitors have the opportunity to shop for one-of-a-kind woodwork at this annual show. A gathering of more than fifty artists who work primarily in mesquite will showcase collectibles, cabinets, mantels, sculptures, musical instruments, and other artwork made from the often maligned tree. (888) 997–3600; www.fredericksburg-texas.com.

Old Gruene Market Days, Gruene. Shoppers especially flock to this community during Old Gruene Market Days. The event includes plenty of arts and crafts, a farmers market, and lots of live entertainment from 10:00 A.M. to 6:00 P.M. More than 125 vendors give you the chance to make holiday purchases along the streets in twenty-five shops and at the arts-and-crafts tent. Look for one-of-a-kind quilts, pottery, wreaths, jewelry, and other special items. During the Christmas Market Days, visitors will find plenty of activity celebrating the season. Enjoy live music at Gruene Hall on Saturday from 1:00 to 5:00 P.M. and on Sunday starting at noon; admission is free. (830) 629–5077; www.gruene.net.

Texas Book Festival, Austin. Held at the Texas state capitol and on the surrounding grounds, this festival draws more than one hundred authors for seminars and signings. (512) 477–4055.

Wurstfest, New Braunfels. Early in November, pull on your lederhosen, take out your beer stein, and join the fun at this celebration of sausage making. One of the largest German festivals in the country, Wurstfest features oompah bands and great German food. (800) 221–4369.

december

Christmas Lighting Tour, Johnson City, Llano, Fredericksburg, Blanco, Burnet, and Marble Falls. The Hill Country joins together for this trail of Christmas lights and festivities. Blanco's historic courthouse square is lit with festive lights, and Marble Falls celebrates with a walkway of lights every evening. Fredericksburg puts on Kinderfest, Kristkindl Market, and candlelight tours of homes. Llano features a Santa Land. Johnson City, the boyhood home of LBJ, is aglow with more than a quarter-million lights.

On the first weekend, there's a special Pickup Truck Parade (only in Texas!), with decorated trucks to ring in the Christmas season. Finally, Stonewall celebrates with an annual tree-lighting at the LBJ Park, a live nativity scene, and pioneer foods served by candlelight at the Sauer-Beckmann Farm. (830) 868–7684 or 644–2252; www.johnsoncity-texas.com.

Christmas Stroll, Georgetown. The courthouse square is lighted with thousands of miniature white lights followed by an evening of shopping, storytelling, and visiting a children's village. The town also hosts a holiday homes tour through several historic structures. (800) GEO–TOWN; www.visitgeorgetown.org.

Fort Croghan Spirit of Christmas Past, Burnet. Held the first two Saturdays in December, this festival is a recreation of a pioneer Christmas. A holiday dinner is served in the Old Country Store, then the festivities move to Fort Croghan, lit by glowing lanterns. Visitors on the candlelight tour are met by carolers and costumed volunteers. (512) 756–8281; www.burnetchamber.org.

Holiday River of Lights, New Braunfels. This drive-through lighting park illuminates almost a mile along Cypress Bend Park with hundreds of thousands of twinkling lights and holiday scenes. Believed to be the first of its kind in the Southwest, Santas, reindeer, giant Christmas packages, holiday trees, and more come to life in lights as visitors drive through the park. More than thirty large luminous animated displays, such as reindeer leaping over the road, lighted tunnels, holiday trees, and a 15-foot lighted teddy bear, enchant visitors of all ages. While viewing the lights, visitors can tune into an FM radio station to hear the sounds of the holidays as well. (800) 572–2626; www.nbcham.org.

Las Posadas, San Antonio. This beautiful ceremony dramatizes Joseph and Mary's search for an inn with costumed children leading a procession down the River Walk. Holiday music selections are sung in English and Spanish. (800) 447–3372; www.sanantoniocvb.com.

Lights Spectacular, Johnson City. One of the biggest displays in the state, this dazzling event features more than 600,000 lights illuminating homes, businesses, and churches, transforming this quiet Hill Country community into a glittering wonderland. The largest light display is on the Blanco County Courthouse, a historic building aglow with more than 100,000 tiny white lights.

Maps are available at the courthouse for a self-guided drive of Johnson City's fantastic home light displays, erected by local citizens who play a big part in spreading the holiday spirit. The community also has "light art displays," illuminated panels with up to 1,200 lights. Also a large Christmas tree in Memorial Park on US 290 is illuminated with thousands of colored lights. (830) 868–7684; www.johnsoncity-texas.com.

Main Street Bethlehem, Burnet. Held the first two weekends in December, this festival reenacts a biblical-era village, complete with live animals and Mary, Joseph, and infant Jesus. (512) 756–4297; www.burnetchamber.org.

A Timeless Christmas in Johnson City, Johnson City. Celebrate the season with lamplight visits to the LBJ boyhood home, thousands of holiday lights, and a chuckwagon camp at the Johnson Settlement. (830) 868–7128; www.johnsoncity-texas.com.

Walkway of Lights, Marble Falls. This virtual tunnel of lights is made of more than one million lights that reflect off the waters of Lake Marble Falls, one of the most spectacular lighting experiences in the region. Stroll beneath the lights evenings from late November through early January. (800) 759–8178; www.marblefalls.org.

Wassailfest, New Braunfels. Merchants throughout the downtown area prepare the traditional English holiday drink of wassail and serve it to the evening guests who enjoy live music, horse-and-buggy rides, and a visit from Santa. Look for open houses, caroling, and bell choirs on this special evening of holiday fun. (800) 572–2626; www.nbcham.org.

appendix a

especially for winter texans

If you're among the many lucky travelers who've adopted the Lone Star State as their winter home, welcome to Texas. You've chosen a destination where you can enjoy the excitement of the West, the zest of Old Mexico, the tranquility of the Gulf, and the history of a rambunctious republic, all in one journey. Some of the best seasons and reasons to see the state include the changing post oak leaves in fall, the glittering Christmas festivals, and the often sunny Texas winter days.

Texas has an excellent network of state parks, most of which provide campsites with hookups. Generally there is a fourteen-consecutive-days limit for camping at each park. The central reservation number for all Texas state parks is (512) 389–8900 on weekdays 9:00 A.M. to 8:00 P.M., and Saturday 9:00 A.M. to noon, or see www.tpwd.state.tx.us/park/admin/res for online, e-mail, and fax reservations.

Winter Texans will be interested in the two different discount programs available at state parks. If you are sixty-five years old or more or are a 60 percent VA-disabled veteran, you are eligible for a free or discounted State Parklands Passport (depending on your age). This sticker, which attaches to your windshield, exempts the holder from the entry fee at all state parks. It is good indefinitely, but you must apply for the passport. Bring identification showing proof of age to any state park or to the Texas Parks and Wildlife Headquarters, 4200 Smith School Road, Austin.

The newest discount program is the Gold Texas Conservation Passport. You pay an annual fee for the sticker, which covers all entry fees and gives discounts on camping. For more information on this program, see Appendix B, "Texas State Parks."

appendix b

texas state parks

Texas has an excellent system of state parks offering camping, angling, hiking, boating, and tours of historical sites. Facilities range from those with hiking trails, golf courses, and cabins to others that are largely undeveloped and exist as an example of how the region once looked.

Reservations are recommended for overnight facilities. Pets are permitted if they are confined or on a leash shorter than 6 feet. The central reservation number for all Texas state parks is (512) 389–8900, Monday through Friday 8:00 A.M. to 6:00 P.M., and Saturday 9:00 A.M. to noon, or see www.tpwd.state.tx.us/park/admin/res for on-line, mail, and fax reservations. For TDD service, call (512) 389–8915 weekdays. To cancel a reservation, call (512) 389–8910.

For travelers sixty-five years or older (or those with at least a 60 percent VA disability), there is the free or discounted (depending on age) State Parklands Passport. This windshield sticker permits free entry into any park.

If you visit state parks frequently, consider purchasing a Texas Conservation Passport, which is renewable annually. It provides free entrance into all parks as well as discounts on all campsites and overnight facilities. With it, you receive a newsletter of upcoming events, a directory of access conditions to special wildlife management areas that require a Conservation Passport, and access to guided tours. The Conservation Passport can be purchased at any state park, at the Smith School Road headquarters in Austin, or at retail hunting and fishing stores. For more information, call (800) 895–4248 or (512) 389–4901.

Admission to wildlife management areas (not state parks) is available with the Silver Texas Conservation Passport.

For more information on Texas state parks, call the Texas Parks and Wildlife Department at (800) 792–1112 Monday through Friday during working hours, or at (512) 389–8950 in the Austin area.

Texas Parks and Wildlife Department also maintains an excellent Internet site: www.tpwd.state.tx.us.

appendix c

guide to tex-mex food

You'll find Tex-Mex food everywhere you go in Central and South Texas. It's a staple with all true Texans, who enjoy stuffing themselves at least once a week with baskets of tostadas, the Mexican plate (an enchilada, taco, and rice and beans), and cold *cerveza*. Unlike true Mexican food, which is not unusually spicy and often features seafood, Tex-Mex is heavy, ranges from hot to inedible, and can't be beat.

cabrito—young, tender goat, usually cooked over an open flame on a spit. In border towns, you'll see it hanging in many market windows.

cerveza—beer.

chalupa—a fried, flat corn tortilla spread with refried beans and topped with meat, lettuce, tomatoes, and cheese.

chile relleño—stuffed poblano peppers, dipped in batter and deep fried.

enchilada—corn or flour tortillas wrapped around a filling and covered with a hot or mild sauce. The most common types are beef, chicken, and cheese, and sometimes even sour cream and shrimp.

fajita—grilled skirt steak strips, wrapped in flour tortillas. Usually served still sizzling on a metal platter, with condiments (*pico de gallo,* sour cream, cheese) on the side.

flauta—corn tortillas wrapped around shredded beef, chicken, or pork and fried until crispy; may be an appetizer or an entree.

frijoles refrito—refried beans.

guacamole—avocado dip spiced with chopped onions, peppers, and herbs.

margarita—popular tequila drink, served in a salted glass; may be served over ice or frozen.

menudo—a soup made from tripe, most popular as a hangover remedy.

mole ("MOLE-ay")—an unusual sauce made of nuts, spices, and chocolate that's served over chicken enchiladas.

picante sauce—a Mexican staple found on most tables, this red sauce is made from peppers and onions and can be eaten as a dip for tortilla chips; ranges from mild to very hot.

pico de gallo—hot sauce made of chopped onions, peppers, and cilantro; used to spice up tacos, *chalupas,* and fajitas.

quesadilla—tortillas covered with cheese and baked; served as a main dish.

sopapilla—fried pastry dessert served with honey.

tamale—corn dough filled with chopped pork, rolled in a corn shuck, steamed and then served with or without chile sauce; a very popular Christmas dish.

tortilla—flat cooked rounds of flour or corn meal used to make many main dishes, and also eaten like bread along with the meal, with or without butter.

verde—green sauce used as a dip or on enchiladas.

appendix d

lcra parks

When it comes to parks, Austinites have only one problem: selecting from a long list of excellent facilities located near the capital city. Many of these parks are the products of the Lower Colorado River Authority (LCRA), a conservation and reclamation district that generates and transmits electricity produced by the powerful Colorado River. The LCRA also manages the waters of the river and assists riverside and lakeside communities with their economic development.

Among travelers, the LCRA is best known for its parks. These sites, which vary from unimproved sites along the riverbanks to full-fledged parks with boat ramps, fishing piers, and camping, are favorite summer destinations. Scattered from the shores of Lake Buchanan, down through the rest of the Highland Lakes, and along the riverbanks of the Colorado River all the way to Matagorda County on the Gulf Coast, these waters offer vacationers a great place to relax.

For more information on LCRA parks, call (800) 776–5272; www.lcra.org.

about the authors

John Bigley and Paris Permenter are a husband–wife team of travel writers. Longtime residents of Central Texas, they make their home in the Hill Country west of Austin, near Lake Travis.

John and Paris write frequently about Texas and other destinations for numerous magazines and newspapers. They also write a monthly column on day-trip travel for San Antonio's *Fiesta* magazine.

John and Paris have authored numerous guidebooks. Their other books include *Shifra Stein's Day Trips from San Antonio, Insiders' Guide to San Antonio, Lovetripper.com's Guide to Caribbean Destination Weddings, Adventure Guide to the Cayman Islands, Adventure Guide to Jamaica, Caribbean with Kids, Cayman Islands Alive!, National Parks with Kids, Caribbean for Lovers, Gourmet Getaways, Jamaica Alive!, Nassau and the Best of the Bahamas Alive!,* and *Texas Barbecue,* named best regional book by the Mid-America Publishers Association.

The team also edits *Lovetripper.com Romantic Travel* magazine, an online look at romantic destinations around the globe.

Both John and Paris are members of the prestigious Society of American Travel Writers.

For more on the couple's writing and travels, see www.parisandjohn.com or www.lovetripper.com.